Approaches to the History of Spain

APPROACHES TO THE HISTORY OF SPAIN

by JAIME VICENS VIVES

Second Edition, Corrected and Revised

TRANSLATED
and EDITED   by JOAN CONNELLY ULLMAN

UNIVERSITY OF CALIFORNIA PRESS
Berkeley, Los Angeles, London   1970

University of California Press
Berkeley and Los Angeles, California
University of California Press, Ltd.
London, England

Copyright © 1967, 1970, by
The Regents of the University of California

Second Edition, 1970
ISBN: 0-520-01299-2

First Campus Edition
ISBN: 0-520-01422-7

Aproximación a la historia de España, first published in Barcelona, Spain, by Editorial Vicens-Vives, 1952. The English translation is based on the 2d edition, published by Editorial Teide in 1960 for the Centro de Estudios Históricos Internacionales of the University of Barcelona.

Library of Congress Catalog Card Number 70-127105

Maps by Alice Alden

Foreword

I do not have the credentials to introduce a historian, much less one of the caliber of Vicens Vives, but I can contribute a few reminiscences that will help the reader to understand somewhat the spirit in which *Approaches to the History of Spain* was written.

I met Vicens Vives in person about the year 1951. Everything by him that I had read — a thorough doctoral dissertation in three volumes on Ferdinand II and the city of Barcelona (published 1936–37), various history textbooks written and published during and after 1942, and his contributions to *Estudios de Historia Moderna*, a historical and bibliographical journal he published in collaboration with his students — had made me imagine him as the meticulous type of historian who concentrates on facts and documents and is not at all disposed to let himself be carried away by rhetorical considerations. This impression was confirmed by our first personal meeting, in 1951, which was followed by others during each succeeding summer until the very sad one of 1960, when Vicens Vives died at the peak of his career and with many projects still to be carried out.

Vicens Vives was a man who did not play with historical facts. His every affirmation was based upon a solid pile of documents. There was a reason why Vicens had a reputation for some years of "devouring" archives, of being a man who could literally go through an entire archive in one fell swoop. He was a born historian, a man for whom the past was a living presence in the traces left behind by men and institutions. But it would be erroneous to think that he simply restricted himself to collecting documents and presenting them in an orderly fashion. A true historian does not merely reproduce the past verbally; he must also, and above all, synthesize it and give it meaning. *Approaches to the History of Spain* bears witness to Vicens Vives' power of synthesis; never has so much been said about this history in so few pages. Vicens was, then, a complete historian, able to proceed from a synthesis to an analysis. He was a man who never overlooked a document, but was also one who knew which facts were essential and would not allow history to become a sheer accumulation of facts.

All that I have said, although it is a great deal, is still not sufficient to characterize Vicens Vives' work and personality. Of these there are three aspects that I should like to emphasize.

In the first place, Vicens Vives was possibly Spain's first truly modern historian. Rhetorical history, into which so many Spanish historians had fallen, or stumbled, completely repelled him; no one was so unrhetorical or so adverse to resounding phrases as Vicens. History that concerned itself merely with ideologies struck him as suspect; under the guise of any ideology whatsoever, a historian might very easily jettison facts and documents. Purely political and institutional history merited somewhat more his respect, but still wasn't really what he wanted. What, then, was Vicens Vives' criterion for the writing of history? Simply the criterion (which had already been cultivated outside of Spain but which reached Spain for the first time, and in its full maturity, through the works of Vicens) that, instead of stopping at major events of greater or lesser renown, one should try to penetrate through them to the firmer subsoil of social and economic developments, as analyzed from a rigorously statistical viewpoint. It isn't that Vicens Vives did not know about the great events, or even that he disdained them; what he did was to consider them in terms of data that Spanish historians have not normally used. For Vicens Vives it was very important, of course, to know whether the Cortes had or had not met in a certain year. But it was also extremely important, and at times even more important, to know how many ships had unloaded cargoes in the city of Barcelona on such and such a date, what the tonnage of the ships was, and, naturally, what merchandise they brought. It seems

Foreword

unnecessary to say that it was also very important to know how men had organized themselves in social groups and what pressures these groups had exerted.

Secondly, Vicens Vives was perfectly aware that, even given all the data and documents one might want, to write history is — in the last analysis — to interpret. This is not just a matter of selecting facts — which might very well be selected not in order to interpret but simply to support a prejudice — nor of more or less vague and profound hermeneutics (more often vague than profound) by means of which a historian penetrates "sympathetically" or "emphathetically" into the men of the past. The kind of interpretation that he advocated and achieved involved a very special operation: to allow one's imagination to flower without ever loosening its roots in the solid ground of facts. There is a Catalan expression which seems made to order as a description of Vicens Vives' attitude, one that might be translated as "to keep your feet on the ground." Vicens, historical writings, no less than his entire personality, are living testimonies to the attitude expressed in the Catalan expression which means not "to beat about the bush" ("andarse por las ramas") and consequently, not to get lost either in the clouds or in a labyrinth. It means simply to be firmly rooted in reality, which is where Vicens was from the beginning to the end.

The third aspect of Vicens Vives' work and personality can be easily deduced from the first two, but it deserves a brief comment. Because he was alert to the reality of the past, had no illusions, and yet was free of any paralyzing skepticism, Vicens Vives was highly interested — and with each year increasingly so — in a part of history that still does not exist: the future. My conversations with Vicens, which were enriched by his always very pertinent references to the past, were almost invariably oriented to the future — the future, obviously, of Catalonia and of Spain. These were not merely daydreams; Vicens Vives was thinking about the future in terms of very specific and very concrete possibilities. Besides being a historian, Vicens Vives was thus, in a way, a politician. Unfortunately, the era in which he lived did not permit him much freedom to maneuver, but he took full advantage of the little he had.

Historians usually get together with historians, and Vicens Vives did not disdain such professional contacts. But he was more frequently in the company of writers, economists, philosophers, scientists, industrialists, workers. All learned from him, but at the same time he learned from all of them. He learned that a human community, which is what makes history, is composed not of any one kind of person but of many kinds, often in mutual conflict. Vicens Vives certainly did not restrict himself to an academic discussion of the problems of Catalonia and of Spain. An academician by profession, Vicens Vives had the least academic personality one could imagine. He did not live in an ivory tower; he lived out of doors, because that was where the history he had done so much to scrutinize and interpret takes place.

The reader has in his hands a work that Vicens Vives considered "minor"; after all, it was originally only an article for an encyclopedia. But the best qualities of an author are often revealed in certain minor works. With no display of documents, with the minimum of facts, yet always the essential ones, *Approaches to the History of Spain* is the work of a historian who, had he set out to do so, could have written a book on each one of its sentences. Instead he preferred to condense a book in each sentence.

This book is thus "essential" in many ways: it goes to the root of the problem; it teaches much more than many a series of voluminous and indigestible tomes. It was an excellent idea on the part of Professor Joan Connelly Ullman, whose abilities as an historian I learned to appreciate during her years at Bryn Mawr College, to translate this work, and an excellent decision on the part of the University of California Press to publish it. Anyone who would like to start learning something about the history of Spain can without hesitation begin with these *Approaches*.

JOSÉ FERRATER MORA

By Way of Prologue

In the prologue which I wrote in October 1952 for the first edition, I described how this book had originated in the meetings then held every Monday in the history seminar room of the University of Barcelona. The group was not very large: a dozen friends, either university colleagues or recent graduates who, in the course of plowing through the arid program of studies then in effect, had lost neither their vocation nor their enthusiasm. These conversations, generally dealing with methodology, proved to be extremely stimulating because of the participants' enthusiasm and because absolute freedom of discussion was an established rule. Endless nuances developed as our discussion ranged from comments on a provocative article in the latest issue of a Spanish or foreign publication to very subtle observations in a general evaluation of the work of Karl Jaspers or Arnold Toynbee, who were then in vogue. We often focused our attention, of course, on the problematical aspects of Spain's history, for we were the first to lament the decadence in the post-Civil War period of this type of research, a decadence due as much to the rigidity of old molds of scholarship as to the blithe ideological intuitions of persons who did not want to be bothered with the hard task of digging into archives.

The enthusiasm of our meetings suggested that it might perhaps be of interest to sketch, in a very few pages, the fundamental structure of Spanish history. My purpose, however, was not to produce a new synthesis of the Peninsula's past, but rather to provide a general account of problems on which friends and collaborators, and all who feel a sincere obligation to penetrate into the historic existence of

Hispania, could base their work.[1] This idea was still in embryonic form when the amiable pressures of a friend, Santiago Nadal, forced me to act. Nadal asked that I collaborate on a dictionary of politics being prepared under his direction, and we agreed that my contribution should first be published as a short book. It appeared in bookstore windows and had an unexpected, splendid success. This discouraged the editors of the dictionary and they decided not to include my article. I state this purely as bibliographical information, but also as a justification for omitting the note that appeared on the frontispiece of the first edition of this book.[2]

I must attribute its success in the bookstores to the fact that for the first time in fifteen years the public had found a book on Spanish history that was impartial. Based on a dispassionate and concrete analysis of events (at times I would summarize a monograph in one adjective), my assertions were presented simply as working hypotheses, in order to have them perfected or discarded by future research. For this reason I had given the book an extremely modest title. I would attempt only to "approach" the true history of Spain, and I would do so without rhetoric or grandiloquence, but rather with the artisan's effort to persevere in his work and to perfect it.

My *Approaches* soon called for a new edition. Hispanists in Germany and North America, where my book had been well received, were particularly insistent in their demands. But an "approach" needed some time to mature before a second edition would be possible. I had to observe for a while: what would be the advances in research; which would be the great works of synthesis; what would

---

[1] Hispania, rather than Spain, is the term preferred by Vicens Vives and other Catalan historians. See, for example, the excellent textbook by Santiago Sobrequés Vidal entitled *Hispania: Historia política y cultural de España,* (Barcelona, 9th ed., 1960). For these historians, Hispania expresses more adequately the heterogeneous origins of the nation, while Spain is associated with the Castilian-based government developed from the sixteenth century on (see, p. 79–80).

[2] The note stated that "with some variations, the text of this work will appear in the *Diccionario de política* which is being prepared by the Argos publishing house."

By Way of Prologue

be the orientation of the various schools; what would be the definitive positions? Thus it seemed prudent to wait a few years, particularly because historical science in Spain, which had only recently emerged from its dreams of rhetorical grandeur, had begun developing three movements. These were a revitalization of the philological-institutional school, an abrupt burgeoning of the socio-economic methods advocated by the *Annales* in Paris,[3] and the elimination (less rapidly than had been foreseen) of the "ideologism"[4] of the post-war period. To these movements we must add the contributions (at times, major contributions) of the foreign historians who have concerned themselves with Spain, as well as the equally forceful interpretative works by Américo Castro and Claudio Sánchez Albornoz — two intellectual lights of exiled Spain.[5]

As a consequence, the seven years that separate the first and second appearances of my *Approaches* may be considered of capital importance in the development of Hispanic historiography in the twentieth century, especially because of the type of publication appearing during that period. Outstanding among these are three general

---

[3] The Parisian historical journal *Annales* was founded in 1929 by Lucien Febvre (1878–1956) and Marc Bloch (1886–1944). The original title, *Annales d'histoire économique et sociale* was shortened to *Annales d'histoire sociale* in 1939, and then broadened to *Annales: Economies, sociéties, civilisations* in 1946, reflecting a shift in emphasis within its general socio-economic orientation. Vicens was an enthusiastic advocate of Febvre's ideas, and particularly of the need for "precise quantifiable data," from 1950, when he attended the Ninth International Congress of Historical Sciences; see Stanley G. Payne, "Jaime Vicens Vives and the Writing of Spanish History," *Journal of Modern History*, XXXIV (1962), 127.

[4] Vicens Vives has defined the term "ideologism" as theorizing about the climate of ideas prevailing at a certain point in history on the basis of an analysis of literary texts or official documents. See the prologue to the first edition of *Aproximación a la historia de España*, pp. 18–20. See also Vicens' review of Américo Castro's book in *Indice histórico español*, vol. II (1955–56), item 6901.

[5] For a discussion of the books by Américo Castro, living in exile in the United States, and Claudio Sánchez Albornoz, living in exile in Argentina, see pp. xxi–xxiv.

histories (by Ramón Menéndez Pidal,[6] Luis García de Valdeavellano,[7] and Fernando Soldevila [8]) and two dramatic interpretations of the Peninsula's past (by Castro and Sánchez Albornoz). There are also several very distinguished sociological contributions (for example, those of Julio Caro Baroja [9]), as well as the achievements in the field of economic, socio-economic, and regional history by the Catalan and other schools. In addition, there have been a remarkable number of monographs, books, and magazine articles, which in content are, in general, far superior to those of the preceding two decades.

Reflecting on this material, I am led to believe — and this is my second point — that we find ourselves in a period of transition. In one way this period is characterized by the liquidation of a series of anachronistic positions (in general, those of the scholarly and philological school of Castilian nationalism), and in another way by the birth of a new concept of writing history, responsive to real life and pulsing with human blood, and incompatible with great abstract themes and with those political and ideological drugs that have poisoned Hispanic historiography.

---

[6] Ramón Menéndez Pidal (1869–1968) edited a multivolume history of Spain. Publication began in 1935, but the most important period was 1950 to 1958 when six volumes appeared, either for the first time or in a second, revised edition. Menéndez Pidal wrote many of the introductions for these volumes, published by Espasa Calpe in Madrid. During this same period he also published a collection of essays on Spanish literary and political history, some for the first time: see *España y su historia*, 2 vols. (Madrid, 1957).

[7] Luis García de Valdeavellano, *Historia de España*, vol. I in 2 parts, *De los origines a la Baja Edad Media* (Madrid: 1st ed., 1952; 2d ed., 1955; 3d ed., 1964). Valdeavellano was a student of Sánchez Albornoz.

[8] Fernando Soldevila, *Historia de España*, 8 vols. (Barcelona, 1952–59).

[9] Perhaps the major work of Julio Caro Baroja during the decade 1950–1960 is *Los Moriscos de Granada: Ensayo de historia social* (Madrid, 1957). In 1962 he published his most important work to date: *Los Judíos en la España moderna y contemporánea*, 3 vols. (Madrid). He synthesized his findings in his speech upon the occasion of his entry into the Royal Academy of History: "*La sociedad cripto-judía en la corte de Felipe IV*" (Madrid, 1963). For additional bibliographical references, see p. 152*n*.

By Way of Prologue

The increasing dissemination of new auxiliary methods (demography, economics, sociology, and statistics) warrants the belief that, within a short time, order will be imposed upon whatever has been capricious and unintelligible in Spain's historical jungle, and that clarity and moderation will sweep away the romantic foliage and baroque obscurantism. In other words, we shall become faithful to ourselves, not take refuge in metaphysical speculation in order to avoid a conscious understanding of our past experience.

In the evolution of this historiographical movement, the Barcelona school has during the past seven years been in the vanguard.[10] We, its members, have toiled without ceasing since January 1953, the same month in which the first edition of this book appeared. During these epic years, through the pages of the *Indice histórico español*[11] and of the *Estudios de historia moderna*,[12] we have struggled to open new horizons for our science and to liberate it from all fetishes; we have broached subjects not previously considered in our historiography, and we have presented without acerbity aspects formerly embittered by disagreement or else systematically avoided.

As we have advanced, we have found numerous collaborators — persons already proceeding in our direction or colleagues who have

---

[10] In the first edition, Vicens cited historians Ramón Gubern, Juan Mercader, and Juan Reglá as other members of the Barcelona school.

[11] The *Indice histórico español: Bibliografía histórica de España e Hispanoamérica*, 10 vols. from 1953 to date, a concise summary of reviews of all publications on Spanish and Hispano-American history. It is nominally published by the Center for International Historical Studies, College of Philosophy and Letters, of the University of Barcelona, and thereby gains exemption from the regular state censorship imposed on commercial publications. However, it is in fact printed and distributed by the Teide publishing firm, formerly owned by Vicens and his brother-in-law, Federico Rahola, and since the death of Vicens by Rahola alone.

[12] *Estudios de historia moderna*, begun in 1951, publishes articles and monographs of original research. Initially appearing under the auspices of the Barcelona Section of the Instituto Jerónimo Zurita, Consejo Superior de Investigaciones Científicas (the official, government-financed research institution), the journal received an annual state subsidy that was later discontinued. It has appeared only irregularly.

joined us along the way.[13] But we have also had to engage in some skirmishes — intellectual ones, needless to say. Victorious or defeated, we bear no grudge toward anyone. We are always ready to welcome historians of good will who come from any camp, group, or school whatsoever. From our circle we regretfully exclude only those persons who leave the arena, carrying with them their political hatreds, and who launch their darts from behind the parapets of comfortable and unearned official redoubts.[14]

I hope I have justified my decision not to reedit this book until now. I might add that, following the inundation of the preceding decade, we now find ourselves in a relatively serene moment. The waters appear to be stilled. Thus I can proceed with my task and push my *Approaches* towards its second appearance, which I hope will be as fortunate as the first.

But before I begin, I must caution the reader about the methodology that governs the book. Here I have no recourse but to show my credentials as a professional historian,[15] and the best way I can show them is to repeat a few paragraphs from the prologue I wrote in 1952, modifying them where I deem it necessary.

We all know — I wrote in 1952 — our reaction some thirty years

---

[13] Among the historians who worked with Vicens Vives are Manuel Ballesteros-Gaibrois and Mario Hernández Sánchez-Barba of the University of Madrid, Guillermo Céspedes del Castillo of the University of Seville, and Antonio Domínguez Ortiz of Granada. Specifically, they collaborated in writing the *Historia social y económica de España y América*, 4 vols. in 5 parts (Barcelona, 1957–59; reprinted in 1961 under the title *Historia de España y América*). Vicens directed the entire work, a comprehensive but uneven pioneer study, and wrote the section on nineteenth- and twentieth-century Spain.

[14] Vicens is referring to the protection offered by such government-subsidized publications as *Arbor*, the journal of the Consejo Superior de Investigaciones Científicas. See the first edition of *Aproximación a la historia de España*, p. 15.

[15] For a complete chronological, annotated bibliography of the publications of Vicens Vives (1910–1960), see *Indice histórico español*, VI (1960), 1–16. For an excellent analysis of Vicens' work, and a description of the difficult political and professional situation in which he worked, see Payne, "Jaime Vicens Vives," *Journal of Modern History*, pp. 119–134.

By Way of Prologue

ago against the narrative method that prevailed as the norm in university lectures and, above all, as a fundamental guideline for historical research. Since then Spanish historiography has sought a new methodological orientation, at times as an outgrowth of movements originating abroad, at other times attempting its own formulation of the study of the past. These developments have not, however, extinguished a devotion to the old narrative system. It still has many partisans in our country because we find it impossible simply to discard the oldest of historiographical methods. We need only to contemplate the extensive lacunae in Hispanic history to realize that we still must sacrifice a few principles in order to maintain a system which, although it has already failed in its objectives, is indispensable for filling in such lacunae. In order for us to profit directly or indirectly from the work of historical narrators, we ask only that they be thorough and exact in their scholarship and that they be knowledgeable about new methods of research. Quite apart from this, it should be emphasized that it is still useful to publish a good collection of documents on any problem in Spain's internal or external history.

I have purposely used both of the foregoing adjectives.[16] Because the narrative method was accused of superficiality — it never reached a conclusion of any significance — its place within the national methodology was taken by one called (for what exact reason I do not know) internal history. Those were the years when German procedures invaded our science. Ernst Bernheim was the idol of our professors.[17] Although the exact results of such a method were not known, everyone surrendered to the almost mythical impact of that name. Ah, internal history! Its dissemination undeniably had great benefits: it put a stop to romantic improvisation, exacted an

---

[16] External history refers to the traditional political or military narratives, internal history to the study of institutions.

[17] Ernst Bernheim (1850–1942) published his compendia of methodology, highwater mark of Leopold von Ranke's "scientific" school, in 1889 (*Lehrbuch der historischen Methode und der Geschichtsphilosophie*), revising it substantially in subsequent editions. Not until 1937 was there a Spanish translation (*Introducción al estudio de la historia*, trans. Pascual Galindo Romeo from the 3d ed., 1908).

impartial criticism of sources, and made indispensable an extensive addition of archival material. All of this was needed and welcomed. But because of the simultaneous development of research in the history of law, the new methodological experiment ended up being a cold and sterile history of institutions.[18] Little by little the human factor, the basis of all historiography, was forgotten. Importance was bestowed upon the framework instead of the contents, upon the conduit of energy instead of the charge which the conduit merely transfers passively. The conduit — the institution — was moved about from one side to the other. These moves filled the texts of conscientious monographs and occasioned formidable scholarly controversies. Today it is sad to contemplate the results that were achieved. One can barely sustain even one of the theses formulated by the great institutional masters at the beginning of the century.

This virus penetrated deep into our medieval field, creating sad havoc when it paired with another, equally dangerous virus, that of pure philology, the myth of the document.[19] Spanish medieval studies are thus today in a dead-end street where words, not men, are debated. In general, medievalists have forgotten that any word is a carryover from an earlier period and therefore cannot provide

---

[18] In Spain the most prominent institutional historian was Eduardo de Hinojosa (1852–1919), a professor at the University of Madrid; he was active in the Centro de Estudios Históricos, part of the pre-Civil War Junta para la Ampliación de Estudios Históricos (the predecessor organization of the present Consejo Superior). In 1924 Hinojosa's students began publication of the influential *Anuario de historia del derecho español*. One of these students was Claudio Sánchez Albornoz, who played a key role in the *Anuario* until he left Spain in 1936.

[19] The techniques of philology were introduced into Spain from Germany by Menéndez Pidal, Director of the Real Academia Española (1926–1936, 1948–1968). Convinced that philology, if used within a broad context, was an important instrument of historiography, he exerted wide influence through his chair at the University of Madrid and as director of the Centro de Estudios Históricos. Américo Castro is one among many who studied with him. For a study of Menéndez Pidal's work in the current historiographical controversy in Spain, see José Antonio Maravall, *Menéndez Pidal y la historia del pensamiento* (Madrid, 1960), pp. 83–160.

By Way of Prologue

them with a perfect image of the new, vital reality they are trying to define. They have also forgotten that any institution, by the simple act of encasing a vital tension or of achieving a new equilibrium of forces, is stillborn or at least inert. The vital content of an institution comes from the men who use it as the means for fighting to achieve their own ambitions. The passage of time only aggravates this problem, because an institutional body either deforms its social ambience in order to continue representing it, or moves further and further away from expressing the true character of that ambience. I exclude the case in which an institution is converted into myth, for then it loses its "objective reality" and its place at the core of institutional history, and finds a new one in the history of ideas.

Accordingly, although institutional history can show us the approximate channels through which biological energies circulate (which undeniably signifies considerable progress over the accounts of successions of kings and battles I mentioned previously), it does not hold the key to the secret of history. Neither regulations, nor privileges, nor laws, nor constitutions bring us close to human reality. These are formulas that establish limits, but nothing more than limits. The expression of life is to be found in the application of the law, statute, decree, or regulation; in the way in which individuals distort the desire of a state, of a corporation, or of an oligarchy to impose a certain order. An institution should be considered not in and of itself, but in terms of the human fervor that stirs in its innermost recesses. In order to understand such fervor as an historical phenomenon, one must discard the legislative caparison and go directly to the human collectivity that it represents — to human desires, petty pride, and profound resentments, because something of all these is in the Lord's vineyard. For this reason I have unceasingly advocated the need for a radical change in how sources are selected for historical research. Instead of the great collections of laws, historians should consult archives where law clashes with life — notarial protocols, consular and commercial records, police archives, law-court decisions, and so on.

However, simply because today neither the philological method nor that of the history of institutions fully satisfies us does not mean we should subordinate them to the more brilliant but far less efficacious method of the so-called history of culture.[20] Obviously an exploration of the ideological, juridical, emotional, esthetic, religious, and moral aspects of any people will have beneficial results. I do not deny its usefulness. What I do deny is that cultural historians make an objective contribution to our exact knowledge of the Spanish people's past.

I find three important defects in their historical publications. In the first place, every history of a culture has until now required a preliminary intellectual scheme — orthodox or heterodox, materialistic or idealistic, unitary or evolutionary. But life flees from any such circumscription. In the immense majority of cases, life in the process of creating itself (I hope it is obvious I do not mean this in any purely biological or teleological sense) lies far beyond the professional historian's concern. In the second place, until now the history of culture has been nothing more than a study of intellectual minorities, and has therefore examined only a microscopic portion of the mentality at work in any specific period of history. Such a viewpoint is exactly like the old myopic concept that limited political history to the study of some few crowned heads and their followers. Finally, cultural history has not discovered a convincing technique for assessing the relative weights of the spiritual and material contributions of a country or a society. This has given rise to innumerable controversies that have converted cultural history from a spearhead for the vanguard of historical science into a spearhead for political troops disposed to seize power.

Considerations such as these justify the fact that from the beginning of my career as a university professor, I have urged my students to restrict themselves exclusively to the writing of history — but to absolute history, to life itself. In order to make my position clear, I wrote in the inaugural issue of *Estudios de historia moderna*: "Fundamentally we believe that history is life in all its complex

---

[20] By the term "culture," Vicens means specifically the artistic and intellectual history of a nation, rather than the broader sense in which it is used by most modern anthropologists or sociologists.

By Way of Prologue xix

diversity. Therefore we do not feel bound by any a priori prejudice against any method, speculative theory, or objective. Materialism we reject as being unilateral, positivism as schematic, ideologism as shallow. We are attempting to capture the living reality of the past and, above all, the interests and passions of the common man."

My experience over the last few years, verified by Spanish and foreign historical publications, leads me to reaffirm this premise. However, if a method is to embrace all of life, it must be carefully defined. To gauge an individual life, one need only know the fundamental principles of the new biographical techniques: the historic moment (the conjecture) penetrating deep within the individual, who reacts to his physical surroundings and to the ambience of his generation according to his psychological potential. But it is much harder to evaluate the past of the common man.

Unless we resort to statistical method as our primary instrument, collective life cannot be deciphered.[21] In history, statistics is no mere accumulation of data; it is an art of applying percentages and constants, averages and coefficients. It defines clearly how many times men repeat the same offense, without necessarily implying that these men would condemn whatever it is they are doing. Statistics establishes those geographical sites in which the greatest number of major events have taken place. Above all, it expresses numerically the material and spiritual interests of humanity, which are what counts in history. Thus it does not bother me to repeat that statistics is "essential for the determination of values, fortunes, and mentalities," and that "unless this is approached through a minute analysis of prices, salaries, political trends, and cultural tendencies, it is possible to understand nothing."

Nothing: let this point be well understood. Let us imagine we are studying an era, a reign, or a country. It is of scant importance to concentrate on outstanding military or political events. Two successive defeats on the battlefield during this century have not diminished the weight of Germany in the European power system.

---

[21] For the background to this insistence on "quantifiable data," see *n.* 3, above, on Lucien Febvre's *Annales*.

By definition, no institutional body reveals the course of history; glorious names have shielded successive moments of splendor and decadence.

And as for the ideological yardstick, one might commit the very grave error of asserting that five, ten, or twenty individuals (whatever their mental stature) actually represent a reign, a society, or a generation. This is simply not true, not of any twenty in the eighteenth century, nor of any one thousand in our century. An intellectual class represents only itself in its literary production. (When an intellectual participates in politics or takes a streetcar, the case is different, for this activity must be evaluated as a function of his new role.) Consequently, one must determine what interests an intellectual serves through the medium of his specific profession. Such interests are the basic human ones: interests directly related to his employment and to the office he holds; the interests of the groups he belongs to; the material and moral pressures exerted by those upon whom he is dependent; psychological complexes such as routine, fear, ambition, and envy; concretely spiritual interests; and so on. Therefore, when trying to establish successive generations in the history of ideas, one must not fall into the error of generalizing by saying "So-and-so thought in that way; everyone must have thought that way." The history of ideas is far more capillary; in order to take full account of this, one must broaden research and consult neutral archives, that is, those archives that candidly reflect our ancestors' "intellectual pluralism."

This leads us back once more to the statistical method. The historian who does not use it is deprived of his best working tool, in the same way that government officials cannot function without the data supplied by statistical services. Even when we know personally the living reality of a country, we must still submerge ourselves in the sea of facts provided by annual publications, to try to take the exact pulse of that country by means of data on population, production, wealth, culture, sanitation, labor, and so on — data, with which the intellectual's pen *never* deals. If this be the case, how much greater would the benefit be if, when examining the societies of the past, we reformulated such data? Historical science, particularly in Spain, would take a great step forward if the statistics of the past were done over. Fortunately we are already working in this field, but the harvest is great and those who can work on it are few.

In redoing the configuration of his own history by using the new methods cited above, the Spanish historian should make some contribution to the methodology of the future. Even the most progressive circles abroad continue to debate this matter. The problem to be resolved is that of integrating demographic, social, economic, and psychological techniques — based on statistics — into a totality that can be termed a "method of the sciences of man."

There are two aspects to the resolution of this problem: the epistemological (about which it is better to allow philosophers the last word), and the distinctively scholarly. About the latter, it is feasible for me to offer an opinion, by resorting not to the metaphysics of the human being or of the event (as is common among present-day Castilian scholastics) but to the simple and modest task of studying material taken directly from the archives. The difficulties involved in this task of original research have led to certain experiments which, although they are at the moment of limited use, will with time be integrated into a more general formula. In recent years these have constituted our most valuable system of collaborating with foreign colleagues, and the one for which we have been most grateful to them.

Before concluding this already extended prologue, I must express my concern about a reaction the reader may have. Perhaps he may find it strange that my *Approaches* does not actively engage in the controversy that today divides Hispanic historians and Hispanists in general, some of whom have declared their support for the thesis of Américo Castro [22] and others for the thesis of Claudio Sánchez

---

[22] Américo Castro (b. 1885), *La realidad histórica de España* (Mexico City, 1954). Professor Edmund King of Princeton University has translated it into English under the title, *The Structure of Spanish History* (Princeton, 1954). Castro's book is a greatly modified version of his earlier work, *España en su historia: Cristianos, moros, y judíos* (Buenos Aires, 1948).

Albornoz.[23] This book is not a critical study, nor is it an essay. It attempts to provide orientation and guidelines for research, and to establish the point at which we have arrived and the point at which we could arrive in the near future. Therefore it has not diverged from its original format of absolute adherence to the practice results of research. If anything in these pages has changed since the first edition, it is not because I have changed my criterion, but because of the progress achieved (after ten years of productive work in the archives) in subject matter and in the formulation of the problems of Spanish history.

Nevertheless, I do not want to abandon this comfortable refuge of a prologue without entering the lists. In my judgment, the work of both masters constitutes a singular and intelligent contribution which we must gratefully acknowledge. To write a history of Spain today without taking into account *La realidad histórica de España* or *España: Un enigma histórico* would be inconceivable.

At this point I do not think it important to discuss the methods of these two authors, which are very different (especially that of Américo Castro) from the statistical method that I have just commended. I would even go so far as to affirm that both of their methods have been largely superseded, although in doing so I am well aware that I will bring down upon myself fulminous rays from each Olympus. What interests me in both these works is the broad presentation of Spain's problems in antiquity and the Middle Ages, and in the modern era up to the seventeenth century. Many facts and events have been discussed (at times with excessive scholarly tolerance on the part of Castro, and with excessive commitment to Castile on the part of Sánchez Albornoz), so much so that Don Américo and Don Claudio — who set themselves a task of sifting — have left a very fine flour of good quality. A hurricane wind has carried off the chaff; let it be noted that there was a lot of it, and that it had had a great historical impact. This invaluable sifting will

---

[23] Two years after Castro's book was published, Claudio Sánchez Albornoz (b. 1893) published *España: Un enigma histórico*, 2 vols. (Buenos Aires, 1956; 2d, rev. ed., 1962); it tends to be a point-by-point refutation of Castro's arguments.

greatly benefit all consciences, particularly when its results are publicized and when they actually affect the conscience of Castile.

As a matter of fact, Castile has been confronted with a grave crisis of conscience since 1898. She would like to attribute the origins of the crisis which is disturbing her to the negative attitude of other Hispanic peoples — for example, to the attitude of Catalans. This is a most understandable reaction, and one that is even salutary for Castile's collective psychology, given the intrinsic conflict between Castile and Catalonia — a conflict that since the eighteenth century has constituted both a vital stimulus for, and the cohesive force of, the Spanish state.

Castile supposedly resolved the crisis of 1898 by an act of nationalistic willpower. Strangely enough, this nationalism was not based on a study of history. The single exception was the group in the University of Madrid that gathered around Ramón Menéndez Pidal and Manuel Gómez Moreno. Neither Miguel de Unamuno nor José Ortega y Gasset turned to history; both approached the Castilian through an experience that was very personal and, simultaneously, eternal.[24] From this approach emerged an unreal Castile that has been perpetuated up until now by all the men of that earlier generation and, even more, by their followers.

But in 1955 this same Castile — in the person of two of her most characteristic historians — considered the possibility that now it may be necessary to plunge into a study of her history in order to resolve what she believes to be an excruciating problem of conscience. One part of the problem is Spain's inability to follow the course of Western civilization in its economic, political, and cultural aspects — capitalism, liberalism, and rationalism. Another is that Castile has failed in her appointed role of making Spain a harmonious, satisfied, and compliant community. Both these themes are interwoven in the pages of the books by Castro and Sánchez Albornoz; although both authors might think it impossible, they are reconciled in this

---

[24] For the effect of these intellectuals on Spanish historiography, see Richard Herr, "The Twentieth-Century Spaniard Views the Spanish Enlightenment," *Hispania* (1962), pp. 183–193.

one gigantic accord. It could not be otherwise, even though Castro tries to explain this failure by the ending of medieval Castile's intellectual pluralism, whereas Sánchez Albornoz tries to explain it in terms of what he calls (it cannot be reduced to a clearer synthesis) "the short circuit of modernity": Castile's paralysis in the sixteenth century, caused by her threefold effort to be a European, colonial, and dynastic power.

The dimensions of the controversy aroused by these historians (which has involved all of us who cultivate this science on the Peninsula) lead one to suspect that it will be productive. It will be particularly so if in its resolution, stereotypes and platitudes are abandoned, and the basic factors of Peninsular history are set forth: men, misery, and famine; epidemics and death; land ownership; the relations between a lord and his vassal, between a government official and the citizen subject to his jurisdiction, between an employer and a worker, between a monarch and his subject, between a priest and a believer, between one municipal government and another, between town and town, between national capital and province, between individual production and national income, between a soul and God. These factors do not differ greatly from those that underlie the experience of neighboring Mediterranean nations; for this reason it is very doubtful that Spain is "a historic enigma" as Sánchez Albornoz believes, or that it is "un vivir desviviéndose" as his opponent declares.[25] This is too much anguish, Unamuno style, for a Mediterranean community with very concrete and compact "epoch-making" problems — the problems of procuring a modest but dignified livelihood for its thirty million inhabitants.

I have strayed so far off the path that I will conclude with a very few words to draw attention to the innovations in the text — two

---

[25] Explaining his term "vivir desviviéndose," Castro writes that many eminent Spaniards "have tried to explain the existence of Spain as a chronic ailment. . . . It has not befallen any other great civilization to live for century after century feeling all the while that the very ground under its feet was missing and creating at the same time such first-class values." *Structure of Spanish History*, pp. 29–30.

By way of Prologue xxv

chapters dealing with prehistoric life, and one dealing with the culminating moment of medieval life. At the end of the book I have added a commentary on each chapter, in which I set forth my opinions on very controversial points or discuss certain very categorical affirmations; these are neither critical nor bibliographical studies, but rather a kind of log of my intellectual itinerary.

JAIME VICENS VIVES

February 1960

Contents

		Page
	FOREWORD by José Ferrater Mora	v
	By Way of Prologue	ix
CHAPTER ONE	The First Settlers	1
CHAPTER TWO	Colonizers and Invaders	7
CHAPTER THREE	Roman Hispania	14
CHAPTER FOUR	The Visigothic Mirage	22
CHAPTER FIVE	The Triumph of Islam	28
CHAPTER SIX	Asturian Legitimacy and the Frankish Intrusion	32
CHAPTER SEVEN	The Caliphate of Córdoba versus the Kingdom of León	36
CHAPTER EIGHT	Return to Europe: Navarre and the Spirit of Castile	40
CHAPTER NINE	The Invasions from North Africa and the Ideal of a Crusade	45

CHAPTER TEN	Hispanic Pluralism and the Pyrenean Empire	50
CHAPTER ELEVEN	Military Expansion on the Peninsula and in the Mediterranean	56
CHAPTER TWELVE	The Medieval Apex	61
CHAPTER THIRTEEN	Beginning of Dissension in Hispania	68
CHAPTER FOURTEEN	The Crisis of the Fifteenth Century	76
CHAPTER FIFTEEN	The Ordering of Hispania by the Catholic Monarchs	87
CHAPTER SIXTEEN	Hispania under the Hapsburg Monarchs	96
CHAPTER SEVENTEEN	The Overthrow of Hispania and the Bankruptcy of the Hapsburg Dynasty's Policy	104
CHAPTER EIGHTEEN	Bourbon Reforms	114
CHAPTER NINETEEN	Politics and Economics in Nineteenth-Century Spain	121
CHAPTER TWENTY	The Crisis of the Twentieth Century	141
Commentary on Bibliography		151
Index		179

Maps

1. The two Spains — a socio-economic view   xxx
2. Roman Hispania under Augustus 7–2 B.C.   18
3. Spain at the beginning of the tenth century   38
4. Modern Spain   142

Genealogical Tables

1. House of Burgundy   48
2. House of Barcelona   52
3. House of Trastámara   71
4. House of Austria (the Spanish Hapsburgs)   89
5. House of Bourbon   112

Map 1

The Two Spains — a Socio-economic View

THE PERIPHERY (the coastal lowlands) has four principal areas of intensive economic activity: Barcelona–Gerona, Valencia–Alicante, Seville–Cádiz, and Oviedo–Santander–Bilbao–San Sebastián. The stippled areas also include all parts of Andalusia, the Levante, Catalonia, and Galicia, where, according to the 1960 census, the population density was more than 160.8 per square mile. Excluded by this factor are Lugo in Galicia, Castellón in the Levante, and Almería and Huelva in Andalusia.

THE HINTERLAND (the central plateau, or Meseta) has, according to the 1960 census, less than 160.8 population density per square mile and includes Navarre, Aragon (with the exception of the city of Sarragossa) León, Extremadura, and Castile. The province of Madrid constitutes an exception, both in terms of population density and because in the post-Civil War period it has become an area of intensive economic activity.

CHAPTER ONE

The First Settlers

Five hundred thousand years before our time, give or take a century, a few groups of Pithecanthropi set their seal of approval on the Hispanic peninsula and established residence. They were not the first hominids to wander about the planet. Those who can almost certainly be considered to be such — the so-called Australopithecines, who made their appearance seven hundred thousand years ago — did not travel very far from their place of origin in southern Africa. Thus only the second wave of humanity reached the Peninsula, and one far more developed than the first; possibly this regeneration had taken place in the equatorial zone and in the Far East.

These Pithecanthropi (certainly a most unflattering name) had wandered westward, reaching western Germany (Heidelberg Man) and Algeria (Atlanthropus). All this is obviously provisional and contingent, for on the basis of two discoveries one cannot write a history of the two hundred thousand years that the Pithecanthropi dominated the earth. But the stone objects which have been conserved for us on the sites where they settled provide us with further data. From them we learn that the impoverished and dispersed groups of the first Hispanic peoples left traces of their existence in various parts of the Peninsula, that they were harassed by their struggle with powerful beasts, that to the best of their ability they defended themselves with fire, and where it was possible attacked by hurling staves, that as they moved about they gathered fruits and roots. The Pithecanthropi did not stray far from sites where flint lodes were to be found, because although they possessed only a weak intelligence, they had already learned to chip that hard stone crudely and to fashion artifacts either by reducing the stone to a core or by striking off flakes. For some time these have been improperly termed weapons (as in the case of the famous hand-axe of the Acheulian culture); actually, their principal purpose — that is to say, their most common use — was to strike and crush other materials.

Calculating on the basis of a sequence of stone-working techniques, prehistorians established stages within that period which they called, and still call, Lower Paleolithic. To recall these stages today is useless, because this problem of technique — which is complex because it involves human beings, not just stones — still confuses the prehistorians, and some time must pass before it can be resolved to everyone's satisfaction. Let us say only that the Hispanic examples of the core and flake tools of the Lower Paleolithic are outstanding, and the bifacial percussion tools of the Acheulian culture, from the San Isidro site in Madrid, fill our archaeologists with pride.

About 200,000 B.C. there was a change in the panorama from which the Peninsula benefited immediately. Neanderthal man, far more capable and active than Pithecanthropus, appeared in the Old World; we are now considering a man endowed with a complex spiritual life, with overtones of religion and magic. Far more attractive than the stereotype usually associated with him (a stereotype resulting from some unfortunate hasty judgments),[1] Neanderthal man was in physical appearance very close to us. The expansion of Neanderthal humanity greatly stimulated culture. For this reason prehistorians have decided to open a new archaeological period, using the term Middle Paleolithic when referring to the period of time when this hominid predominated.

The Neanderthal men entered the Peninsula through the Pyrenees and occupied almost all of it. A curious fact is that fossil

---

[1] Prehistorians attempted some years ago to reconstruct Neanderthal man on the basis of the scant fossil evidence available; they produced a hunchbacked, bent-legged, low-browed brute. Subsequent reconstructions have depicted him as a fully erect biped, who may or may not have been an ancestor of modern man.

The First Settlers

remains have been found inland along the Mediterranean coastal corridor from Bañolas to Gibraltar, as well as on the Atlantic promontories of Portugal, whereas deposits of stone objects abound in the vicinity of Madrid and at the mouth of the Tajo river. This indicates once again that archaeological discoveries have not yet been reconciled with the human and cultural realities of that era. And it would be truly interesting to establish the relationship between them, because the Neanderthal hunter achieved the first technical synthesis, developing core and flake tools into a complex of craftsmanship in which small tools, especially "triangular points" and side-scrapers, predominated. This technique has been termed Mousterian — another strange name.

Neanderthal man took still another step forward. He learned to affix a stone to a reinforced staff — that is, to make a spear. It had taken him almost a hundred millenia to achieve this enormous technical advance, which was as long as he had taken to organize a rudimentary funeral cult.[2] As we can see, the rhythm of history had accelerated notably.

We have logged four hundred thousand years; our narrative could not be more condensed. At this point we welcome the entrance onto the Peninsula of our direct ancestors — Homo sapiens, bands of men who had fully developed the skill of hunting.[3] This migration may have begun about 40,000 B.C., a far more accessible date.

---

[2] From an archaeological point of view, the importance of Neanderthal man's burying his dead is that fossil remains were more likely to be conserved and are easier to relate to a culture.

[3] Most scholars today believe that the first man of modern physical type, who had evolved in Eurasia, and in the late Paleolithic moved westward, entered the Peninsula through the Pyrenees from Europe and not across the Straits from North Africa. Both this man (Cro-Magnon) and his culture (Aurignacian) take their names from type-sites in southwestern France. Spain has scant skeletal evidence of this racial substratum, but it does have many artifacts of Aurignacian culture proper and its later variants (Périgord and La Gravette type-sites). But scholars who deny the ability of this first modern man to cross the Straits in the Paleolithic believe it is possible that he invaded later (in the Mesolithic) and fused with the earlier, larger group to form the Iberians. For bibliography, see pp. 151–154.

The arrival of bona fide men, with well-developed crania and anatomical features identical with our own, gave rise to a far more interesting social dynamic. The first and most numerous invaders — Périgord and Cro-Magnon man, racial varieties of Homo sapiens — were adventurous hunters who carried out far-ranging expeditions to capture animals. The weather was cold and harsh, and game was far more evasive than in the previous period. Fortunately, Homo sapiens succeeded in solving a series of technical difficulties and produced a complete instrumental repertory of stone tools. His great discovery was the chisel. With it he accomplished marvels. He carved superb blades, knives, bits, burins, and points. Furthermore, he learned to work horn and bone, and with these devised harpoon and lance points. His great technical conquests, however, were the javelin and the arrow. With these he was able to conquer the world and proclaim himself king of creation.

Archaeologists do not agree about the protagonists of these changes. Happily ensconced as they were in the so-called Upper Paleolithic, they used to believe in the existence of three cultural stages, corresponding to three peoples: Aurignacian (Asiatic), Solutrean (African), and Magdalenian (Nordic).[4] Now the horizons are more complex, and I expect them to become even more so as new research is carried out, for the thirty thousand years of this era constitute a long period of time, and we are not able to distinguish clearly what Aurignacian man did from what Solutrean man did. Possibly the former were more sedentary and the latter less so.

---

[4] Vicens refers less to "peoples" than to the regions where the three major cultures of Paleolithic Europe presumably originated. Distinguished according to successive techniques of stone working, the three take their name from type-sites in southwestern France. The Eurasian origin of the culture of Aurignac (30,000–15,000 B.C.) is far less controversial than that of Solutré (19,000–15,000 B.C.). Rejecting the earlier theory that it originated in North Africa and was brought north by a well-armed "Capsian Man," most scholars agree that it evolved from Aurignacian culture but disagree about whether the evolution occurred on the east coast of Spain or in southern France. The rich culture of La Madeleine (15,000–9,000 B.C.) originated in the Franco–Cantabrian region.

The First Settlers

Perhaps the Solutreans were nomadic tribes, who often traveled on the Peninsula intermixed with tribes of Périgord man. In any event, Solutreans apparently preferred to settle in five regions: Catalonia, the Southeast (Alicante, Murcia), the area along the Cantabrian sea, New Castile, and the mouth of the Tajo river. At least, such are the findings to date — the result of chance discoveries and of the size of the teams of prehistorians at work in the respective regions.

Without any doubt, the paramount fact of the Upper Paleolithic is that men of the Magdalenian culture settled along the Cantabrian mountain range, from Navarre to Asturias. On the northern side of the Pyrenees, they spread out through the Garonne river basin as far as the upper valleys of its tributary, the Dordogne. These human beings, forming a compact cultural group, were great innovators. They have been given credit for the technical advances to which I have referred, including the bow.

And to these men belongs the credit for having developed the art form of painting and drawing on the walls of caves. This was the fruit of a society that had become specialized and hierarchical; new weapons made hunting usually productive, and so it was possible to free a group from work and allow it to devote itself to magical practices intended to ensure good expeditions for their companions. Even today, for all of us who contemplate this art with no preconceptions, it remains a question mark. It was a fully realized and unprecedented achievement, the best examples of which are the cave paintings at Ruffignac, Lascaux, and Font de Gaume in France, and at Altamira and Castillo on the Peninsula. This artistic province is usually termed Franco-Cantabrian. An examination of its geographic location shows that it might be more appropriate to rebaptize it the Aquitaine-Cantabrian area, even though scattered examples are to be found in other areas of France and Spain.

This is what the Magdalenian peoples were able to contribute to culture. Unfortunately, their artistic contribution could not be cumulative. With them, the aesthetic fever spent itself, and cave painting gradually decayed until it disappeared into schematic forms. Only in the Mediterranean precoastal region, in a still undetermined period (possibly after the Magdalenian era — that is to say, between about 7,000 and 3,000 B.C.) were there any successors to the great Aquitaine-Cantabrian animal paintings. These were vivacious, expressionistic paintings, in which the human figure acquired the role of protagonist, testifying to his existence and to his society. Deriving possibly from the Magdalenian art of Lascaux, this new style would be zealously perpetuated by Périgord tribes in the eastern part of the Peninsula, and would characterize their settlements along the entire Mediterranean precoastal corridor from Catalonia to Andalusia.

During those nebulous years of the Old Stone Age, the notion begins to emerge of an Aquitaine-Cantabrian province and a Mediterranean province. The significance of this idea is simply that it is one way to explain a possible relationship among the twenty-five or, at the most, fifty thousand human beings who inhabited the Peninsula at that time.

CHAPTER TWO

Colonizers and Invaders

The culture of the great hunting peoples of the Upper Paleolithic began to disintegrate in the West in the seventh millennium B.C. because of profound changes of climate. We witness the same process on the Peninsula. Many places in the land became deserts and lost their populations. Only the coasts and some mountain zones offered a chance of existence to minor fauna and to the dispersed tribes who pursued them. The Pyrenees were inhabited by groups of mountain folk who worshiped painted pebbles (the Azilian culture),[1] while along the Cantabrian and Atlantic coasts we find a population of shellfish eaters ("Asturian Man").

In the Mediterranean coastal zone, particularly in the lower Ebro river valley and in Almería, the tribes who survived used small stone instruments to hunt stag and wild boar. The name of these tribes has been much debated. In the belief that they were related to the peoples of northern Africa, they were called *Homo capensis*;[2] today it is preferable to consider them an autochthonous people, a prolongation of the Périgord man of the Upper Paleolithic. Such complications should not trouble us. The important developments are the cultural decline of the Peninsula during the Mesolithic era, and the slow differentiation of the inhabitants into homogeneous geographic areas.

In Mesopotamia and Egypt, meanwhile, the intellectual and tech-

---

[1] The term Azilian is derived from the excavation site at Mas d'Azil, in the French Pyrenean department of Ariège.

[2] Capsa (the Latin name for Gafsa in western Tunisia) is the type-site of an epi-Paleolithic culture found also in eastern Spain.

nical revolution that inaugurated the modern history of humanity had begun. We now find ourselves at the year 5,000 B.C. Within a short period of time there were decisive conquests: domestication of animals and stock raising, agriculture, pottery making, the building of shelters, casting of metal, navigation of rivers and oceans. Intellect had triumphed over magical formulas. As a result of the Neolithic Revolution (as it is rather inappropriately called), the Near East would become the capital of the world for four millennia. Material and technical innovations (especially in agriculture and metallurgy) would come from those lands, but so would the great religions. Little by little, in successive waves, these forces would integrate the Mediterranean world. Initially, this process was carried out mimetically, then through intermediary colonizers. Finally, the peoples of the East themselves dared to sail as far as the feared and distant West. And at this point the peoples on the Hispanic peninsula would be fully incorporated into the civilization created along the shores of the eastern Mediterranean.

The first infiltrations onto the Peninsula of the new way of life may possibly be dated about 3,000 B.C. Archaeologists have discovered the remains of groups of men who lived in caves or in huts made with branches; they had learned how to raise livestock and how to farm in a very rudimentary way by using hoes and sharpened sticks. These men of the early Neolithic belonged to the same human type that had predominated on the Mediterranean coastal since the time of Périgord man. There is no invasion to record, much less one coming from North Africa, which at that moment was as backward as the Peninsula in relation to the cultural developments of the Near East. This leads us to suspect that the first Neolithic reforms were transmitted in a very slow fashion, via the Mediterranean or even across Europe (in this case, starting out from the Danube river basin).

A few centuries later, colonizers from the East exerted direct influence on the Peninsula. From that area of the Mediterranean came navigators who settled in Liguria, Provence, Catalonia, and Valencia; they made new material contributions — above all, a characteristic type of pottery (decorated with impressions of the

Colonizers and Invaders

Cardium shell).[3] This impact was followed by a far more decisive and penetrating one — that of the "people of Almería," as they were called. From the acropolis they erected in the region of Almería, they gradually spread knowledge of an authentic Neolithic agriculture toward Catalonia in one direction and toward Andalusia in the other. It penetrated most profoundly in Andalusia, moving on from there toward Portugal. Only after a long delay did such substantive achievements reach the center and the north of the Peninsula.

We now find ourselves approximately at the year 2,500 B.C. Andalusia had entered a period of full development under the tutelage of tribe chiefs, who were able to accumulate wealth and occasionally ordered the construction of monumental tombs — a distant reminder of Pharaonic Egypt, the nucleus (albeit now forgotten) of the new Hispanic culture. But this culture did not reach its maximum splendor until a short time later, when navigators from the East, entering through Almería, brought copper metallurgy and the megalithic religion to Spain. During these years, perhaps on the eve of the second millennium, the first Hispanic peoples were wrenched out of the Old Stone Age and set on the path they would follow during their recorded history.

The impact on the Peninsula of a third wave from the East — one related, perhaps, to the hegemony of Crete in the Aegean — led to an astounding cultural florescence. These missionaries of the megaliths, the great cathedrals of that era, demonstrated not only the process and art of obtaining copper but also a religion of high moral values, presided over by a cult of the dead, the dispensers of all fertility, and by a cult of fire and lightning, which purified and consecrated. They carried their gospel as far as Portugal and Castile, which at that moment acquired their first cultural solidarity, and

---

[3] Cardial Ware, the first pottery made in Spain (Neolithic, 5,000–2,500 B.C.), derives its name from *Cardium edule*, the seashell most often used to incise designs on broad-base bowls and jugs. It resembles ware found in the eastern Mediterranean and in Italy. Pericot and Bosch Gimpera believe that it inspires the Bell Beaker pottery (see p. 10).

moved on to Brittany, Cornwall, and Ireland. In all these regions, megaliths triumphed in various styles: passage graves with cupolas, dolmens, galleries, and cists.

Under the influence of megalithic culture, southern Spain achieved her first golden age. A series of powerful chieftains, who had established their residence in Almería (at the site of Los Millares)[4] and in the rich agrarian regions of Andalusia (near the present-day cities of Carmona, Antequera, Seville, and Huelva), governed an active and diligent people skilled in a great variety of art crafts. The bell beaker (*vaso campaniforme*), an imitation of the fine baskets woven by the peasants of the Guadalquivir valley, was created by this culture. Some people would like to relate the diffusion of the bell beaker to the diffusion of a brachycephalic people coming from Asia Minor. Such a hypothesis, which enormously complicates the cultural picture of Hispania at the end of the Neolithic era, quite possibly need not be accepted. Perhaps a group of nomadic artisans set out from Andalusia itself, or from the Mediterranean coast, and was later to be found at all strategic crossroads of the international trade in that era: in Catalonia and in Alsace, on the lower Rhine and in Moravia, in Saxony and on the lower Elbe. The spread of the bell beaker corresponds to the cultural potential generated in Andalusia by her conversion to megalithic culture.

The Pyrenees constituted another zone conquered by a megalithic people. Groups of mesocephalic shepherds, distant precursors of present-day Basques, colonized the mountain range from the Basque country to Catalonia, erecting dolmen monuments everywhere. Thus a new cultural area can be delineated, an area of transition situated between Languedoc and the Ebro river valley; in many ways this recalls the Aquitaine-Cantabrian area of cave art and its residuum, the Azilian culture.

Following this era of megalithic brilliance, Peninsular peoples

---

[4] Los Millares is an excavated site of a major fortified settlement of the Copper Age, near Santa Fe de Mondujar in the province of Almería. The carbon–14 technique has been used to date one tomb (2430 B.C. ±120), one of the first dates in Spanish prehistory to be established by this technique.

Colonizers and Invaders

gradually degenerated. A cultural decline can be observed in Portugal and Andalusia, along the Mediterranean coast and in the Pyrenees — not to speak of the central plateau (la Meseta)[5] and the Cantabrian periphery. The Peninsula would be revived by bronze metallurgy, introduced between 1900 and 1600 B.C. by a people who also settled in the region of Almería and from there spread their knowledge of the new bronze techniques, together with a series of artistic, martial, and cultural archetypes, to the east coast, the center, and the south. Possibly these people did not move about, but instead, as was usual in such cases, were groups of colonizers working through a system of trading stations. In either case, their role in spreading civilization was the same. Archaeologists, who have entitled this the culture of El Argar,[6] have once again failed to be precise.

Peninsular affairs achieved Mediterranean stature at the time of the culture of El Argar. The states of the Near East needed tin to manufacture their weapons and tools, and tin was to be found only in the far distant West or else on the Hispanic steppes. This induced Phoenicians to make their appearance in the life of Tarshish, a land rich in silver, minerals, and exotic objects. Tarshish is the biblical version of Tartessus, the rich capital of Andalusia. The Phoenicians settled along the coast, specifically in Cádiz,[7] at the beginning of the first millennium B.C., and initiated a series of advantageous commercial and cultural contacts that made a deep impression in eastern Mediterranean ports. In all of them, the fabulous treasures of the West were discussed.

The Greeks, to a certain degree the successors of the Cretans,

---

[5] The central plateau, or *meseta*, corresponds roughly to the tablelands of Old Castile and New Castile.

[6] El Argar in Almería, twelve miles from the coast, is the type-site of a relatively advanced, semi-urban Bronze Age culture.

[7] Cádiz (derived from the Phoenician name, Gadir) is traditionally believed to have been founded about 1100 B.C., which would make it the oldest city in western Europe. Recent historians have favored a much later date — ca. 800 — on the ground that it is unlikely that Cádiz was founded before Carthage was in the eighth century. However, the attraction of Spain's metal deposits makes the prior foundation of Cádiz credible.

decided to repeat the maritime adventure of the Phoenicians, and so, sailing directly from Asia Minor or from their colonies in Italy, Magna Graecia, and in Provence, they plunged into Spain (sixth century B.C.). One of their principal settlements was Emporion (on the gulf of the Rosas river in Catalonia), the Iberian keystone of the Greek West.[8] Phoenicians and Greeks transformed into a mighty force the wealth of the Iberians, a generic term for the inhabitants of the Mediterranean coast from Catalonia to Andalusia. Concurrently, an event of indisputable importance occurred in the interior.

The Celts had entered through the Pyrenees (900 to 650 B.C.). After they had occupied a large part of the Peninsula, possibly as far south as the Tajo and Jucar rivers, they disseminated knowledge of the technique of iron metallurgy acquired in their homeland on the Danube. This invasion had immediate effects on various material and cultural factors in the life of the Peninsula. Furthermore, in certain locations this warrior caste imposed itself upon a population of farmers, while in other places it merged with the natives. We are very badly informed about this entire development and we always will be, for Celts introduced the incineration of corpses and Iberians adopted the custom. And so the dead have been silenced forever.

Linguistics and archaeology, when applied to the problem, only create bones of contention. One group of authors views the Celts as the predecessors of the Germanic peoples on the Peninsula, with everything this might presuppose about the Visigoths and their unitary monarchy. Others view the Iberians in the south and the east as the archetypes of subsequent Hispanic idiosyncrasy. Nothing could be less convincing. Both the Celts and the Iberians were very

---

[8] Emporion (in Spanish, Ampurias), founded by Phocaean Greeks ca. 580 B.C., was far less important commercially than their colony of Massilia (Marseille). But after their naval defeat by the Carthaginians (Alalia, 535 B.C.), the Greeks were forced to abandon their trading colonies in southeastern Spain. Meanwhile the Celts cut Massilia off from interior trade. Emporion now became the entrepôt for trade with the West, particularly overland to metal-rich Andalusia.

complex groups; no psychological canon be applied to either one of them, and still less one that is merely intuitive and generalized — the Iberians as farmers and urban dwellers, a tractable and rather inconsistent people; the Celts as shepherds, rustic, crude, and violent. We know only that their languages, like their attitudes to life, were different. But still another millennium was to elapse between these Iberians and Celts and the future *Hispani*.

At the moment when Rome was about to make her appearance, the Peninsula still looked very primitive. The only exceptions were Andalusia (or Turdetania) and the Mediterranean area (or Iberia), where foreign cultural and economic influences had been most intensive. A powerful separatism was manifested everywhere, as much among the chiefs of the rich Iberian populations along the Mediterranean coast, as among the Celtiberian and Celtic princes in the interior. Within the latter group, the Lusitanians (in Portugal) stood out, both because of their greater economic potential and their discordant social structure.

As for the north, along the Cantabrian Sea and in Galicia, it remained primitive and distrustful of any novelty. Until the tenth century, the recuperative forces of the nation would be kept in reserve in this area.

CHAPTER THREE

Roman Hispania

The vicissitudes of the Second Punic War (third century B.C.), by means of which Rome and Carthage settled the question of who would dominate the western Mediterranean, converted the Hispanic peninsula for the first time into an arena of importance in universal history. In order to offset the Roman victories in Sicily, the Barca family of Carthage (Hamilcar, Hasdrubal, and Hannibal) feverishly adapted the Hispanic peninsula for use as a strategic base.[1] Its inhabitants were thrust into the great Mediterranean conflict with no premonition that when it ended, their social and cultural panorama would be completely transformed.

For when the Romans launched their counterattack against Hannibal's overwhelming campaign in Italy, they sent to the Hispanic coasts not only an army led by the Scipio family,[2] but also a complex

---

[1] A primary objective of the Barca family was to prepare for the overland invasion of Italy, for which they had to secure men and provisions on the Peninsula and protect the future rearguard of their armies. Therefore, Hamilcar (270?–228 B.C.), his son-in-law Hasdrubal (d. 221 B.C.) and then his sons Hannibal (247–183 B.C.) and Hasdrubal led troops inland from their coastal bases, beginning the conquest of the Iberian peninsula which the Romans would complete.

[2] The prestige of the Scipio family was closely linked to military campaigns in Hispania. P. Cornelius Scipio (d. 211 B.C.) and his brother Gnaeus were killed fighting on the Peninsula. In 212 the son of Cornelius, P. Cornelius Scipio — later called Africanus — captured Cartagena; he eventually defeated Hannibal. Africanus' adoptive grandson, Scipio Aemilianus (185–129 B.C.) returned to conquer Numantia, the last Hispanic city to resist Rome.

mentality — one that drew its inspiration from the distant shores of the Aegean and its nuances from the temperament and customs of the Latium. Once the Legions had triumphed over the Carthaginians, thanks to the skill of P. Cornelius Scipio, they went on to incorporate within the nascent Roman Empire a colony — Hispania. Simultaneously they initiated the country into the most complex perfections of Hellenic culture, whereof the inhabitants had savored only the first fruits in the period immediately following the establishment of Greek colonies on the east coast of the Peninsula.

Like any process of thoroughgoing colonization, the Roman conquest of Peninsular soil aroused violent opposition among the natives. There is no need to seek in this a singular patriotic ideal; it was merely the response of the native to the novelties and expropriations imposed by foreigners. Endowed with a superior organization, the latter rapidly overcame the successive uprisings which fame has elevated to the rank of epic greatness.

The pacification of the central plateau, however, did turn out to be far more difficult than that of the Mediterranean and Andalusian regions, where an old tradition of interchange with foreign peoples had prepared the terrain to accept Roman domination. On the central plateau, protected by easily defended mountain accesses — such as those leading into the rugged terrain of the Celtiberians — the Romans had to combat a pertinacious hostility, the tone of which intensified as the Legions moved inland from their bases on the coast. This fact explains the tenacious resistance, first of the Lusitanians and later of the Numantines. Rome was forced to modify her recruiting system in order to subdue the city of Numantia, whose independence was vanquished by Scipio Aemilianus in 133 B.C. This is a basic date for the Roman colonization of the Peninsula; the subjugation of Asturians and Cantabrians, carried out one hundred years later by Augustus Caesar, was more a large-scale police action than a war.

In the course of their seven centuries of domination, Roman conquerors and colonizers made their presence felt even in the farthest confines of the country, and this presence was translated into tangible factors: renovation, construction, and beautification of cities; opening of communication systems; cultivation of agricultural soil; exploitation of mines. The policy of public works was financed by meshing the Hispanic economy into the great Mediterranean commerce of that era in metals, wines, olive oil, and grains.

Those who profited most from this activity were the great capitalists in Rome, a fact that must be taken into account. Within the Hispanic provinces, the economic prosperity of the first and second centuries (A.D.) redounded to the benefit of the ancient tribal chiefs, transformed into powerful landowners under the auspices of Roman legislation, and to the benefit of foreign bureaucrats, who used their savings to acquire rural estates on the Hispanic periphery (particularly along the Guadalquivir river). This development, whereby geographical and technical factors merged with Tartessian traditions and Rome's economic needs, gave rise to one of the basic socioeconomic structures of Spanish history: an agrarian economy based on large landed estates (latifundia). At its height, this system combined the use of slave labor with the development of a program of day laborers, employed only for a season.

Thus a privileged social class gradually took shape, the class of *seniores*, who from their urban property, or from their country estates and rural *villas*,[3] dominated the mechanism of Hispanic colonial society. They held in their hands the wealth of the country, not only from the exploitation of agriculture, but also from ownership of stocks in mining and thermal enterprises and in companies exporting olive oil and grains. After the second century (A.D.), through a process of historical evolution, this group would reduce its membership and augment its power.

Beneath this nucleus of aristocrats lived a great mass of farmers and shepherds, undoubtedly the largest group in the country. Almost no one has been concerned with their social position or with their way of life. In some regions of Andalusia, along the Mediterranean coast, and in the Ebro river valley, farmers were reduced to slavery. On the central plateau, semi-free peasants resided in villages

---

[3] The *villa*, usually the seat of a seignorial domain, was a town possessing special privileges that distinguished it from a *pueblo* (town) or *aldea* (village).

belonging to large landowners. Shepherds lived in Galicia and along the Cantabrian coast. In all, they constituted some six million human beings, over whom a nearby city, a newly installed colony, little by little exerted influence.

From the city these farmers and shepherds would accept administration, technical progress, and (with far greater difficulty) the new language and oriental religions. In contrast, they always rejected the juridical system that chained them to their lords, either as slaves or semi-free laborers initially, as villeins bound to a lord in the last phase of the Empire. Opposition between the countryside and the city is a constant in the dynamics of Hispania. It explains why some pastoral tribes ferociously maintained a liberty that they more than once confused with banditry. In fact, some peoples in the north never did become cogs in the political and bureaucratic machinery installed by Rome. A brave and indomitable people, they took up a position on the fringe of the Hispanic community — not because they adapted themselves to its ways, but because they were forced to live there.[4]

The city dwellers constituted a third world that must be inserted between that of the aristocrats (*seniores*) and that of the farmers and shepherds (*humiliores*) — two worlds closely interlocked yet possessing little solidarity. Rome's success in colonizing Spain must be definitively attributed to these Hispanic urban dwellers. There were only a few colonies of Romans, and they were badly distributed in space and in time; therefore the direct participation of Romans was so small that it cannot possibly be considered a factor of importance when speaking of the Romanization of Hispania.

The Hispanic cities extended over a relatively broad area of the Peninsula. Although there were not too many of them, and they were not themselves very brilliant, they fulfilled their role as vertebrae of Mediterranean culture on the Peninsula. They were incorporated into the juridical system of Rome in successive stages, until in A.D. 212 they received from Emperor Caracalla full rights of

---

[4] For a more complete explanation of this point, see José María Millás Vallicrosa (b. 1897), *Nuevos estudios sobre historia de la ciencia española* (Barcelona, 2d, rev. ed., 1960), pp. 32–33.

Map 2

Roman Hispania under Augustus 7-2 B.C.

citizenship. The inhabitants were thus linked together, not by means of any sentiments of "hispanization" but by an imperial idea. In the course of the first and second centuries (A.D.), Hispania was thoroughly transformed into a Roman province, and this phenomenon was due exclusively to the mental attitude of her citizens. Everything reminded them of Rome: the enriched local magistrate, the bureaucrat, the educator.

From these cities — most of which had roots in the cultures of Almería, of El Argar, or of Iberia — young Hispani set out, attracted by the dazzling center of Rome. In that City, greatest of all cities, a few became successful and bedecked themselves with the laurels of fame in politics or literature. But the distinguished names of the Senecas and Lucan,[5] Martial and Quintilian,[6] as well as those of the Emperors Trajan and Hadrian,[7] represent only the foam which yesterday, as today, concealed a sea of repeated and anonymous failures. As a result of the good fortune of the first group, and the reverses of the latter, the urban element slowly forged the notion of a common conscience, linked with the idea of Rome. The mentality of the Hispani, or Hispano-Romans, thereby made its appearance. Rather than a social class (as certain resolute institutional historians of the Germanic school have claimed), the Hispani constituted a mentality that was urban and peripheral;[8] because this is important, it is worth repeating.

These same cities constituted so many seedbeds where the Gospel took root and fructified. Reaching the Mediterranean coast in the middle of the first century (a probable mission of St. Paul), the doctrine of Christ prospered in that urban medium, which was already dominated by the power and culture of Rome yet was empty of a higher mystical ideal; it had found no fulfillment in the superficiality and skepticism of the imperial cults. As elsewhere in the West, the dissemination of Christianity in Spain brought on a conflict with the traditionalism of peasant religiosity; only with exhausting slowness did it win the battle against pagan rites. But the

---

[5] In the Silver Age of Rome, the Hispano-Roman family of the Senecas gained high renown: Marcus Annaeus Seneca, the rhetorician (54 B.C.– A.D. 38), and his more famous son, Lucius Annaeus Seneca, the Stoic philosopher (5 B.C.?–A.D. 65). The latter's nephew, Marcus Annaeus Lucanus, wrote poetry (A.D. 39–65). All three were born in Córdoba.

[6] Quintilian, the author of two books on rhetoric (A.D. 35?–100), was from Logroño in the north of Spain. Martial, the epigrammatist (A.D. 40–102), was also from the north, from Calatayud.

[7] Trajan (A.D. 53–117) ruled as Emperor 98–117. His nephew, Hadrian (A.D. 75–138), succeeded him as Emperor 117–138. Both men were born in Italica, near Seville. Of all these men, probably only the writer Martial and Quintilian had any Hispanic blood; the others were merely born in Spain of Roman parents.

[8] Vicens employs the term peripheral here and throughout the book to refer to the coastal areas — richer agriculturally, more densely populated, and in more direct contact with foreign cultures — in contrast to the hinterland (the meseta or central plateau). See map 1.

cities ended by imposing themselves on the countryside, and the periphery imposed itself on the central plateau, so that by the end of the second century Hispanic Christians were offering up to their Lord the same bouquet of martyrs for the faith as the Eastern churches. In this fashion, Christianity, introduced together with Latin and its sequitur of Mediterranean culture, completed the work of Romanization. In certain cases, as in that of the indigenous peoples in the north, one has reason to suspect that the spirit of Rome became firmly established in the land only by means of this new religious ideal. In certain notable cases, this evangelization would bear no fruit until well along in the Middle Ages.

In the first few centuries during which Christianity spread throughout Hispania, its attitude toward Rome was very different from the attitude it adopted after the Edict of Milan in 313. Christianity had expanded by openly opposing all state religions and, above all, by opposing the imperial cult. Therefore it did not constitute an element linking Hispania to Rome, but was rather an element of dissidence among the underprivileged in urban society.

This verified statement obliges us to revise many contemporary ideas about the role which Rome played in unifying Hispania. Neither the Emperors, nor the Senate, nor minor Roman administrative officials ever viewed Hispanic problems as a separate matter, nor did they encourage any tendency in that direction. They and the gilded Hispanic youth felt only the greatness and the unity of the City and of her universal dominions. But of necessity, in the course of their transactions, they initiated a series of measures that contributed to the development of a certain sense of community among the inhabitants of Hispania. We cannot include here the imperial cult (a cult which was practiced by a skeptical bourgeoisie of businessmen in the first century A.D.), nor the administration of the provinces (which was in the hands of Romans and tended more to separate than to unite the Hispani). The forces of unification came from the technicians and communication engineers, from city planners and sculptors, from teachers and bureaucrats, who were sent out by Rome; such forces were translated into beautiful cities, perfectly paved roads, bridges and viaducts, and to some degree into administration. All of this — we repeat — was on the periphery of the peasants' world; many of the things taught to them — things such as law, and language (which was immediately adulterated into specific individual patterns, differentiated according to regions) remained a dead letter.

Hispania's historic personality actually did not begin to develop until the onset of the crisis of the third century. Between 264 and 276 the Hispanic provinces were barbarically devastated by Franks and Suevi, their principal cities sacked and destroyed, the countryside razed without mercy. Slowly the country rallied from that calamity; those cities able to recuperate surrounded themselves with walls and fortified towers. A new world began, outwardly functioning in accord with the drastic measures of the absolutist Emperors, yet inwardly beginning to form a new society, which, because of bonds of legal and personal servitude, was subject to its most powerful members. And at this point, while urban life decayed and the nation turned rural, the Hispanic people began to move along the path of their history — not that of great history, which neither explains nor justifies anything (such as the useless reorganization of imperial administration at the beginning of the fourth century, which placed the diocese of Hispania *under* the prefecture of Gaul), but the history constituted by the smallest ephemerae. One example might be the change in attitude which led the Christian bishops of Hispania to establish an ecclesiastical organization in the image of the Roman organization — that is, to absorb the state-oriented, hierarchical, and cultural spirit of Rome and, in short, to accept the Christianization of the Empire and official protection as consummate facts.

Thus at the end of the fourth century, the Church crossed the frontier that had formerly separated it from the Empire and was transformed into the fundamental bulwark of the ideas of authority and universality that Rome had imposed on Mediterranean lands. As a result of this concept of the world, and as a result of the actual experiences of the bishops (unexpectedly transformed by the invasions into "defenders of the cities"), the Empire outlived itself in Hispania.

CHAPTER FOUR

The Visigothic Mirage

The invasion of the Germanic peoples through the western passes of the Pyrenees — the eternal route of Europe's great racial contributions to Hispania — took place in the year 409. This was not the first such invasion, nor were there a significant number of invaders. Yet these relatively few men had the advantage of a decisive factor: once Rome's defenses along the frontier on the Rhine had been incapacitated, the inhabitants of her Hispanic provinces found themselves powerless to confront the military bands that the invaders had formed. This explains why Vandals, Suevi, and Alans were able to plunder extensively and with great ease, and why the sensation of terror (crystallized in the accounts of contemporaries), when coupled with the memory of the harsh treatment by the Franks barely two generations earlier, led to a general air of defeatism. Salvation could be expected only from venerable Rome, but she was experiencing identical hardships and suffering equal horrors. Rome was now nothing more than a myth.

This Roman mirage would be used to advantage by another Germanic people — the Visigoths — as the means for establishing their hegemony on the Peninsula during the fifth and sixth centuries. There has been a clearly erroneous impression that Visigothic Hispania began in 415, when Ataulf led his troops as far as Barcelona and established an ephemeral capital there.[1] The Visigoths

---

[1] In 418 the Romans signed a pact with Wallia, Ataulf's successor as chief, which granted the Visigoths the right to own lands in Aquitaine and a semi-autonomous jurisdiction over them. In exchange, the Visigoths assumed responsibility for restoring the three Hispanic provinces

The Visigothic Mirage

actually operated during the fifth century from a base in Toulouse, France, as a "federated" army in the service of Rome. In Hispania this army drove the Suevi into a corner in Galicia, and ousted the Vandals from Murcia and Andalusia. But its principal field of activity was the south of France, a rich agricultural complex over which Euric (466-484) succeeded in imposing his authority. Simultaneously Visigothic chieftains, either as auxiliaries of the Roman Empire or on their own behalf, took possession of important redoubts on the central plateau of Spain. The Mediterranean periphery, still linked with the world of the legitimate Empire (at first that of Rome and later that of Constantinople), proved from the beginning to be far more opposed to any such substitution of power. Consequently, when the Visigoths sought refuge beyond the curtain of the Pyrenees from the Franks (who defeated them at Vouillé in 507 and expelled them from Gaul), although they did vacillate somewhat between Barcelona and Seville, they did not establish their capital in the rich and cultivated regions along the Tarragonian, Carthaginian, or Baetican coastline, but in the heart of the Peninsula — in Toledo. For the first time, the central plateau became the political center of the Peninsula.

This event augmented the differences that already existed between the eighty or one hundred thousand Goths who occupied the interior high plateau of the country (Segovia, Soria, Burgos, Madrid, Toledo, Valladolid, and Palencia), and the three or four million Hispani who lived along the Mediterranean coast from Septimania to Baetica.

A good number of the Hispani, with armed support from the Eastern Empire, freed themselves of the barbarian menace and began to play a role once more in the culture and economy of the Mediterranean. Stretching from Cartagena on the Mediterranean to the Algarve in Portugal (an area called Byzantine Spain in the textbooks), this piece of liberated Hispania reconstituted her forces and

---

to the Roman empire. In the absence of effective Roman control, the Visigoths gradually interpreted their obligations in Hispania to include the right to govern the area and thereby to establish a basis for their subsequent claim to be the legitimate successors of Rome.

prepared for the great historic occasion of the Hispanic retaliation against the Visigothic invaders — not, certainly, a military retaliation, but rather one of vitality and culture.

The Germanic people's last great effort to assimilate the Hispani was carried out by Leovigild (568–586). Actually this monarch had already succumbed to the Hispanic mentality, a consequence of the events during the preceding two generations when Gothic aristocrats had ceased to be chiefs of military bands and had become wealthy property owners, to some extent related by marriage with the Hispanic landowners. Leovigild was the first Germanic sovereign to don royal insignia, Roman style, and the first to consider his dominions as being an imperial legacy. His campaigns eliminated the Suevi redoubts in Galicia, where a few chieftains, using titles of nobility, had maintained their power. Simultaneously, he forced Cantabrians and Basques to acknowledge Visigothic sovereignty. Leovigild also set out to subdue southern Spain, which was still linked to the Byzantine Empire, but although he acquired the Guadalquivir valley by means of military operations, he was unable to win the favor of his new subjects.

In 582 a wave of insurrection roused the Hispani, and became all the more critical when Hermenigild, Leovigild's own son, took over as leader. After innumerable vicissitudes the rebellion was suppressed. Hermenigild fell as a sacrifice, a martyr in the fight for the Catholic faith and, obviously, for what that faith represented as the affirmation of a spirit and of a culture.

This tremendous experience turned out to be definitive. In 585 Hermenigild was executed; his father (Leovigild) died the following year; in 587 his successor, Reccared, was converted to Catholicism; in 589 the Third Council of Toledo publicly solemnized the change in the dogma of the Visigothic state, which until then had supported the Arian doctrine. Within a four-year period the revolt of the Hispani, extinguished by arms, had triumphed within the very conscience of the ruling Germanic minority. From that time on, this clan (composed of some two hundred families at court and some ten thousand men and women spread throughout the rest of the country) became an almost closed oligarchy. It arrogated the

The Visigothic Mirage

highest offices, the command of the army, the leading posts in the provincial administration.

But the Hispani kept the country going. They were the ones who shaped the legislation, the spiritual life, and the relative economic splendor of the Visigothic monarchy during the seventh century. The gateway to these advances was opened by St. Leander and St. Isidore, the two giants of the Hispanic intellectual world of southern Spain.[2] Because of the Hispani the last stage of Gothic domination over the Peninsula acquired a markedly unified character; after Islam's effortless, demolishing offensive in the eighth century, the memory of this unity would survive among some scattered groups.

Therefore, if Visigothic epigonism on the Peninsula managed to survive despite its own incapacity, it was because of the broad social support offered by the Hispani and, singularly, by the Church and the aristocracy of large landowners. This bond of common interests (for the fusion of blood was always very difficult) had a fatal effect upon the lot of the lower classes of society, especially in the countryside, where slavery and tenant farming had survived. And this was true despite the development of ties of personal dependency characteristic of the Germanic mentality. This development ran parallel to that of monarchs' approving grants of immunity to specific sectors of the population: nobles, churches, and monasteries. All this, when combined with the feeling of social insecurity nurtured in the wake of the invasions, created a pre-feudal atmosphere very similar to that of Merovingian France.

The collapse of the Hispano-Roman municipality, initiated before the barbarian invasion, was consummated in this period because of the debilitation of the money economy and the gradual cessation of mercantile activities; only a few ports along the Mediterranean coast showed any commercial initiative. The urban class, the verte-

---

[2] St. Isidore (560–636) succeeded his brother St. Leander (550?–601?) as Bishop of Seville. St. Isidore is most renowned for his great etymological encyclopedia (written between 627 and 630), the most complete compendium of classical and ecclesiastical knowledge of that era. In his famous prologue to *History of the Kings of the Goths, Vandals and Suevi*, he views Gothic Hispania as heir to Rome's Empire.

brae of Roman Hispania, was thereby extinguished. Its members became dependent upon the protection of Visigothic nobles or of Hispanic lords. Only one escape route remained open to them — the Church, the only truly free body in that era. In their monasteries or episcopal sees, ecclesiastics embarked upon the silent and tenacious task of remaking a world whose glories they perceived but could only crudely interpret.

It was the clergy who gave definitive legal form to the Visigothic state, thanks to the work of legislative unification begun by Chindaswinth and finished in 654 by his son, Recceswinth.[3] The value of the *Liber judiciorum* is not only that it shows a determination that Rome shall survive in a world which is absolutely foreign and impervious to it, but also that the Church required just such an instrument to use in mediating between the Hispanic people and the Gothic oligarchy. The only previous contact between these two groups had been that of owner with serf. However, the haughty Visigothic aristocrats, firmly established in the land, had made such a profound impression that even their baptismal names were imitated. The nobility of the early Middle Ages would build upon this base of personal psychological triumph.

The relationships of power, however, differ greatly from those derived solely from social admiration. Between the Visigothic monarchy and the people of Hispania lay unfathomable abysses. One way of covering these over, of building a bridge, was through the Church. Qualified to represent the people to the throne, and the throne to the people, the Church acquired a place within the state apparatus as a legitimate intermediary between the king and his

---

[3] Chindaswinth, who ruled from 642–653, and his son, Recceswinth, began preparation of the *Liber judiciorum* in 649 in order to provide a common civil and penal law code for Hispani (judged by Roman law) and Visigoths (judged by Germanic law). In the early Middle Ages it was the law code of the Kingdom of León; in the thirteenth century, translated into Castilian (*Fuero Juzgo*), it was the law code of Castile. Eduardo de Hinojosa believed that the *Liber*'s origins were Germanic customary law (*El Elemento germánico en el Derecho español*, Madrid, 1910). Since 1953 Alfonso García Gallo has argued it is basically a Roman law code modified by Germanic custom.

The Visigothic Mirage

subjects. It was in this way that the monarchy acknowledged the legislative authority of the Councils of Toledo. Yet this development cost the Church a great deal of her essential autonomy in such matters as the independent selection of bishops, and she drifted into a conformist attitude that may perhaps have been the principal cause of the distintegration of the Visigothic monarchy. In any event, the experiment was not wasted. After a lapse of time, the Visigothic precedent would be revived as the historic basis for demanding the Catholic unity of the State.

A fragile edifice, Visigothic royalty was unable to overcome its own contradictions — economic, social, ethnic, and religious — when confronted by even the slightest threat from abroad. In 711, amid general indifference, it collapsed.[4] The Gothic oligarchy capitulated in many areas. Some survivors of the old administration found refuge in the Cantabrian north. The Visigothic masses who had settled in Castile were, after the lapse of a century, moved to Galicia. There they were peacefully absorbed by a people who would become the future Galicians and Portuguese.

---

[4] There are two traditional accounts of the Visigothic debacle. One is that after Roderick was elected king of the Visigoths in 710, his defeated opponents (sons of the previous king, Witiza) formed an alliance with the Muslims and fought at their side in the battle of Guadalete, where King Roderick was slain. A variation on the same theme (calling upon foreign allies to resolve a domestic problem) is the legend that King Roderick had dishonored a Visigothic lady, Caba; her father, Count Julian, invited the Muslims to invade, as a means for avenging Caba's honor.

CHAPTER FIVE

The Triumph of Islam

In 711, after various preliminary trial incursions, the great Muslim wave swept over the Peninsula. Islam, which had slowly gained possession of the southern coastline of the Mediterranean until it finally reached ancient Mauretania (Morocco), undertook the task of subjugating the Hispano-Visigothic kingdom with sparse forces and confused objectives. Its rapid triumph following the victorious battle waged on the shores of the Guadalete river must be ascribed not only to the Muslims' superior training in military techniques, but also to the disintegration of the fragile political and institutional structure of Gothic society. Unable to perform its mission of armed defense (which had been assigned to the Germanic military nobility), the Visigothic state collapsed when confronted with the simultaneous upheaval of the Hispanic masses.

We lack the accurate details which would provide a clear picture of what happened during the Hispanic uprising from 711 to 715, the five critical years during which the country fell — like a ripe fruit — into the hands of Tarik and Musa, the generals of the Caliphate of Damascus. But it seems quite possible to me that a majority of the Hispanic people would be opposed to the domination of the Gothic ruling classes, and that they would even take part in a rebellion against the nobility and landowners.

There was a vigorous resurgence of Spanish separatism following the Visigothic catastrophe. Some cities and certain chieftains willingly accepted a regime of local autonomy under Muslim protection — as did Theodemir in Murcia. From this profound social transformation emerged Islamic Spain. It was not a Spain alien to her traditions, an adversary deserving of destruction (as it was adjudged to be from the twelfth century on), but was as authentic as Visigothic Spain had been. The Arabs, Syrians, and Berbers who constituted the first armies of conquest (as usual, few in number) contentedly settled in the country and during their generation made no attempt to modify its system of intellectual values. Their fundamental concern was to secure the greatest possible share of the lands confiscated from the Visigothic public domains and large private properties. These aspirations provoked sharp clashes among the invaders themselves until an Umayyad prince, Abd-ar-Rahman, arrived on the Peninsula.

A fugitive from the disaster suffered by his family in the Caliphate of Damascus, Abd-ar-Rahman I (756–788) extinguished the endemic civil war waged by the different racial groups who made up the Muslim troops. Then he organized the Islamic regime in Spain, severed the political bond which had previously linked the governors (Emirs) with the East, and established the bases for a new state which was to last for two and one-half centuries, through periods of overbearing power and others of obscure decline.

As against the bands of Christian shepherds in the Cantabrian mountains who remained invincible (an inevitable and by now traditional phenomenon), Abd-ar-Rahman I wanted his state to represent the one and only viable Spain. To achieve that end, his successors were forced to restrict the freedom enjoyed by those natives of Hispania who, scorning the advantages that such an act entailed, had not abjured the Catholic faith. They were called Mozarabs, to distinguish them from the renegades (*muladíes*).[1] Mostly city dwellers, they were survivors of the ancient bourgeoisie and of the artisans of the Roman era who had remained faithful to their beliefs. Firmly organized by the Visigothic Church, whose principal hierarchs resided in territory conquered by the Muslims,

---

[1] Hispani who converted to Islam (Spanish, *muladíes*; Arabic, *muwalladun*) spoke Arabic (primarily, if not exclusively) and adopted Muslim customs. So did the Mozarabs, the Hispani who remained Christian and continued to speak a vulgar Latin. But, as indicated in the Arabic term from which their name derives (*musta'ribun*, meaning one who is "Arabized"), Mozarabs imitated much of the superior Islamic culture and learned Arabic for their business and public activities.

the Mozarabs proved able to resist every attempt to assimilate them. Even after the battle waged over the Adoptionist heresy[2] at the end of the eighth century (the outcome of which signified the end of the subordination of Asturian bishops to the Visigothic hierarchy), Mozarabism stood firm. In the cities of Andalusia during the time of Emir Muhammad I (852–886), it led many of its members to martyrdom, or stimulated rebellions such as the one in Toledo in 853. Under these circumstances, Mozarabism ceased to be a dogmatic distinction and became an indigenous dissident movement that had an effect even on the renegades. The political expression of this complex of objectives is to be found in the rebellion of Umar-ibn-Hafsun, a renegade of Gothic ancestry, in the mountains of Ronda (899–917), and in the triumph of the indigenous element in Saragossa, Toledo, Mérida, and other cities of Islamic Spain.

Mozarabism is a factor, therefore, which one cannot discount when evaluating the historical life of Spain during the first three centuries of Muslim domination. In the forefront of various wars and political events, it represents a way to understand both the spiritual substrata of Emirate society and the problematical relationship between Muslims and Christians. The Mozarab form of Vulgate Latin, its religious rites, art, culture, and poetry spread slowly from Andalusia to the north; in varying degrees of intensity, these reached Asturias, León, Castile, Portugal, Aragon, and even Catalonia. At times Mozarabs en masse crossed the frontier separating Islam from Christianity and under the protection of the Asturian armies established communities in territories these armies had conquered and were in the process of repopulating. Of special impor-

---

[2] Adoptionism was a heresy that developed among the Mozarabs, based on certain terms in their liturgy and in the apocalypse of St. John, which implied that Jesus was not divine but the adopted son of God. It is historically important because the head of the Hispanic Church, resident in Muslim-held Toledo, defended it (784–805), while Charlemagne denounced it, possibly in an effort to gain control over the Church in northern Spain. Asturian Christians did reject Adoptionism and the authority of the primate in Toledo, but they also rejected French ecclesiastical direction; instead the Asturian Christians organized a national church.

tance were the migrations at the end of the ninth century, after Alfonso III the Great had extended the limits of his state southward as far as the shores of the Duero river. We can imagine the technical role which such social groups must have played in the midst of a primitive society of Cantabrian shepherds and warriors. The Mozarab spirit probably influenced the transformation of the Kingdom of Asturias into the ambitious and traditionalist Monarchy of León.

But we must not, however, so exaggerate the impact of the Mozarabs as to argue that even the Emirs and the administrators of Córdoba spoke their special dialect. The opposite interpretation seems now to be far more substantiated. Three centuries after the conquest, the world of the Arabic-speaking Mozarabs had become thoroughly Arab; only occasionally did Mozarabs in Córdoba remember their Gothic origins. Even the artisans who crossed over to the north had only a vague, tenuous idea of what they represented; their technical triumphs can in no way be regarded as a spiritual hallmark, as evidence of a Roman or Visigothic spirit among the Christians.

In contrast, during those same three centuries Islam had achieved a sensational triumph — it converted to the Muhammadan doctrine all the peasants living south of the Duero river in the western sector of the Peninsula, and all the peasants living south of the Pyrenees in the eastern sector. There can be no doubt about this phenomenon; it is the axis around which will revolve the future problems of Hispania — beginning with the repopulation, the reconquest, and the successive failures to assimilate the Moriscos.[3]

By the middle of the tenth century, Hispania was a country with a Muslim majority. Al Andalus was preparing to live through a period of singular splendor, while in the Christian North, deep and taut roots were beginning to give forth runty but robust shoots.

---

[3] Morisco is the term for Muslims living in Christian territory who were forced to accept Christian baptism or leave Spain, from 1502 in Castile and from 1525 in Aragon. Most complied, nominally, but retained the Arabic language and old customs. Unable to assimilate the Moriscos, Spain ordered their expulsion in 1609.

CHAPTER SIX

Asturian Legitimacy and the Frankish Intrusion

After the Islamic invasion, the political continuity of the Visigothic state was broken, and the economic, juridical, and spiritual structure of its society was destroyed — nothing more could be expected of that regime. It was now the responsibility of a new camp, whose definitive boundaries would be established by the conversion of the peasants to Islam. At that moment the Spains, in their pluralistic unity, were born. Along a line from Galicia to Catalonia — at the most, they were like great rocks jutting up out of the waters, bearing witness to the Islamic tide — these enclaves of Christians began their career in history. We must not imagine them brandishing their weapons in heroic fashion. It is better to see them from the viewpoint of the Emirs of al-Andalus: as indomitable bands who from the mountains threatened cities and crops, lines of communication, and the rearguards of armies.

It is a historic paradox that Asturians and Cantabrians, who had always been the groups most obstinately opposed to joining the Peninsular community, should have constituted themselves as the perpetrators of the Hispanic tradition. The groups of warriors from King Roderick's army who took refuge in Asturias [1] may have played a role in this transformation; they supplied leaders for the mountaineers' innate drive for independence and their fight against the Emirs seemed aimed at recapturing the Visigothic kingdom lost

---

[1] The most famous warrior was Pelayo, who established — in however crude a form — the basis for the Asturian monarchy; he ruled from 718–737.

at Guadalete. Since the twelfth century, tradition has taken pleasure in this account of the events, even exaggerating the details. However, the guerrilla activities recorded throughout the eighth century have more the character of the old expeditions of the mountaineers against Roman legions, or against Gothic hosts, than of any ideal of a reconquest.

Yet there is one important fact. The Asturians, or perhaps the Hispani administrators and clergy who had taken refuge there, laid claim to a specific monarchic principle — legitimacy. Although for nearly two centuries this claim had practically no political value, it did make it possible for them to conserve an element that was decisive for their ultimate objectives. This could be plainly seen when the first political difficulties in the Islamic world permitted the Asturian principality to emit some flashes of glory, first in the time of Alfonso I (739-757) and again in that of Alfonso II (791-842).

Dominating the lands of Galicia and Asturias from atop the high passes of the mountains of León and the Cantabrian range, these kings made possible the development of a small and virile cultural world, presided over by a few clergymen. It was the latter group that prepared to cut the umbilical cord which still bound the Asturian ideal to the Mozarabs. Decisive milestones in this process were the battle over Adoptionism (to which I have already referred) and the establishment by Alfonso II of the cult of the Apostle St. James in Compostela (Galicia). However, it is not necessary to go to the extreme of presenting St. James (Santiago) as an anti-Muhammad.

From the middle of the ninth century, through the pens of the scribes who drew up the documents, Asturian legitimacy proclaimed its role as heir to the Visigothic world and, specifically, to the unifying idea of a Hispania under a single monarchy. From 850 to 910, during the reigns of Ordoño I and Alfonso III the Great, this ideology made substantial progress. However, the Pyrenean mountaineers, who had been equally successful in confronting Muslim armies, did not know about the role that the Asturian kings had assumed in the fight against Islam. From Navarre to Urgel in Catalonia, Hispanic communities had remained free of Islamic domination. But along this Pyrenean front there was present an element that was to affect the course of its future history — the Franks.

Through a series of fortuitous circumstances, it became the responsibility of this Germanic people in the eighth century to put an end to Arab expansion in Western Europe (the victory at Poitiers, 732), and to organize the last remnants of the Roman world behind an imperial façade, planned and supported by the Roman Church (the Carolingian Empire, 800). As an extension of the first task, Frankish warriors (outfitted by the governors of Aquitaine) went to the aid of the exiled Hispanic peoples and resettled them on their lands south of the Pyrenees. These objectives, heartily endorsed by Charlemagne himself, were expanded to include the destruction of the Muslim frontier by means of the conquest of Saragossa, an important Mozarab redoubt. But when this great project failed (778),[2] the Franks had to resort to immediate tactical solutions. Therefore they carried out a systematic conquest of Catalonia. Although the Franks were unable to expand beyond this region, their intervention in the ancient territory of the Visigoths had extensive repercussions. On the western side, Navarre's individualist spirit grew until, in the middle of the ninth century, Navarre created its own monarchy under Iñigo Arista. On the eastern side, Charlemagne incorporated within his Empire the Catalan counties which had come into existence in the course of his campaigns between 785 and 801; they were organized into a poorly defined political body called the Hispanic March. There Frankish nobles lived side by side with Visigothic exiles and Hispanic emigrés; below them lived a native population which was quite turbulent as a result of the wars. The Hispanic March protected Europe at the Pyrenees against any possible return of Islamic power; because of this defensive character, it was trans-

---

[2] In retreat from their rout at Saragossa, the Franks were crossing into France through the Basque area of the Pyrenees when they were suddenly attacked at Roncesvalles; many Frankish nobles, including Roland, were killed. The *Chanson de Roland* attributes the attack to Muslim troops; although some may have participated, most of the attacking troops were Basques, angry because Charlemagne, afraid to leave a hostile fortified city in the rear of his retreating army, had burned the walls of Pamplona.

Asturia and the Franks

formed into a military redoubt of the first order, in which the nascent European feudal organization had a privileged field of expansion.

The agricultural colonization of the countryside, the vigorous systematization of vassalage, the dissemination of culture from monasteries in the south of France, and even France's political subordination to Rome, created in Catalonia a society which was different from that of the brave Asturian mountaineers, from that of the great Muslim potentates, and from that of the self-absorbed Mozarabs. An independent dynasty of counts was established in Barcelona by Guifred the Hairy (874–898), who was the descendant of a family that had come from Carcassonne in Languedoc. Despite this dynasty, and despite the fact that they never forgot the urgent problem of defending themselves daily against the powerful Muslim raids, the Catalan counties for two centuries obviously marched to a tune called by France.

CHAPTER SEVEN

The Caliphate of Córdoba
Versus the Kingdom of León

Islam reached its political, economic, and cultural zenith on the Peninsula at the beginning of the tenth century. The introduction of new Persian and Nabatean agricultural techniques, together with the development and improvement of an irrigation system, converted the Guadalquivir river valley, the Genil river depression, and the basins of the Mediterranean coast from Málaga to Tortosa into admirable orchards, cultivated by a growing population of slaves and serfs — a fatal degeneration of the primitive equalitarianism and democracy of the desert.

In the cities (especially in Córdoba, Seville, and Málaga), artisans were busily engaged in weaving silk, working metal, and making pottery, in response to the growing demands of European feudal society. Almería was one of the wealthiest ports in the West, the key to commercial contact between al-Andalus and the Caliphate of Baghdad. Córdoba, the capital of this world, radiated prosperity and elegance. Gold circulated in abundance; Muslim coins, scaling the frontiers of the Christian world, indicated how far the direct influence of Spanish Islam extended.

This wealth was the basis for the reorganization of Islamic power in Spain carried out by Abd-ar-Rahman III (912–961), who founded the Caliphate of Córdoba (929).[1] In order to calm for all time the

---

[1] The title Caliph designates a Muslim ruler with absolute authority in religious matters as well as in civil affairs; his power is limited only by the prescriptions of the Koran. Before 929, the year that Abd-ar-Rahman II proclaimed himself Caliph with the title of "Commander of

provincial separatism and rebellious spirit of nonconformist elements, Abd-ar-Rahman instituted a unified regime under the auspices of his newly acquired authority in religious matters and, even more effectively, by increasing the troops in his army. The Caliphate's economic and military superiority allowed Abd-ar-Rahman III to extend his influence to Morocco in the south and to drive back the armies of León and Navarre in the north. During his reign and that of his successor, al-Hakam II (961–976), al-Andalus was without any doubt the most powerful state in Europe. Her brilliance dazzled the barbarian courts of Europe.

But the military state instituted by Abd-ar-Rahman came too late to eliminate or even to confine the Christian kingdoms on the northern frontier. The Kingdom of Asturias had extended to the shores of the Duero river since the reign of Alfonso III. His son, Ordoño II, abandoned the mountain valleys and established his residence on the high plateau at León (914) — the junction point of the roads to Galicia and Asturias, and of the roads to the frontier regions of the Duero and Ebro rivers. From this center, the kings of León were able to withstand the attacks of the Caliphate armies with varying success; this sustained fight was enhanced by several notable feats of arms (the triumph of Abd-ar-Rahman III at Valdejunquera in 920, and of Ramiro II at Alhandega in 939).

But leaving to one side the outcome of wars, we should devote our attention to a human development of far greater importance — the repopulation of the Duero tableland. The monarchs of León granted extensive privileges to all who would go to repopulate its ancient or newly founded cities and fortified *villas*; this gave rise to an intense process of democratization in the frontier zone. It also engendered a spirit destined to play a celebrated role in Spanish life — the Castilian spirit.

León drew nourishment from her gilded dreams of a restoration, inherited from the Asturians' claim to monarchic legitimacy. Court

---

the Faithful," Muslim rulers in Spain employed the title Emir, exercised only civil and military powers, and recognized the supreme authority of the Caliphs in Baghdad in all religious matters.

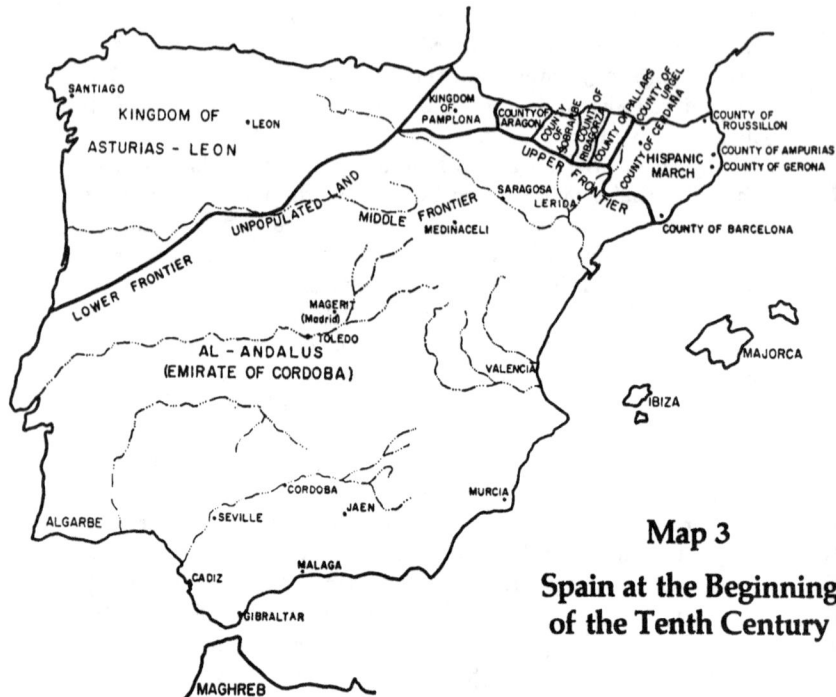

Map 3

Spain at the Beginning of the Tenth Century

clerks engaged in composing chancery documents even used the word *imperator*, although in a sense too ambiguous to be correctly interpreted by modern historical criticism. But when faced with the realities of daily problems, the kings of León failed deplorably. They were incapable of establishing an effective military organization, such as that of the feudal system in force in Europe; incapable of integrating the interests of the mountaineers who had nurtured the monarchy with those of the small agricultural proprietors who defended it on the shores of the Duero river; incapable of absorbing the stimulating democratic militarism engendered in the Castilian zone. Thus they allowed themselves to be dragged into a series of civil disputes that embellished the second half of the tenth century and reflected these regional discrepancies and social conflicts. This situation enabled Castile — in the person of Count Fernán González (961) — to gain her independence from León, and enabled both Navarre and the Caliphate to intervene extensively in the affairs of León.

But most importantly, the Muslims believed the moment had come to vanquish their Christian opponents. Such was the dream and the venture of Hisham II's prime minister, al-Mansur. He transformed the military system of Abd-ar-Rahman III into a true dictatorship, maintained by a professional army of slaves.[2] By draining off the financial resources of al-Andalus into military expeditions, al-Mansur was able to strike extremely telling blows against his adversaries in the north. León, Santiago de Compostela, Barcelona, and many other cities and monasteries in León, Castile, and Catalonia, learned to know a Muslim who granted no mercy. Yet even though the Christians were powerless to resist the Caliphate hordes in the open field, or even from behind the walls of their cities, the frontiers underwent scarcely any modification. This proves that at that moment the borders between Christianity and Islam already marked human limits — population limits — and not strategic positions.

The summer campaigns (*aceifas*) of al-Mansur, which ended in 1002, reduced to bankruptcy the two Hispanic powers of the tenth century — the Caliphate of Córdoba and the Kingdom of León — just at the time of the general recovery of Western Europe. Spain was about to inaugurate an era of profound social, political, and cultural transformations.

---

[2] Some of the slaves were Negroes from Africa, but many were "Slavs," persons of Slavic birth, Franks, and others from the North. Most slaves were eventually freed and settled in Spain; some achieved great political power, particularly during the eleventh century, when they controlled the "Party Kingdoms" in southeastern Spain.

CHAPTER EIGHT

Return to Europe: Navarre and the Spirit of Castile

Having surmounted the calamities of the hundred years that boast the name "the Century of Iron," amid the ruins left by the second wave of invasions (Normans, Magyars), Europe came to life again and bestirred herself to carry out a thorough rehabilitation. The Cluniac reform constituted the motive power of this movement: it represented not only a spiritual reaction against feudalism but also the beginning of the reactivation of Europe's agrarian economy. These influences reached the Christian states of Spain through the Cluniac monasteries of southern France, which established chapter houses from Navarre to Catalonia. In the course of the eleventh century these influences were to be reinforced by the pilgrimages to Santiago de Compostela. The famous road, leading from the basin of the Garonne river to the sepulcher of the Apostle in Compostela became a passageway for commerce, art, and culture, and even made it possible for the kingdoms on the central plateau to establish a direct link with the spirit of the West.

In this vast process of cultural renovation (which would give rise to the Romanesque), Navarre was in a privileged position not only to receive from but to transmit to the rest of Christian Spain, for the routes of pilgrimages and commerce that united Western Christianity with Hispanic Christianity passed through Navarre. To this fact must be attributed the surprising political turn of affairs that brought Navarre to the forefront of the Christian states of the reconquest, a change occurring in the brief space of one generation and culminating in the reign of Sancho III the Great (1000–1035).

Sancho's successful intervention in the affairs of León enabled him to become lord of Castile, and many counties in the Pyrenees accepted his sovereignty and acknowledged him as their king. Sancho's glory even extended to Catalonia, at a moment in which the latter was beginning to recover from the clash with al-Mansur and from the de facto break with France. This was the era of Bishop Oliba,[1] when the Catalan consciousness became aware that it was forming its own unique personality. One generation later Ramón Berenguer I the Elder, Count of Barcelona (1035–1076), would define the peculiar juridical and social character of the country in his famous legal code, the *Usatges*.

The spirit of Navarre — a combination of the spirit of the Hispanic mountaineers with that of Europe — was carried to the central plateau and took hold in Castile through a successful maneuver by which Sancho's son succeeded to the throne of Castile (Ferdinand I, 1035–1065).[2] This eliminated León from her position as the principal kingdom on the high plateau of the Duero river and elevated Castile to the front rank of Hispanic politics.

We have here a transcendental moment in Peninsular affairs in which Castile actually made her appearance in history. The Castilian people — of Cantabrian and Basque blood — were in agreement that their society was to be open, dynamic, and bold, as are all social structures on an advancing frontier. A people of shepherds and peasants, they led their flocks beyond the Duero river (the area of Coria in Extremadura) or they worked the fertile plains of the

---

[1] Oliba, Bishop of Vich, was abbot of the famous Benedictine monastery of Santa María del Ripoll from 1008 to 1046. Founded as a pantheon for the Counts of Barcelona in the ninth century (on the ruins of a Visigothic monastery), it used its rich endowment to patronize translations of works from Arabic into Latin from the mid-tenth century on. Here Gerbert of Aurillac (later Pope Sylvester II) studied mathematics, ca. 967. Ripoll reached its apogee under Oliba, who patronized Catalan poets writing in Latin, continued translations from Arabic, and sponsored the writing of a general history of the principality, which contributed to the development of Catalan nationalism.

[2] At his death, Sancho elevated the county of Castile to a Kingdom and bequeathed it to his second son, Ferdinand.

Arlanzon or Carrión rivers; and they would exchange their shepherd's crook or plowshare for sword and bow, either to defend themselves against the invader or to strike a blow for booty beyond the mountains of the central range. In the midst of these clashes (trivial perhaps, but psychologically decisive) Castile forged her warrior temperament, her will to command, and her ambition to achieve a great destiny. Thus emerged a revolutionary country with no closed social classes, in which a villein, if he were fortunate enough to obtain booty, could easily become rich and elevate himself to the rank of gentleman. An adventurous, reckless, improvident land of leaders, Castile was incomprehensible to the quiescent people that the Leonese had become by the eleventh century.

The Navarrese-European framework — Cluniac monks, craftsmen, and ministerial clerks, Frankish immigrants — endowed the new kingdom of Castile with sufficient solidarity to carry out her first enterprises. Of no little significance, these demonstrated the explosive and expansionist tendencies which characterize so many pages in Castilian history. As the Caliphate of Córdoba disintegrated into Islamic separatist states (the "Party Kingdoms" [3]), Castile spread out her tentacles in all directions, from the Atlantic to the Mediterranean.

Ferdinand I had established certain military and political premises which were carried out by his son, Alfonso VI (1065–1109): reduction of the most important "Party Kingdoms" (Badajoz, Seville, and Toledo) to the rank of tributaries; territorial ambitions in the Ebro river valley basin (Saragossa) and along the Mediterranean coastline (Valencia). Once Alfonso VI was settled on the throne (after a second war that demonstrated León's reluctance to recognize Castilian hegemony in the Duero area), he advanced the Castilian armies to Toledo, which he conquered in 1085, and on to the Guadiana river. For Spanish Islam, this break through

---

[3] The "Party Kingdoms" (*reinos de Taifa*, from the Arabic word for band or faction) were twenty-three splinter states, organized around major cities, into which al-Andalus was subdivided after the collapse of the Caliphate (1030). Often at war among themselves as well as with the Christian states, they were finally conquered by a new wave of Muslim invaders, the Almoravids.

her defenses jeopardized her immediate future and forced her to consider the problem of the imminent invasions from North Africa. One year later, at the battle of Sagrajas, the Almoravids stabilized the struggle between the Christians and Muslims in Spain, and nullified the results of Alfonso VI's conquest of Toledo.

Throughout this struggle, Alfonso VI cut a figure as a great monarch. He repopulated his rearguard, the area between the Duero and the Tajo rivers, by granting numerous franchises to all who would settle there (primarily Galicians, Asturians, and Cantabrians); the result was the appearance in this region of the powerful Councils of Castile, presided over by a patriciate of minor aristocracy; the *hidalgos*[4] and *caballeros villanos*.[5] A warlike people, they lived off the products of their flocks and of the lands they possessed within the jurisdiction of the Council (*el alfoz*). The most typical cities in Castile emerged from this repopulation: Ávila, Arévalo, Segovia, Guadalajara, Alcalá, Madrid, and (on the far side of the frontier of León) Zamora, Salamanca, and Plasencia.

Along the Tajo river, starting at Toledo, Castilians were confronted with a major problem: the incorporation en masse of alien elements that resisted assimilation — the Muslims and the Jews. Both groups constituted the merchants and artisans of the cities, and the Muslims were also skilled cultivators of the fertile plains. In short they were people of superior culture, the product of a rich and complex economy.

Let us exclude for the moment the intellectual and emotional relationships among Moors, Christians, and Jews — relationships

---

[4] In the twelfth century *hidalgo* replaced the earlier term, *infanzón*, to designate minor birthright nobility (*grandes* constituting the first rank). A royal grant of hidalguería conferred only the privileges and exemptions of this social status, not land: usually possessing little wealth of his own, the hidalgo was at best of modest means. From the thirteenth century, kings created many hidalgos in an effort to offset the political power of the grandes.

[5] *Caballeros villanos*, a distinct social class from the late tenth to the thirteenth centuries, were wealthy residents of Castilian cities who served as cavalry at their own expense (primarily from livestock profits); in exchange, kings granted them (but not their heirs) the privileges of hidalgos.

which from the twelfth century on constituted a problem of such force that it cannot be ignored. The initial Castilian attitude toward the subjugated peoples appears to have been one of transigence and comprehension. Such an attitude was nurtured by the dynasty's European background, by the elimination of the Mozarab residue which had been treasured by León, and by the possibility that a broad gesture of reconciliation might put an end to the war with Islam. This criterion was translated into propagandistic titles of sovereignty (Emperor of the Two Religions, Emperor of Spain, and so on), adopted from the neo-Gothic ideal of the Chancery of León. Modern philologists have attempted (obviously projecting exaggeratedly) to determine "the manifest destiny" of Castile in these titles.

The Castilian destiny has also been sought in still another development, that expressed by the figure and military feats of el Cid Campeador who in 1090 conquered Valencia and governed the city in the name of Alfonso VI.[6] However, the history of this figure deserves a basic revision, because the epic poem that narrates his activities (*El cantar del Mío Cid*) is more modern than was believed.[7] Moreover, he may be a composite of two different heroes: el Campeador, from a legend from the Duero river area (a harsh vassal of Alfonso VI, a conqueror of Andalusian Moors, a man involved in monetary payments and tributes), and el Cid, a Mozarab figure, a protagonist in the minor separatist disputes in the Ebro river basin, in Catalonia, and in Valencia (tolerant and human, a sentimental and fabulous hero).

---

[6] Rodrigo Díaz de Vivar (1043–1099), known as el Cid Campeador (*cid* from the Arabic word, *sayyid*, meaning lord), was born in a village near the Castilian capital of Burgos. Exiled from Castile in 1079, he fought in the pay of Muslim rulers, particularly in that of the king of Saragossa. But his basic loyalty was to the king of Castile, in whose name he conquered and governed Valencia. After his death, his wife Jimena defended Valencia for three years until it fell to the Almoravids.

[7] Antonio Ubieto dates *El Cantar* ca. 1207 (see below, p. 164). Menéndez Pidal, editor of the definitive text, dates it ca. 1140 and even believed that there was an earlier version written right after the death of el Cid (*En torno al Poema del Mío Cid*, Buenos Aires, 1965).

CHAPTER NINE

The Invasions from North Africa and the Ideal of a Crusade

With the advent of the twelfth century, the Muslims launched their counteroffensive on the Peninsula. This was an event of extremely long-range significance for it lead directly to the development of a Crusading spirit, which imbued the Castilian ideal from that time forward and transformed it into a "divine" force. It also consolidated the political situation of a pluralistic Spain, which was defined by the presence of three kingdoms — Portugal, Castile, and the Crown of Aragon.

The course of events which might have resulted from the capture of Toledo — rapid elimination of the Islamic political domination of Spain, assimilation of Muslims and Christians, and restoration of the Gothic monarchy in the Kingdom of Castile — was brusquely interrupted by the invasion of the Almoravids.[1] They were fanatical warriors from the Sahara desert who, after they had seized control of Morocco, moved on to Spain to aid in the defense of the "Party Kingdoms." From 1086 on, they fought against the Christians with an intolerance of such fundamental intransigence as had never be-

---

[1] Almoravids derive their name from a rigidly orthodox Islamic reform movement, originating among a clan of nomadic Berber tribes from the Sahara known as the Sanhaja. Starting in a *ribat* (a house of retreat, thus: al-Murabitun, "the people of the ribat"), it imposed orthodoxy on the Sanhaja (late, ninth-century converts to Islam) and inspired them to conquer Morocco and west Algeria (1055-1080) and Spain. Entering as allies of the "Party Kings" to halt the Christian Reconquest (1086), they conquered al-Andalus in their own name (1090-1110). Marrakesh (Morocco) was the political capital of their empire, but Seville was the cultural center.

fore been associated with the flag of the Caliphate. Although their successors in the Hispanic arena — the Almohads[2] (from 1146 on) — were more educated and tolerant, they adopted the same militaristic tendency to reduce all men to mere vassals.

This spiritual harshness, exalted on the crest of military victories (Sagrajas, 1086; Valencia, 1102; Uclés, 1108), caused their opponents in Castile and León to react in the same manner. In this era, at the beginning of the twelfth century, the ideal of the reconquest emerges as the violent elimination of the Muslims from the lands of Spain, as much because the Muslims were considered "usurpers" of the Visigothic state as — and this is an essential fact — because they were considered adversaries of the Catholic faith. Carried along the same path by her own mystical enterprise of rescuing the Holy Lands, Europe not only failed to check Hispanic Catholicism but inspired it with her own aspirations. For this reason the Holy See, from the twelfth century on, acquired a prominent and at times decisive role in the making of Spain.

During the generation that followed the defeat at Uclés, the Castilian kingdom struggled against its own weakness. The vital stimulant received during the preceding century was now transformed into internal disorders that became all the more perceptible when the adversary redoubled his attacks along the Tajo frontier. The aristocracy, which had profited from the conquests of Alfonso VI, made constant demands upon the monarchy, thereby inaugurating a process that would culminate in the great civil wars of the fifteenth century.

---

[2] Almohads (al-Muwahhidun, "Unitarians") was the name taken by a confederation of Berber tribes led by the Masmuda from the Atlas Mountains. Claiming the Almoravids had failed to preserve Islamic unity, they conquered the empire, extended it eastward to Tripolitania (1125–1159), and regained control of al-Andalus; theirs was the largest Islamic empire in the West. The Almohads carried out the only radical suppression of Judaism and Christianity in the entire history of Islam before they too succumbed to Hispano-Muslim civilization. Defeated by the Christians in 1212 (las Navas de Tolosa), by 1269 they held only the ports of Algeciras and Gibraltar. (Granada was ruled autonomously by an Hispano-Muslim dynasty, the Nasrids.)

Invasions and Crusade

Along the Atlantic façade there was also marked unrest. The recently established County of Portugal directed its energies toward securing independence and dragged into this movement Galicia, wealthy as a result of the pilgrimages to Santiago and the great monasteries. Still another cause of Castile's structural weakness was the fact that the repopulation of the Duero tableland [3] had emptied the Cantabrian provinces of their manpower reserves; the new frontiers therefore were settled with exasperating slowness. The countryside around Salamanca is one of many examples that could be cited. In summary, Castile became less and less active, then perceptibly paralyzed.

Such are the basic conditions which apparently determined the profound crisis in Castile during the reign of Queen Urraca (1109–1126). This crisis, whose epicenter was Galicia, led to the fragmentation of the state at the death of Urraca's son, Alfonso VII, when León reclaimed her independence under Ferdinand II.

Portugal achieved her independence in 1143 by making the country a fief of the Papacy and by disavowing the right to carry out a neo-Gothic unification that was claimed by the Chancery of Castile. Under Alfonso VII (1126–1157) the Chancery had created an imperial title for Castile that was a blend of the ideology of León, of a desire to counteract the aspirations of Frederick Barbarossa of Germany, and of the political realities of the Peninsula (that is, Castile's occupation of Saragossa in 1134 and the subsequent rendering of homage by the monarchs of Aragon to Castile in exchange for this ancient Moorish kingdom). But the empire proclaimed in León in 1135 — an empire that had been given a new format — was but the flower of a day, for it was contradicted by the course of events and, above all, by the structural weakness of Castile. Therefore, Castile was unable to resist the violent demands of León and Portugal for independence. The reality of that moment was best expressed in the treaty that Alfonso concluded with Ramón Beren-

---

[3] For the significance of the repopulation of the Duero tableland, unoccupied during the eighth and ninth centuries, then slowly repopulated during the tenth and eleventh centuries, see pp. 37–39.

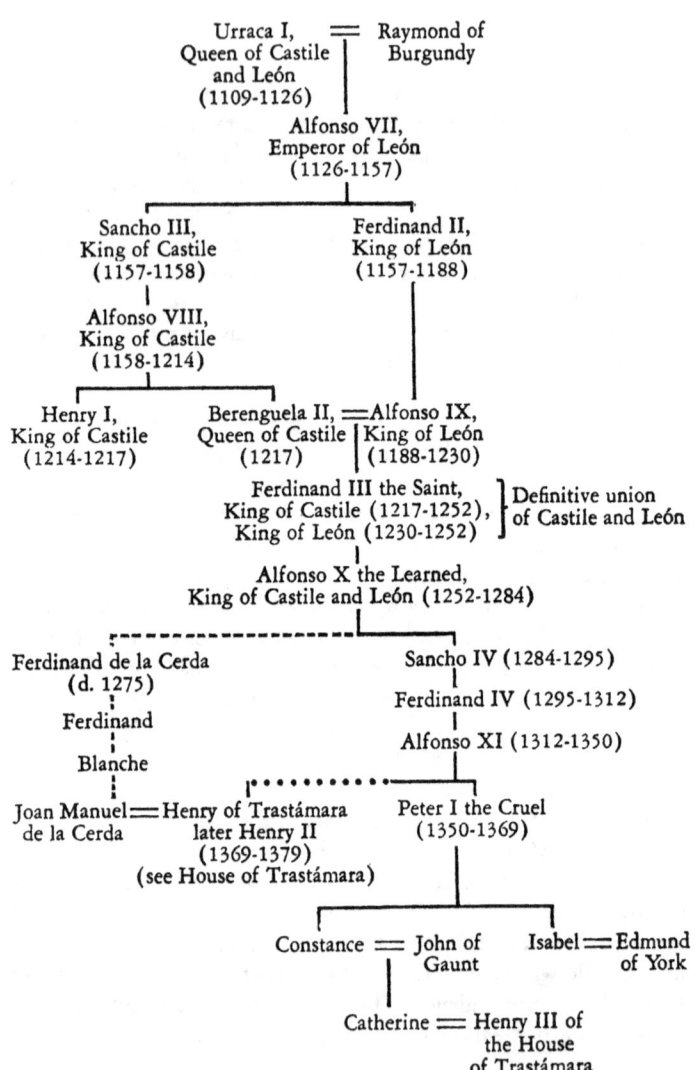

TABLE 1. The House of Burgundy, which ruled in the kingdom of Castile-León from 1126 to 1369, was established by the marriage of Urraca (daughter of Alfonso VI) and Raymond (son of the Count of Burgundy) in 1087. It ruled until 1369, when Peter I was killed by his bastard half-brother, Henry of Trastámara.

Invasions and Crusade

guer IV of Barcelona (the Treaty of Tudellén, 1151), which set fixed limits to their respective zones in the future reconquest of the Peninsula.

The destruction of the neo-Gothic ideal, and the substitution of that of a Crusade, was reflected in two phenomena that occurred in the second half of the twelfth century. One was the participation of various Peninsular kingdoms in common enterprises, such as the conquest of Almería in 1147 and of Cuenca in 1177; their importance is obvious, for they demonstrated that each state could benefit from common enterprises and thereby established the bases for the collective success of Christian arms in the battle with the Almohads at Las Navas de Tolosa (1212).

The second phenomenon involved the military orders who settled along the Muslim frontier zone, in Aragon as well as in Castile.[4] These military-religious organizations occupied extensive regions in the southern half of the central plateau, where they introduced a system of latifundia and a livestock economy that were antithetical both to the initial type of Castilian colonization on the high plain of the Duero (that is, agrarian communities governed by town councils) and to the Islamic agricultural tradition. Moreover, the harsh spirit of religious intransigence that characterized the reconquest in Spain from that time forward crystallized in this zone dominated by the military orders.

---

[4] Military orders were organized in response to the Almohad invasion (1155-1175), when armies of nobles and of the fortified cities of New Castile proved unable to defend the frontier, much less conquer new land. The three principal orders (nominally subject to the Cistercian rule, although most members did not take religious vows) were the Calatrava (founded 1158), Alcántara (1166), and Santiago (1170). They played a major role in the reconquest, and then in the recolonization, of Extremadura and La Mancha (a development paralleling the contemporaneous settlement of eastern Germany by Templars and the Knights of St. John). Until the reign of Ferdinand and Isabel, between 1476 and 1499, military orders retained the right to govern the land they had conquered, to tax its produce, and to control the Church in that region (through appointment of the secular hierarchy).

CHAPTER TEN

Hispanic Pluralism and the Pyrenean Empire

The Aragonese monarchy, a branch of the dynasty of Navarre, came into existence at the death of Sancho III the Great.[1] With its poverty and its sparsely populated territory, it was certainly a monarchy with very few pretensions. Yet from the days of its founder, Ramiro I (1035–1063), Aragon possessed the virility of the Pyrenees, and it drew for inspiration upon a primordial, indigenous reservoir that had hardly been touched by Roman culture. Reactivating quite ancient geo-historical laws, this nation of shepherds began to assault the fortified redoubts which denied their flocks access to the sub-Pyrenean plains. This turned out to be a very difficult enterprise, and became even more so when the Muslims living in the Ebro river basin were opportunely reinforced by the Almoravids.

During the reign of Sancho Ramírez, the Aragonese seized the cities of Barbastro, Graus, and Monzón, but Huesca resisted until 1096, when Peter I gained possession of it. Not until the reign of Peter's successor, Alfonso I the Warrior (1104–1134), did Aragon acquire the powerful allies she needed in order to achieve her objectives — nobles from the French Pyrenees and knights of the military orders of Palestine. With these reinforcements, she successfully stormed Saragossa (1118) and defended her conquest with the victory at Cutanda (1120). This gave the Aragonese access to the fertile

---

[1] When Sancho III died in 1035, he divided his reigns among his sons, leaving Navarre to his first-born, García IV, and Castile to Ferdinand I; to Ramiro, a bastard son, he left several counties, including Aragon, which he elevated to the rank of a kingdom.

plains of the Jalón and Jiloca rivers. At a single stroke, the general outlines of historic Aragon had been constituted (the Kingdom of Aragon, a mountain region, and the Kingdom of Saragossa, a river valley).

The political viability of a state confined within the Iberian depression was very slight.[2] For some time (throughout the reigns of Ferdinand I and Alfonso VI), Castile had been eyeing the rich prize of Saragossa; therefore, when Alfonso the Warrior died, leaving no heir, King Alfonso VII of Castile immediately put forth a claim. He went to Saragossa and forced it to acknowledge his rights (1135). But this attitude turned out to be self-defeating, for it pushed the Aragonese into the arms of the Catalans, with whom they had maintained good frontier relations.

In 1137 Count Ramón Berenguer IV of Barcelona signed a marriage contract with the Infanta Petronilla, daughter of Ramiro II, and began to rule by right of his position as Prince of Aragon. The Castilian affair was resolved by having Alfonso VII withdraw his troops from Saragossa and by having Aragonese royalty render homage as vassals of the Castilian monarchy for the western sector of the so-called "Kingdom of Saragossa." A Catalan decision thus contributed to the birth of the Crown of Aragon,[3] not a hypothetical tendency of Aragon to occupy the seacoast of her river basin.

---

[2] In order to expand beyond the Ebro river valley, Aragon had to ally with either Castile on the west or Catalonia on the east. The events leading to the unification with Catalonia are more complicated than Vicens' narrative suggests. When Alfonso the Warrior died in 1134, leaving no heir, he bequeathed the kingdom to the military orders. But the nobles of Aragon elected the brother of Alfonso, Ramiro the Monk, to be king. In the ensuing disorders, the Muslims began to recover some of the land lost to Alfonso. Meanwhile, Ramiro was released from his priory, married and had a daughter, Petronilla; when she was one year old, he agreed to a marriage between her and the twenty-two-year-old Count of Barcelona, Ramón Berenguer IV, possibly in an effort to thwart Castilian penetration. Then, either because of Aragonese opposition to his rule or from personal preference, Ramiro retired to his priory, while Ramón Berenguer ruled Aragon as the royal consort.

[3] The Crown of Aragon is the title of the union of the Principality of Catalonia and the Kingdom of Aragon; Ramón Berenguer presided as

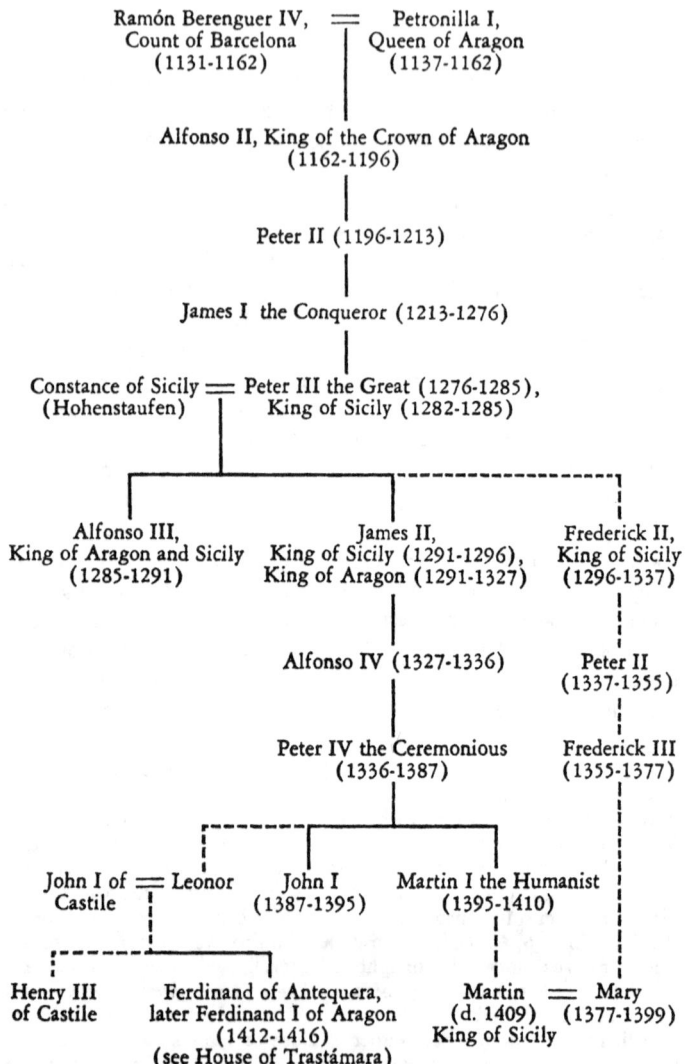

TABLE 2. The House of Barcelona, which ruled in the Crown of Aragon (Aragon and Catalonia, then later Valencia and the Balearic Islands) from 1137 to 1410. (Broken lines indicate branches of the family that were not of the ruling line.)

Pluralism and Pyrenean Empire

The Counts of Barcelona were accustomed to the coexistence of various sovereignties within Catalan territory (the counties of Barcelona, Urgel, Roussillon, and so on). Therefore they worked out a formula of mutual respect for the individuality of the two states — Catalonia and Aragon — who were united on that occasion, under a system whereby each retained complete autonomy. Furthermore, French sovereignty over the counties of Catalonia, combined with the discrete but resolute attitude of the Papacy, to some degree forced acceptance of this formula of coexistence. Ramón Berenguer IV avoided proclaiming himself either King of Catalonia or King of Aragon, contenting himself with the more modest title of Prince. Whatever be the cause, the solution devised at that critical moment later turned out to be extremely fruitful, when the problem arose of how to govern Valencia and the Balearic Islands, and when the even more extensive and complicated problem arose of how to govern the Mediterranean possessions of the Crown of Aragon in Italy. In this fashion, the communal system of Catalonia, derived from her juridical understanding of the concept of a contractual relationship, led to political pluralism. In contrast, Castile rejected this possibility and thereby intensified the dilemma already posed at the death of Ferdinand I and again at the death of Alfonso VII — unification with, or separation from, León. Here were two different concepts of how to organize the Peninsula which, in the course of succeeding centuries, would be forced into a confrontation.

Castilian idealism and Mediterranean realism were also in opposition from that time forward. Nothing illustrates this point better than comparing the actions of Alfonso VII of Castile with those of Ramón Berenguer IV of Barcelona. All official literature (documents, chronicles, ceremonies) favor Alfonso; all political results redound to the credit of Ramón Berenguer. The cancellation of the imperial phantasm, the birth of a viable Spain forged with a Portuguese, Castilian, and Catalan-Aragonese trident — such were the

---

Prince and royal consort, but it was his son by Petronilla, Alfonso II (1162–1197), who ruled as the first king of this union. By military reconquest the Crown of Aragon incorporated the Kingdom of Valencia, the Balearic Islands, and eventually Sicily.

unquestionable merits of Ramón Berenguer. He propounded a pluralism that never excluded an awareness of a unity of purpose in Hispanic affairs.

In the fight against Islam, the unification of Aragonese and Catalan efforts made it possible to destroy the last bulwarks defended by the Muslims in southern Catalonia. Within a short time, Lérida and Tortosa fell and Tarragona could be repopulated. But the reconquest was not the only pursuit. It was but the vertex of a triangle whose other angles pointed toward the Mediterranean and toward the south of France.

Once again the sea became a productive commercial route. Catalan navigators were now free to set out to Egypt along the same route that Italian merchants had followed — and that is exactly what they did. As for the south of France, the revival of trade and the movement of merchandise from the Mediterranean to the Atlantic through this region had showered it with wealth and cultural refinements. Languedoc and Provence glittered with the unrivaled splendor of their knightly courts and animated cities. Under these conditions, and given also the affinity of languages, it was natural for Catalans to allow themselves to be tempted by the paradise of Languedoc — to encounter there poets from whom to learn and treasures in which to participate.

A trans-Pyrenean policy was natural to both the Kingdom of Aragon and the House of Barcelona. But it was Ramón Berenguer III (1096–1131) who had provided it with a clear objective when he married Dulce of Provence and opposed the expansion of the Counts of Toulouse into Provence or Languedoc. He also announced his designs on the Balearic Islands, and with the aid of a fleet from Pisa conquered them, albeit only briefly. His son, Ramón Berenguer IV, continued these same policies. The Catalan fleet supported Alfonso VII of Castile when that monarch directed an expedition against Almería (1147). In the south of France, numerous lords of Languedoc acknowledged the sovereignty of Barcelona. This expansion reached its apogee in the reign of Alfonso II of Aragon (1162–1196), who returned to gather up the Provencal inheritance and was on the verge of creating a Pyrenean kingdom that would have included the valleys of the Ebro and the Garonne.

The events of this dynamic century transformed the Catalan mentality. This feudal, peasant, Romanesque people of other times gave way to a brilliant and expansive society of colonizers and merchants. With the harsh parsimony that characterizes their history, the Catalans stored up enormous moral and material reserves that would, in the thirteenth century, enable them to climb in one leap to the front ranks of Mediterranean politics.

CHAPTER ELEVEN

Military Expansion on the Peninsula and in the Mediterranean

A century of great Christian conquests of Islamic territory was inaugurated at the battle of Las Navas de Tolosa (1212), where the Almohad resistance was shattered by the combined efforts of the countries in the north of the Peninsula — Castile, Aragon, and Navarre. This military supremacy became even more effective when at last the principal states were permanently consolidated under two rulers: Castile and León again united under Ferdinand III in 1230; Catalonia and Aragon had already done so as described.

The Portuguese were the first to occupy the southern seacoast (Tavira, 1238), but it was the Castilians who derived the greatest benefits from the collapse of Almohad power. Castile took possession of Andalusia (Córdoba, 1236; Jaén, 1246; Seville, 1248; Cádiz, 1250), excepting only the mountainous region in the southeast (Granada). Simultaneously, Ferdinand III succeeded in establishing a Castilian protectorate over the Kingdom of Murcia (1244) just as Catalan-Aragonese troops, having taken by storm the walled cities of Valencia (1238) and Játiva, were headed in that direction. The Treaty of Almizra in 1244, signed by the two great monarchs of the reconquest (Ferdinand III of Castile and James I of Aragon), established definitively that Murcia would become part of the Castilian Crown. However, it was the troops of James I of Aragon which held that city for Castile when, shortly afterward (1266), Murcia revolted against Alfonso X (the son-in-law of James I). This extraordinary increase of territory considerably augmented the power and wealth of both Christian monarchies. But the organization of the conquered territory of Andalusia was very different from that of Valencia.

Military Expansion

In Andalusia Ferdinand III of Castile proceeded to distribute land among the nobles who had aided him in the venture, leaving intact the system of latifundia that had been in effect under the "Party Kings," the Almoravids, and the Almohads. The revolt of the Muslim peasants and their expulsion in 1263 facilitated this policy, one of grave significance for the future. Enormous estates thus passed into the hands of an aristocracy coming from the north who from that moment on constituted one of the most powerful elements within the state; it was not counterbalanced in any way by the bourgeoisie, almost nonexistent and dispersed among the cities of the north.

To this development must be added still another: the predominance of a livestock mentality due to the continuation of the early medieval system of migratory flocks,[1] a system that rapidly expanded and for the summer.[1] This livestock economy rapidly expanded in territories dominated by the military orders (New Castile and Extremadura), and in western Andalusia. Still another factor was the lack of a merchant fleet (shipping was in the hands of the Genoese) which might have carried Andalusian merchandise — the products of her agriculture and crafts — within the range of European markets. Whichever the principal factor among those cited might be, historical evidence proves the sensational collapse of the Andalusian economy in the generation following its conquest by Castile.

In contrast, the occupation of Valencia by the Crown of Aragon was carried out in a completely different fashion. Although land was redistributed here also, the nobles benefited only in a few mountainous regions near Aragon — specifically, in the area where the flocks from the Pyrenees moved back and forth and where the wool caravans traveled on their way to the Mediterranean. The rest of the land was repopulated either by Catalan knights, who settled in cities or *villas* near the estates gratuitously bestowed upon them by James I, or by Catalan farmers, who were in large part natives of

---

[1] This economy, unique in medieval Europe, involved owners joining forces to move enormous herds over extensive territory for winter and summer grazing in order to produce on a large scale. Initially these were herds of cattle, but after 1300 they were almost exclusively flocks of sheep.

Lérida and who quickly adjusted to the Muslim's special system for cultivating orchards. These people brought with them the democratic spirit of the agrarian communities of New Catalonia (which had been established and repopulated in accord with liberal *fueros*);[2] the monarchy helped to strengthen this spirit by conferring broad charters on the neo-Valencians and by granting this kingdom the same system of autonomous government that prevailed in the relationship between Aragon and Catalonia. This skillful social and political mechanism promoted the economic development of this region retrieved from the Muslims, all the more so because in Valencia the Moriscos were happy to continue working and because the Catalan merchant marine was able to transport the goods produced by Valencian farmers and artisans.

This experiment in large-scale colonization was not the only one carried out by the Catalans. The Balearic Islands (conquered by James I in 1229) simultaneously benefited from the same type of social and economic policy. However, in the Balearics most of the colonists came from Ampurdán and the Costa Brava in Catalonia. The city of Mallorca (today Palma) was soon converted into a maritime emporium of the first order.[3] A maritime policy prevailed in the Crown of Aragon from that point on, and not because of some hypothetical influence exerted by the monarchy after its continental policy had been checked by the Castilian expansion in the direction of Murcia.

Even though the drive to Languedoc was halted at the battle of Muret (1213) — where Peter II the Catholic, father of James I, died — the Catalans profited enormously from that cataclysm, which put an end to an exuberant civilization and an important commer-

---

[2] A *fuero* is a royal charter incorporating the inhabitants of an area (an urban site and its surrounding lands in the Middle Ages; a region such as Navarre or the Basque provinces in the modern era). In Aragon, as in Castile, this royal grant of laws and liberties early acquired a special connotation in which the "immunities" or exemptions from general laws or taxes outweighed the rights or responsibilities conferred on the inhabitants.

[3] For further information on the repopulation of the Balearic Islands, see pp. 63–64.

cial route. Many Albigensians, fleeing the persecution of French Crusaders, must have found refuge in Catalonia. And their gold, combined with the energies of the people of the Principality of Catalonia, served as the springboard whereby Barcelona merchants vaulted into the great spice trade with the Near East — with Alexandria, Rhodes, Constantinople. The monarchs of the Crown of Aragon were forced to yield to this collective impetus, subjecting themselves to expeditions far more hazardous than any trivial frontier quarrel with Castile over Murcia. The Catalan dynasty's profound respect for the national drive to the Mediterranean is shown in the Treaty of Corbeil (1259), signed by Louis IX of France and James I of Aragon. Under this treaty, France lost her sovereignty over the Catalan counties, but the monarchy of the House of Barcelona abandoned its recent ambitious plans for expansion in Languedoc.

The successor of James I, Peter III the Great (1276–1285), was plunged into a gigantic struggle with the two major powers of that era — France and the Papacy — when he reclaimed the Kingdom of Sicily in the name of his wife, a claim obviously reinforced by the needs and the demands of Catalan merchants.[4] Sicily capitulated to the King of Aragon in 1282, after a series of naval operations that revealed the Catalan fleet's potential in the western Mediterranean. But the most surprising aspect of this daring enterprise was the way that Catalans were able to respond when the French Crusaders invaded their homeland. This time Muret was not repeated; on the contrary, the foreign troops were routed and suffered serious losses (1285).

However, the danger that threatened the monarchy had very profound political and social consequences. For example, Peter the Great was obliged to concede privileges to the nobility of Aragon (Privilegio General) and to the nobility and bourgeoisie of Cata-

---

[4] Peter III was married to Constance, daughter of Manfred, the last Hohenstauffen King of Sicily (1254–1266). In 1262 Pope Urban IV offered Sicily to Charles of Anjou, brother of Louis IX of France. Charles defeated and killed Manfred (1266), but his harsh policies provoked in 1282 a revolt known as the "Sicilian Vespers," which Peter III of Aragon used to justify an invasion in the name of Constance.

lonia. This led to the consolidation of a special climate of liberty, reflected above all through the Cortes. But we must not deceive ourselves too greatly about this development. Liberty, yes, but only for the aristocratic classes in the countryside and in the city. In contrast, this same development imposed upon the peasants a dangerous system of servitude that would, with the passage of time, create a tense agrarian situation in Catalonia.

CHAPTER TWELVE

The Medieval Apex

Within five decades that span the thirteenth and fourteenth centuries, the peoples of Spain lived through the culminating period of their medieval history; in more modern terms, they entered the golden phase of an urban patriciate. Although one certainly cannot talk about this as a period of peace, neither can one talk of serious military encounters.

The Crown of Aragon continued her commitment to a policy of expansion in the Mediterranean. Castile took up a position as sentinel of the Straits of Gibraltar; her objective was to prevent any new Islamic assault against the country. Although far less brilliant than that of Aragon and Catalonia, the Castilian venture was equally tenacious and costly.

In the Mediterranean James II of Aragon (1291–1327) signed a peace treaty with his adversaries, the Papacy and France — first at Agnano (1295) and then at Caltabellota (1302). The basis for this agreement was recognition of the Crown of Aragon's sovereignty over the islands of Corsica and Sardinia and recognition of Frederick, brother of James II, as King of Sicily.[1] The conquest of Sardinia, delayed until 1327, confirmed the Catalan and Aragonese

---

[1] The Kingdom of Sicily remained nominally independent of the Kingdom of Aragon from 1302 until 1377; it was, however, ruled by a branch of the House of the Counts of Barcelona. After 1377, when the last monarch of the Sicilian branch died, it was ruled by a member of the Aragonese branch but as a separate kingdom. Not until 1416 was it formally incorporated into the Crown of Aragon.

possession of the strategic island route (the Balearic Islands, Sardinia, Sicily).

The world watched the feats of the Almogavars [2] as they moved on from one conflict to another. They defended the Byzantine Empire against the first attacks of the Ottoman Turks (1302–1305). In the illustrious Duchies of Athens and Neopatria they established themselves as overlords and thus transformed the site of the famous epics of classical antiquity into segments of Catalan feudalism (1311–1388).

This heroic moment for the Crown of Aragon coincided with an intensification of her policy on the Peninsula. More than that of any other king of the House of Barcelona, the policy of James II was to intervene openly in Hispanic affairs, either by aiding the monarchs of Castile (for example, in the task of defending the Straits) or by taking advantage of that kingdom's frequent internal difficulties to force it to cede portions of frontier territory. The most outstanding case was the acquisition of what is now the Alicante region of the Kingdom of Valencia, including the city of Cartagena, through the Treaty of Ágreda in 1304.

Meanwhile, Castile kept watch upon the Marinids, who had replaced the Almohads as the rulers of Morocco. These Muslims could cross the Straits of Gibraltar with supreme ease, because they had access to the Peninsula through the ports of Gibraltar, Algeciras, and Tarifa,[3] and through them to the fertile fields of lower Andalusia. In a retreat they could count on support from the Kingdom

---

[2] Almogavars, fierce mercenaries lightly clad and armed, primarily from Catalonia, led the conquest of Sicily. Chartered as the Catalan Grand Company in 1302, they were sent to fight for the Byzantine Emperor against the Turks but rebelled when he assassinated their leader, Roger de Flor. In 1311 they conquered the Duchies of Athens and Neopatria; some members of the Company ruled them autonomously, although nominally subject to the King of Sicily, until 1388.

[3] The Marinids, the Berber successors of the Almohads, retained Tarifa until 1294, Algeciras until 1344, and Gibraltar until 1411, when it was conquered by the Kingdom of Granada. The Guzmán, Castilian nobility, conquered Gibraltar in 1462, retaining it as a family appanage until it was incorporated into Castile (1502).

of Granada, provided that the latter had less to fear from an alliance than from their enmity.

In any event, the problems of the frontier with Granada and the sea frontier forced Castile to be constantly on the alert. The sea was often guarded by Catalans, Portuguese, and, above all, by Genoese. As a matter of fact, it was through Genoese efforts that the Straits of Gibraltar were opened up, thanks to the action of Admiral Micer Benito Zacharías during the reign of Alfonso X. After repeated attempts, Castilian troops took possession of Tarifa and Algeciras. Gibraltar was taken, then lost. In short, there was no respite until 1340, when Alfonso XI won a victory on the shores of the Salado river. This battle closed the era of the invasions of Spain, initiated by the Almoravids two and a half centuries earlier.

Such is the surface of the events. Their innermost structure is far more interesting and revealing. In the first place, the Hispanic peoples appeared fatigued by their great military and repopulating effort in the first half of the thirteenth century. The same generation that had conquered Seville and Mallorca had had to assume the task of populating Andalusia, the Balearic Islands, and the Kingdom of Valencia.

Statistics are lacking, unfortunately. Yet one can easily understand the recession experienced by the Peninsula about 1270, when — following the expulsion from Andalusia of the Moriscos, and the reduction or flight of their counterparts in Valencia — the country was forced to proceed with fewer, and with less competent, men. The problem was resolved by having some men abandon their homelands and having others occupy the best lands and crafts — provided always that the lords would agree. This population upheaval altered the nature of Castilian society: it feudalized the northern part of the central plateau, depopulated the lands of Old Castile, enabled the knights to predominate in the town councils of Castile, and stirred the greed of the nobles who settled in Andalusia.

In the Crown of Aragon, this rapid colonization of the lands to the south most seriously affected Catalonia. Her men settled as far away as Murcia, even though it was a Castilian city. If to all this we add the repopulation of the Balearic Islands and the military expeditions in the Mediterranean, we can understand the exhaustion manifest also in Catalan activities following the reigns of the sons of Peter the Great.[4] But in contrast to Castile, the strength of the urban patriciate in Catalonia was so great that she managed to emerge safely from the quagmire of social disorder created by the displacement of population. Barcelona, Perpignan, Valencia, and Palma de Mallorca were the centers of the new social artery created by the urban patriciate. However, one must not forget either the refeudalization of the countryside — by the establishment of a peasantry bound to the soil in Catalonia (*els pagesos de remença*) and in Mallorca (*els foráns*)[5] — nor the tension created by a nobility which, as in Castile, had profited from the distribution of land.

The orientation of the economy of the Crown of Aragon was also very different from that of Castile. The war against France stimulated in Catalonia a great woolen-textile industry whose output was intended to supply the new markets on the Peninsula and, above all, the trade with Sardinia, Sicily, and North Africa. To textiles Catalans added spices and cast iron, coral, and leather for export. All of this increased production and served to counterbalance the inflationary tendencies caused by the demand for consumer goods.

The economic evolution of Castile was completely different. The lack of any industrial activity, the existence of an insatiable market for luxury goods, and the needs of the public treasury plunged Castile into an infernal circle of inflation and debasement of the coinage, and a permanent deficit in the balance of trade. Because of this — and despite the protectionist measures that had been decreed by Alfonso X — monarchs were forced to allow foreign merchants

---

[4] Peter III the Great (1276–1285) was followed to the throne by his son, Alfonso III, who died in 1291 leaving no heir. Peter's second son, James II, succeeded to the throne and ruled until his death in 1327.

[5] The term *foráns* (literally, foreigners) refers to the Catalan peasants transported to Mallorca to resettle the land. After the reconquest of the island of Mallorca (1232), almost the entire native Muslim peasantry emigrated to North Africa.

to reside in the principal cities, and to compensate for the outflow of money by organizing the sale of wool. This was the great solution, at the very moment when Flanders and Italy were becoming great wool purchasers; to base the monarchy's fiscal system on the flocks that moved back and forth from summer to winter pasture, flocks that had become enormous because of the great human vacuum that existed on both of the central tablelands. This is the way that the Mesta [6] was born, and this is the way that the dramatic paralysis of Castilian agriculture was initiated. The wool trade very quickly enriched Burgos, converted the Cantabrian fleet into an instrument of Castilian maritime power, and stimulated the birth of textile industries which, if they had not been suffocated by the financial interests of the nobles, might have given rise to a major economic boom in the fifteenth and sixteenth centuries.

But in order to finance the needs of the monarchy, being unable to live within their income, the kings of Castile were forced to resort to the purses of the Jews. Two centuries earlier the Jews had been eliminated from the money markets of Italy and France, and one century earlier from the market in Catalonia. In such countries credit operations had been absorbed by bankers. By contrast, a capitalistic economy had matured only very slightly in Castile and therefore Jews continued to prevail. Kings, nobles, military orders, ecclesiastical communities, and town councils were forced to submit

---

[6] The Mesta, an association of Castilian stockmen (almost exclusively sheepowners), was established under royal authority between 1260 and 1265 to secure entrée for northern flocks into the newly conquered winter grazing lands of Extremadura. The charter of Alfonso X in 1273 conferred extraterritoriality on Mesta flocks and herdsmen, and extensive grazing rights along three sheepruns (seventy yards wide) from northern Castile to Extremadura. Thereafter kings taxed the profitable wool trade through the Mesta; in return, stockmen extracted major political and economic concessions. Julius Klein's classic study *The Mesta: A Study in Spanish Economic History, 1273-1836* (Cambridge, Mass., 1920) has been significantly modified by Charles Julian Bishko in his article "The Castilian as Plainsman: The Medieval Ranching Frontier in La Mancha and Extremadura," which appears in the anthology *The New World Looks at Its History* (Austin, 1963), pp. 47-69.

to the harsh terms imposed by Jewish moneylenders, who cannot be blamed for imposing such conditions, given the difficulties of collecting the taxes turned over to them and given the bad faith of one group or another in paying the stipulated sums. A necessary cog in the economic policy of that time, these rich Jews aroused the hatred of bishops and aristocrats, who, in turn, transmitted this hatred to the common people in the cities by inciting them against the industrious Jewish communities. A profound economic crisis would be enough to allow this resentment, accumulating for generations, to explode in irreparable fashion.

This impassioned differentiation within the urban society of Castile was something completely isolated from the harmony that existed at that time among Muslim, Jewish, and Christian intellectuals in the major cultural centers. It is a commonplace to refer to the work of the School of Translators of Toledo, especially during the reign of Alfonso X, as a channel of Western culture.[7] But within the last few years it has ceased to be a commonplace, and has become a vibrant and poignant controversial matter, to learn how much impact the Jewish and Muslim mentalities had upon the innermost recesses of the Christian mentality. The theory that in the fourteenth century Castile was a dwelling place (*morada*) for the three religions apparently describes a spiritual structure that occurred only in very special cases. But I believe it cannot be denied that these were profound influences, that the higher cultural

---

[7] The School of Translators of Toledo, founded by Raimont de Sauvetat, Archbishop from 1125 to 1152, reached its apogee under Alfonso X (1252-1284). The Archbishop had reorganized the Muslim *madrasa*, the official center for the advanced study of religious sciences: commentary on the Koran, Islamic law, history, theology, philology, and grammar. Many of the texts used by these scholars were translations into Arabic (done at Damascus and Córdoba) from Hebrew, other oriental languages, and Greek. The School of Toledo continued this tradition of translating, now from Arabic into Latin, and employed for this purpose Arabic-speaking Jews (as the Muslims had done). Thus both works from classical civilizations, and some research in medicine, mathematics, and astronomy from Baghdad, were transmitted to the newly founded universities of Europe.

The Medieval Apex

level of the Jews, and the superior technical skills of the Mudejars [8] and the Moriscos, ultimately left their mark upon the basic resources of Christian society.

Castile was thus confronted by her most difficult problem, one that she would have to endure until the beginning of the seventeenth century — the problem of assimilating, or of expatriating, the religious minorities.

---

[8] Mudejars were Muslims authorized under royal charters to live in territories conquered by Christians (from the Arabic *mudajjan*, "permitted to remain"). Constituting a semi-autonomous community, they spoke Arabic and followed Islamic customs until forced to accept baptism or leave Spain (1502 in Castile, 1525 in Aragon). The legal status of the Mudejars had been abolished but as nominal Christians (known as Moriscos), they maintained their corporate way of life until expelled from Spain in 1609.

CHAPTER THIRTEEN

Beginning of Dissension in Hispania

Victory over Islam was complete, with the single exception of the Kingdom of Granada, which for two centuries would keep alive an antiquated but nonetheless dangerous animosity within the spiritual infrastructure of Castile. As soon as this victory was attained, throughout the length of the Peninsula the nobility pressed its demands upon the monarchy. This problem, a common phenomenon in the Europe of the fourteenth and fifteenth centuries, concerned the need of the aristocracy (feudal or seignorial) to secure a dominant political position that would consolidate its advantageous economic situation. The monarchs of all Western European nations found the bourgeoisie to be a powerful support in counteracting the nobility's schemes for hegemony — even though in the last analysis this would redound to the benefit of those who gave the aid. But the point is that the bourgeoisie was a cushioning element in the clash between aristocracy and royalty. Events in the Crown of Aragon reflected this European development.

On the central plateau, the low density of the bourgeois class (evident since the time of Alfonso XI) made it inevitable that in Castile the clash between the two antagonistic forces would reach catastrophic dimensions. Except for Castile's defense of the Straits of Gibraltar (to which I have already referred), from the death of Ferdinand III until the accession of the Catholic Monarchs her historic fabric was woven with a weft composed of sordid conflicts of personal interests. To measure the full extent of these interests is to become cognizant of the wide pendulum swing of Castilian history, where periods of great creative exaltation are followed by

Beginning of Dissension

stages of profound malaise, devouring unrest, and inability to achieve an integrated society.[1]

During the reign of Ferdinand III and the first years of the reign of Alfonso X, Castile had realized her full potential. The impressive factor is not the military conquests of that period, but rather the broad response to European movements (Gothic art, which inspired the construction of the cathedrals of Burgos, Toledo, and León, and the movement that led to the establishment of a university, located first at Palencia and then at Salamanca)[2] and the spirit of mutual understanding and intellectual tolerance of the old and the new, of the Muslim and the Christian. This enabled Castile to perform the same role of transmitting knowledge that Catalonia had played in the tenth century, when Gerbert of Aurillac, the future Pope Sylvester II, studied mathematics at the monastery of Ripoll.[3] However, the mission performed by Castile in the thirteenth century through the School of Translators of Toledo[4] was far more comprehensive and of far greater consequence for the future of Western society, into which it injected a renovating shot of Greek science and philosophy.

But such brilliant beginnings were corroded by the pressure of social and economic circumstances. Certainly Castile lacked neither ambitions nor ideals nor aspirations to greatness. Alfonso X revived

---

[1] For details see Vicens Vives and Jorge Nadal Oller, *An Economic History of Spain* (translated by Frances M. López-Morillas, Princeton, 1969). Published originally in 1959, it provides the background for problems which Vicens discusses in this text.

[2] The University of Salamanca began as a center for studies organized under episcopal direction between 1208 and 1212 and connected to the Cathedral of Palencia. About 1218 Alfonso IX of León issued a royal edict establishing a similar center in Salamanca. In 1243 Ferdinand III merged the two, granting the school at Salamanca an academic fuero of privileges and rights. In 1254 Pope Alexander IV granted Salamanca the status of *studium generale*, thus ranking it with Paris, Bologna, and Oxford.

[3] For background on the monastery of Santa María de Ripoll, see p. 41n.

[4] For background on the School of Translators of Toledo, see p. 66n.

hopes for an empire, although now these were founded on a claim to the Crown of Germany: in the days of the Great Interregnum — when the Holy Roman Empire lay prostrate in the trail blazed by the Hohenstauffens — Alfonso presented himself as a candidate for the Crown.[5] Castile's desire for hegemony over the other kingdoms on the Peninsula acquired new vigor with Peter the Cruel and John I; the former confronted Aragon, the latter Portugal. But such ventures were debilitated by the increasing boldness with which the nobles fought to achieve their political and economic objectives.

In this social struggle the decisive event was the terrible encounter at Montiel (1369)[6] — an event that could have been predicted from the preceding two generations, in which a period of disorder, instigated by ambitious infantes and angry princes of the Church during the minorities of kings, caused the monarchy to institute equally drastic purges. The last levee separating the nobility from power was sacrificed at Montiel. The bastard branch of the Trastámaras (founded by Henry II, who had slain Peter the Cruel) started out under the handicap of having to capitulate to the aristocrats who had supported the revolutionary movement; the nobles were assured of not only the full extent of their privileges and new grants of land, but also extensive financial benefits, not least among which was the consolidation of the authority of the Mesta. This powerful organization, which controlled the seasonal pasturage of Spanish sheep, enriched the state by proceeds from the tax on cattle and by export duties; it also doubled the fortunes of the nobles in

---

[5] Alfonso based his claim on rights inherited through his mother, Beatrice of Swabia. He first presented his claim in 1256, and vigorously defended it despite papal opposition and opposition from the Castilians, among whom it was unpopular, partly because it was costly. In 1273 he finally withdrew in favor of Rudolph of Hapsburg.

[6] In 1369, in a tent outside the castle of Montiel (Extremadura), Peter the Cruel, King of Castile, was murdered — either by his bastard half-brother, Henry of Trastámara, or by Henry's aide-de-camp. This ended the attempt of Peter the Cruel, allied with Jewish businessmen and Genoese merchants living in Castile, to curb the political and economic power of the landholding nobles and to renovate the economy by promoting industry in the cities of Andalusia.

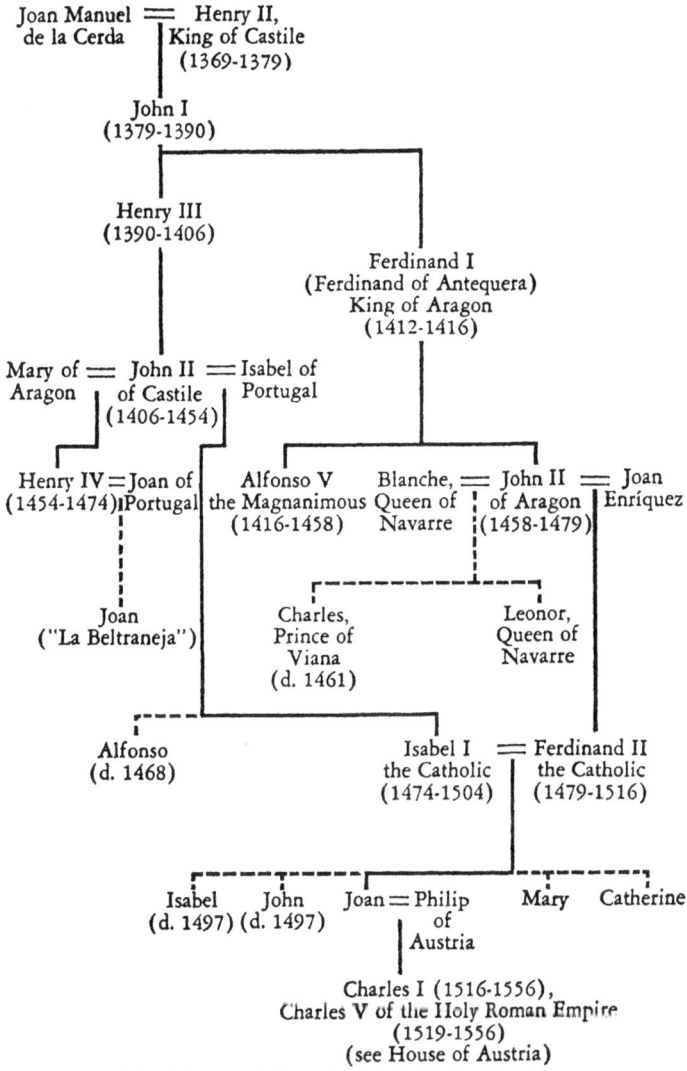

TABLE 3. The House of Trastámara, which ruled in Castile from 1369 to 1516, and in Aragon from 1412 to 1516, was founded by Henry (bastard son of Alfonso XI), who was married to Joan, heiress to the rights of succession claimed by the descendants of Ferdinand de la Cerda (the eldest son of Alfonso X, who died during the lifetime of his father). Under the principles of Roman law proclaimed in the *Siete Partidas*, the throne should have passed to Ferdinand's son. But Alfonso X's second son, Sancho IV, contested this claim and succeeded his father as king. (Broken lines indicate branches of the family that were not of the ruling line.)

Andalusia and Extremadura. The appearance of the spectre of famine and the devastating havoc of successive waves of the Black Death that began in the middle of the fourteenth century (1348, 1362, 1371, and 1375) also helped to thwart the brilliant beginnings of economic recovery in Castile under Peter the Cruel. The sum total of all these interrelated events permitted the ascendency of the *grandes* [7] of Castile — the pivotal axis of future national turmoil.

Two additional topics should be added to those already discussed; both could be explored in much greater depth. The first concerns the stimulus of the Mediterranean, which reached Castile through merchants from Genoa and through the trade of Seville; she responded by carrying out her first navigations in the *Mare Nostrum* and by attempting under Peter the Cruel to secure a port (Cartagena) on the eastern coast in order to export Castilian wool. The other is the first transplanting of Catalan institutions to the central plateau of Castile, carried out by Henry II of Trastámara, who had become familiar with them during his exile in the Crown of Aragon.

Portugal and the Crown of Aragon were confronted by problems identical to those of Castile, but were able to resolve them in a very different fashion. Aside from the fact that the development of their economies had varied from that of Castile, both countries undertook a stimulating program of maritime expansion that made it possible to solve the problem of the demands of the aristocracy in a less rigid way.

In Portugal two equally decisive factors were the national reaction to the Castilian attack of 1385 (broken at the battle of Aljubarrota) and the conversion of Lisbon into the preferred port for refueling in the trade between the Mediterranean and the Atlantic. Then came a policy of expansion in North Africa (the conquest of Ceuta and Tangier) that led on to the Atlantic adventure in which such magnanimous efforts were expended.

In the Crown of Aragon, a somewhat similar process took place.

---

[7] Vicens implies an ironic play on words: *grandes* can be translated not only as Grandees (the highest rank of Castilian nobility) but also as "great men."

Beginning of Dissension

At the beginning of the fourteenth century (as we have seen), with Catalonia in the vanguard, Aragon reached her historic zenith. As the immediate heir to the heroic generation of Peter the Great, the dynasty pursued an ambitious policy that recognized no limitations on the compass card.

During the century under discussion, the principal objectives of the Crown of Aragon were to pacify Sardinia, to reincorporate the Balearic Islands (which, together with the county of Roussillon, had been separated under the provisions of the will of James I), and to prepare for the annexation of Sicily (ruled since 1302 by a minor branch of the House of Aragon). Enterprises such as these — in which the kings of Aragon struggled against Genoa, her persistent and indomitable rival — demanded an accumulation of enormous human, military, and economic resources and, above all, patient perseverance immune both to the inevitable reverses and to the exaltation of victory.

The great organizer of the Catalan-Aragonese Empire was Peter IV the Ceremonious (1336–1387), conqueror of Mallorca and Sardinia. But his work was not completed until the following generation, when, in an effort that was to some degree beyond the capabilities of the nation, Sardinia was definitively vanquished in her repeated attempts to gain independence (1409) and the Throne of Sicily was incorporated into the senior branch of the House of Aragon.

This potential for expansion was reflected, simultaneously, in the dynasty's policy on the Peninsula. Contact with Castile was accentuated in the course of the fourteenth century. There were frequent frontier fights, intermarriages between dynasties, and commercial exchanges. For a few years James II became the arbiter of Spain and took advantage of his hegemony to extend the borders of the Valencian territory southward. Peter the Ceremonious was confronted by a Castilian counterattack: the troops of Peter the Cruel seriously menaced the Aragonese, demonstrating the military efficacy of Castile. But the political and diplomatic retort of Peter the Ceremonious was equally impressive; he exploited to the utmost the antagonism existing among the aristocratic parties of Castile and succeeded in forcing a life-and-death confrontation between his rival and the latter's half-brother, Henry of Trastámara.

By the end of the fourteenth century, one could have foreseen that the end result of this period of conflict would be the merger of these kingdoms under a common monarchy. But one could not have foreseen whether Castile or Aragon would dominate in such a merger.

Despite the spectacular nature of the Crown of Aragon's foreign policy during the fourteenth century, in the eyes of a historian it fades into the background when he contemplates the vital forces within the lands which composed that kingdom. A swarm of merchants underwrote the maritime expansion, sending the sailors of Barcelona and Mallorca from the Sea of Azov to the coasts of Senegal, or else to the shores of England and Flanders. Barcelona maintained consuls in the principal Mediterranean ports and in the great Atlantic emporiums. Sicily, Sardinia, and the center of the Barbary Coast were her fiefs. Nor should it be forgotten that Catalan merchants competed with Venetian and Genoese merchants in the traffic in spices between Alexandria and Toulouse in Languedoc, and in the trade in Mediterranean products between Naples and Brugge. Until 1420 they occupied second place in Brugge, center of the Nordic commerce, as well as a leading position in Alexandria, key to the markets of the Far East.

The wave of prosperity that pervaded the Crown of Aragon (for Valencia and Saragossa benefited from the stimulus with which Catalonia and Mallorca galvanized the joint enterprises) consolidated the authority of urban oligarchies within the governments of the increasingly powerful municipalities. These were open oligarchies, which admitted enriched merchants, and a new social group of bankers, on a par with the original patricians. From within this oligarchy the ideal of a contractual state [8] slowly took shape —

---

[8] Pacto has been translated as "contractual relationship" or "contractual state," the terms used by J. H. Elliott in his discussions of the crisis of this constitutional principle in 1640. Furthermore, Elliott sat in on the history colloquy in Barcelona, where Vicens Vives and his colleagues dis-

Beginning of Dissension

an ideal that would constitute one of the most authentic contributions of the urban patriciate of Catalonia to the politics of the quattrocento.

At that moment, because of the bourgeoisie's economic power, the Catalan-Aragonese monarchy was powerful enough to humble the nobility of Aragon, which had grown insolent because of its Privilegio General, conferred by Peter the Great at a difficult moment in his war with France and the Papacy.[9] At the battle of Epila (1348) it subjugated the Aragonese aristocracy and reduced it to those exact limits set by its military responsibilities and political exemptions.

Despite the largess of the dynasty, the Catalan-Aragonese nobility declined continuously after the end of the fourteenth century. Except for some few great magnates in the Pyrenees (the Counts of Pallars, Urgel, and Cardona), a few in Aragon (the Count of Híjar), and some in Valencia, the aristocracy possessed scarcely any landholdings or economic power of great significance. On any scale with their Castilian peers, even the greatest nobles of the Crown of Aragon would rank only very modestly. The result was that responsibility for the major political decisions of the country devolved upon the bourgeoisie.

As for the rural classes, a prolonged period of disorder aggravated their discontent, which dated from the time when the Black Death killed more than one-half of their members. Some became wealthy, others, steadily more impoverished. In both cases, the new circumstances induced them to present some elementary demands for personal liberty. Beginning in 1390, a great clamor for emancipation vibrated throughout the Catalan countryside.

---

cussed the concept of *pactismo*. See Elliott, *The Revolt of the Catalans* (Cambridge, 1963), p. 5 and *passim*.
[9] For the Privilegio General conferred by Peter the Great, see p. 59.

CHAPTER FOURTEEN

The Crisis of the Fifteenth Century

The word crisis sums up the history of Spain in the quattrocento. Once again this was not something peculiar to the peoples on the Peninsula, for the other nations of Western society were prey to the same turmoil. The waning of the cultural values of the Middle Ages and the emergence of a new spiritual and artistic movement — the Renaissance — merged in the course of this century with a phase of economic depression whose roots are to be found in the fourteenth century: decline of agriculture, withdrawal of capital from overseas trade, wars that razed the major economic regions, and, above all, the outbreak of the Black Death (1348) — a scourge that lingered on in Europe, lashing it severely, until the seventeenth century. Pestilence and death, followed by the abandonment of fields and industries, interlocked with misery and famine, created an infernal circle of depopulation and inflation. These factors sharpened the social conflicts between peasants and lords, artisans and patricians, nobles and monarchs, particularly during the last decades of the fourteenth century, when prices fell, commercial and industrial activity was paralyzed, and the lower classes accused their superiors of oppression and misgovernment. Beginning in 1380, Flanders, Italy, France, and England showed the effects of these blows, and so did the peoples of Spain.

The first violent reaction of the Spanish masses turned into an attack on the Jews. The anti-Hebraic movement had begun in the middle of the fourteenth century as a release for pent-up emotions and economic discontent. But the pogroms of 1391 developed into an extremely serious affair. Beginning in Seville, they spread through

Crisis of the Fifteenth Century

Andalusia and La Mancha, where there were widespread persecutions. Then they vaulted over into the most prosperous wool-trading cities of the North (Toledo, Madrid, Burgos, Logroño) and finally subsided on the Mediterranean seacoast in the Crown of Aragon: the Jewish quarters of Barcelona, Valencia, and Palma de Mallorca (to cite only the major urban areas) were looted.

This movement created a schism between the Christian and Mosaic communities, and an inevitable and dangerous mutual distrust. Above all, it led to the formation of an indecisive minority, composed of those Jews who converted to Catholicism between 1391 and 1415. Known as *Conversos* and numbering approximately one hundred thousand, they were influential because of their financial connections and their intellectual prestige. Within a short time they had become a magnet for all the hatred of the "Old Christians," not only because they continued to maintain contact with the Jews, but also because they had difficulty in adjusting to a new set of values in their daily activities, from their way of eating to their way of dressing. Very soon they were accused of being heretics and were called Judaizers and "swine" (*marranos*). This hostility was kept alive by Grandees, knights, and ecclesiastics — in general, the aristocratic classes whose vanity kept them perennially short of money. But in Castile as in Aragon, the Trastámara kings protected the Conversos, because they were both an indispensable source of financial aid in difficult moments and an administrative apparatus that the kings could not easily do without. In Catalonia the lending of money had been entrusted to bankers and solvent banking institutions, and therefore conditions were more favorable to the Conversos. There was never a demand in Catalonia for an Inquisition against Judaizers as there would be in Castile from the mid-fifteenth century on.

The contraction of the economy had immediate repercussions in the social sphere. The least complex were those unleashed in Castile, where the ambition of the nobility was to seize power in order thereby to protect their enormous fortunes: latifundia, properties extorted from the Crown, the grants by complaisant kings and regents of land and stipends (*juros y soldadas*[1]). To insure this wealth, they sought appropriate legal measures (the right to entail their estates and seigniory in gross), and financial concessions (the Mesta and its highest offices, collection of customs duties on goods transported by land or sea, taxes on livestock [2]). For these sublime aspirations the aristocracy plunged Castile into the chaos of four civil wars, the last an extremely violent one.

In contrast, the conflict in Catalonia developed more slowly, and encompassed all social classes: from 1395 on, unrest was evident among the peasants; from 1435 on, among the urban lower classes; and about this same time, among the patricians and nobility. This led to three simultaneous subversive movements: that of serfs against their lords; that of guilds and artisans against the patricians; and that of patricians and nobles against the authoritarian monarchy. Alfonso the Magnanimous supported the cause of peasants and artisans in Catalonia (but not that of the *foráns* in Mallorca),[3] so that in 1455, when he resolved the problem of the people's demands, he prescribed truly democratic measures. But these incited the privileged classes to retaliate; taking advantage of the circumstances, they would end up taking part in the uprising against John II in 1461 and 1462.

The social upheaval brought to the fore the problem of how to organize the peoples on the Peninsula. They were by then bound

---

[1] *Juros* were originally rights of perpetual ownership granted by medieval kings to nobles for lands they conquered. The term later came to mean an annuity paid from state revenue, granted in perpetuity, by a king to a noble. From the reign of the Catholic Monarchs, a juro was an annuity paid from state revenue in repayment of a loan by an individual to the Crown. *Soldadas* were royal payment for service, in money or in a temporary grant of land with seignorial privilege.

[2] Royal taxes on livestock, combined in 1343 as the "servicio y montazgo," became the principal source of Crown revenue. Servicio was a levy on each migratory flock, voted initially by the Cortes as an extraordinary surtax but soon converted into a regular tax. Montazgo was a fee paid to the Crown for the right to graze on mountains or pastures on royal lands.

[3] For the *foráns* of Mallorca, see p. 64.

by so many ties that the political arrangements consecrated in the twelfth century could not be continued. Castilian and Aragonese magnates crossed their common border and intervened directly in their neighbors' political problems. The ships of Biscay and Andalusia constituted the light fleet of the Catalan and Mallorcan maritime force during this period. And when Louis XI attacked Roussillon in 1473, Barcelona residents were the first to dream of the Castilian lances which their prince and heir apparent might bring to them from Segovia.[4]

The Renaissance monarchy of the Peninsula was in the process of creation — a monarchy that would bear the hallmark of Castile, not because of any mystical foresight, but because of empirical facts: her expanding population; the freedom of action that royalty could legally claim in Castile; the revenue which, despite the economic recession, the transhumant flocks of the Mesta continued to provide. The unification of the various kingdoms on the Peninsula under a single monarchy was preceded by a historic tradition and by political marriages between dynasties; some of these were cordial relationships, others hostile.[5]

The historic tradition was strengthened by the Humanist ideal. Rejecting Visigothic Spain as it had been conceived by Asturian legitimists and by the Leonese chancery, Humanism looked farther back for inspiration — to Roman Hispania, with its system of two large provinces (*Hispania Citerior* and *Hispania Ulterior*), which tallied with the division of territory left as a legacy from the struggle against the Muslims.[6] Catalan Humanists particularly cherished this concept — as for example, John Cardinal Margarit Pau. It is curious that Castile at this time was ratifying the name *España*, appro-

---

[4] For a discussion of the marriage in 1469 of Prince Ferdinand of Aragon and Isabel of Castile, see pp. 83-84.

[5] One example of a marriage between the dynasties of Aragon and Castile that failed because of "hostility" is the second marriage of Urraca, Queen of Castile (1109-1126), to Alfonso I, King of Aragon (1104-1134). Wed in 1109, Urraca and Alfonso were so incompatible that the marriage was annulled five or six years later.

[6] For a map of Roman Hispania, see p. 18.

priating a term that had originated in foreign commercial circles (first in Avignon and then in Flanders) and that distorted the traditional medieval idea of Hispania as an association (*mancomunidad*).

Marriages between dynasties prepared the advent of monarchical unity — the *Monarchia Hispania* — from the moment in which they made it possible to establish the same family, the Trastámaras, on the royal throne of Castile and of Aragon.

The death of Martin the Humanist, last king of the Crown of Aragon from the lineage of the House of Barcelona, led to the Compromise of Caspe (1412),[7] which broadened the scope of the Catalan political theory of a contractual state. The result was the designation of Ferdinand I, grandson of Henry II of Castile, as the new monarch of Aragon. For Aragon this was a beneficial turn of events, because it enabled her to take advantage of the fabulous wealth concentrated in the hands of this minor branch of the Trastámaras (through their contacts with the Conversos of Burgos and Medina del Campo,[8] the Order of Santiago, and the money of the Mesta). This money was used to win over the factions in Valencia and Saragossa that had rebelled against James Count of Urgel.[9]

---

[7] Martin the Humanist died on May 31, 1410, leaving no legitimate heir. Among the many pretenders to the throne, the two strongest were Ferdinand of Castile (a Trastámara, but on his mother's side a grandson of Peter the Ceremonious of Aragon) and James Count of Urgel, in Catalonia (a great-grandson of Peter the Ceremonious). The Cortes of the Crown of Aragon convened in February 1412 to decide which was the legal heir. When they could not agree, they selected a commission which met in Caspe (March-June 1412) and chose Ferdinand of Castile.

[8] The Trastámaras had invested in commerce, which brought them into contact with Conversos, who loyally aided them with money and advice. Vicens Vives, *Juan II de Aragón, 1398–1479: Monarquía y revolución en la España del siglo XV* (Barcelona, 1953), pp. 28–29.

[9] James Count of Urgel was closely identified with Catalan interests because of his title and his family. When Martin the Humanist died, James was acting as his representative (*lugarteniente*) in Saragossa; in support of his pretensions to the Crown of Aragon, he seized power, but Valencia and Saragossa rebelled against him. Even after the decision of Caspe, James continued to fight for his rights, but he was finally captured, and died in prison in 1433.

Crisis of the Fifteenth Century 81

The rebellions had been directed not so much against the Pretender himself as, above all else, against the inability of the Barcelona bourgeoisie to find a formula for reconciliation with the Pyrenean aristocracy, a formula that would solve the political dilemma which confronted the Crown of Aragon in connection with the problem of the succession: either a contractual state with its ultimate consequence of an aristocratic republic, or royal authoritarianism with its inevitable sequel of social, political, and administrative reforms.

The establishment of the same dynasty in Castile and in Aragon is no small factor in the developments leading to a unified monarchy of Las Españas. However, we must discard the romantic idea that the sovereigns of one or the other of the two branches did not rest until they had achieved this goal. Quite the contrary: the name of Aragon was never so hated by Castilian nobles as during the reign of John II of Castile. Nor was there any Castilian who so greatly condemned and despised the intrigues of his countrymen as did Alfonso the Magnanimous.[10]

Yet there was a group that, without either a doctrine or a program, went marching on in pursuit of unity — that of John II of Aragon, who was also King of Navarre and one of Castile's great magnates.[11] Caught between the sword of Louis XI of France and the wall of the Catalan Revolution, John saw no other recourse for salvation than to reply upon Castilian aid. Such was the pragmatic

---

[10] Ferdinand I of Trastámara (1412–1416) was succeeded by his eldest son, Alfonso V the Magnanimous (1416–1458), who was born and raised in Castile. Alfonso died leaving no legitimate heir and was succeeded by his brother, John, who had also been born in Castile.

[11] John II (1458–1479) was King of Navarre by right of his marriage to the Queen, Blanche. He inherited his great Castilian landholdings from his father's branch of the Trastámara fortune and from his fabulously wealthy mother, Leonore de Alburquerque. While Alfonso V reigned in Aragon, John and his brother, Henry, fought in Castile to defend the family lands from John II of Castile and from his minister Alvaro de Luna. In 1445 at Olmedo, John and Henry — the Infantes of Aragon — were defeated by Castilian forces led by Alvaro de Luna.

objective that sustained the project of a marriage between his son Ferdinand and the Castilian princess, Doña Isabel.

This project was to encounter considerable difficulties. Since the middle of the century, civil wars had laid waste the kingdoms of the Peninsula. In Portugal this was simply an episode, liquidated by the action on the battlefield of Alfarrobeira. But in Castile and in Navarre it became an endemic evil, a continuous series of partisan disputes that little by little consumed the resources of both countries.

The arrogant nobility of Castile split into two camps in the reign of John II (1406–1454) as a result of the passions generated by ambitious opponents: the Infantes of Aragon versus the Constable, Don Alvaro de Luna, who intuited the efficiency of an authoritarian monarchy but did not know how to sacrifice his own interests for the ideal that he was attempting to serve. The defeat of the Aragonese faction at Olmedo (1445) consolidated the position of their rivals, who thereby gained access to the means of power and to the very substantial wealth that the Infantes possessed in Castile. This power and wealth became a constant source of suspicion and jealousy, of intrigues and surprise attacks, which were not attenuated by the execution of Don Alvaro de Luna (1453). But the fate of the king's favorite did arouse a terror of death, which was added from that moment on to the old concerns of groups and factions, and made them want to seek all kind of guarantees as protection against a similar fate.

In this atmosphere Henry IV began to rule (1454–1474). His projects for the reform and restoration of his country, truly revolutionary insofar as they would have undermined the power of the Grandees, were in conflict with his own temperament — sentimental, tolerant, and excessively flexible. The Court's program, which the Conversos supported with their money, roused all Grandees against Henry IV. Disregarding their factions, they reached agreement on a joint plan of action which would ensure their interests — that is to say, possession of lands, privileges, and annuities.

In 1465 at Avila Henry IV was deposed and his stepbrother,

Alfonso,[12] was elevated to his place. But the revolutionary bloc disintegrated because of opposition from the people, widely demonstrated throughout Castile, and because of the inevitable mistrust among the leaders of the aristocratic movement. The death of the Pretender, Alfonso, made possible what appeared to be a general reconciliation in the interview at Los Toros de Guisando (1468); the rebels recognized the government of Henry IV on the condition that he admit their own leader, Princess Isabel, as his successor to the throne. Despite agreement upon this formula, tranquility was not restored to Castile.

In the following year, Isabel's marriage to the son of the Aragonese monarch brought up for discussion once again not only the future fate of the parties locked in combat, but also the general orientation of Castilian policies. At that moment, Castile could choose an Atlantic or a Mediterranean orientation. The first would have had the support of France, whose alliance with Castile dated back a century. The second might have led to a rapprochement with Burgundy, whose markets were crowded with Castilian wool vendors. Actually, there was no intellectual decision. The dramatic choice was made by force of arms.

The effectiveness of Isabel's marriage to the son of the Aragonese monarch depended upon the outcome of the desperate situation of King John II in Aragon. His brother and predecessor on the throne, Alfonso the Magnanimous (1416–1458), had been a great figure in the Mediterranean, bestowing upon the cautious Catalan-Aragonese policy the dynamic and imperialistic mark of his Castilian lineage. During his reign, the efficacy of collaboration between the two most important peoples of the Peninsula had been demonstrated in the conquest of Naples and in the extension of political influence in the eastern Mediterranean basin. But the symptoms of future

---

[12] Henry IV's father (John II, 1406–1454) had married twice. Of John's marriage to Mary of Aragón, Henry IV was the only surviving child. The children of John's second marriage, to Isabel of Portugal, were Alfonso (who died in 1468) and Isabel, who married Ferdinand of Aragon.

evils also made their appearance: unsteadiness in action, lack of fixed objectives, and the exhaustion of the nation in enterprises beyond her immediate capacities.

This policy created an atmosphere of unrest in Catalonia where the principles of a contractual state, based on an oligarchy of nobles and bourgeoisie, were stated with increasing precision (in the Cortes from 1454 to 1458) in the face of revolutionary outbreaks by the urban lower classes and peasant masses. In 1455 artisans and guilds won positions of authority in the Barcelona city government and this, together with the demands of serfs for lands and liberty, led to the storing up of a great quantity of explosive material in Catalonia; the tense relations between John II and his son, Charles, Prince of Viana, served to ignite the explosion.[13]

Since 1451 father and son had fought in Navarre, where they represented respectively, the peasant and seignorial party of the river basin (la Ribera) and the pastoral, traditionalist group from the mountains. This conflict, fomented by Castilian gold, was resolved in favor of the monarch, but he was incapable of pacifying the nation. In 1460 John II and the Prince of Viana reached an agreement that the latter broke within a few months by involving himself in indiscrete negotiations with Castile to arrange a marriage. Exasperated by (false) accusations, the monarch ordered the arrest of his son in Lérida (1460). This act kindled the Catalan Revolution.

During the first stage of the revolution, a unanimous Catalonia succeeded in subjugating the monarchy: it wrested from John II liberty for Prince Charles, and even more important, a code of broad political concessions that transformed Catalonia into a crowned republic (the Capitulations of Villafranca del Penedés, 1461).

But when the Prince of Viana died a few months later, demagogy easily took hold of a highly susceptible people; it was at this level that the civil war was launched. At the side of John II fought part

---

[13] Charles was John's son by Blanche, Queen of Navarre, who died in 1441. She asked Charles not to claim Navarre until John's death, but he rebelled in 1451, unsuccessfully. When John became King of Aragon in 1458, Charles was his legal heir. But John favored Ferdinand (born in 1452 of his second marriage, to Joan Enríquez of Castile).

of the nobility, almost all the clergy, and — although it may seem surprising — the majority of the peasants. Opposing him were the lower nobility, the patriciate, and some of the artisans (who, in tribute to Charles of Viana, discarded their monarchical position of 1460–1461).[14] Barcelona emptied her treasuries into the fight to such an extent that the king could withstand the revolutionary coup of May 1462 only by seeking the protection of Louis XI of France.

Thereupon the Catalans dethroned John II and proclaimed Henry IV of Castile as King of Aragon. The Castilian Crown was now provided with an obvious opportunity to extend its dominions as far as the Mediterranean, but succumbed instead to French pressures and to treacherous advisors. A Catalan attempt to secure the support of Portugal and Burgundy by appointing Peter, Constable of Portugal, as "King of the Catalans" collapsed within a short time, following a series of military and political reverses for the Portuguese paladin.

In 1466 Barcelona might have capitulated to the Aragonese monarch (after the defeat at Prats del Rei and the surrender of Tortosa) if the Francophile party had not imposed the candidacy of René of Anjou to succeed the deceased Constable of Portugal. The election of René, who was Count of Provence, was equivalent to the indirect election of his nephew, Louis XI of France, and to opening the gateway of the Pyrenees to that country.

Louis XI therefore abandoned the cause of John II. His troops achieved resounding success, so much so that they might have established themselves in Catalonia and even dismembered the Crown of Aragon had it not been for the complicated and astute diplomatic moves of John II to defeat the Catalan revolution. He set in motion the power of England, Brittany, Burgundy, and Naples, and when he considered this insufficient, the power of Castile. When Barcelona surrendered in 1472 — salvaging the theoretical principles of the revolutionary movement — it was an index of the success of John II's anti-French program.

---

[14] For the basis of the alliance in 1460–1461 between John II and the artisan class, see pp. 81–84.

The last round of the game was played out on the Castilian card table. Henry IV, eternally enamored of peace, had with difficulty maintained an equilibrium, by balancing the Grandees of Castile against each other, Aragon against France, his daughter against his sister. At his death the inevitable conflict broke out. A war of succession began that involved not only a juridical problem — that of the respective rights of Princess Isabel and Princess Joan [15] — but also the vastly greater problem of the role that Castile would play in the organization of the Peninsula and in international politics. France and Portugal supported Princess Joan. Aragon and her allies (Naples, Burgundy, and England) supported Princess Isabel. The youthful efficiency of Ferdinand of Aragon, the reformist orientation of the Aragonese and Catalan intervention in Castile, and the military support of experienced Mediterranean technicians assured victory for Isabel's party.

Having eliminated the principal source of her political discord — the duplicity of Trastámara influences within the country — Castile could be organized to prepare for her role as the sustaining force of Hispanic society.

---

[15] Joan (1462–1530) was the daughter of Henry IV and of his Queen, Joan of Portugal. The supporters of Isabel claimed that Joan was actually the daughter of the Queen by a lover, Beltrán de la Cueva; for this reason, she bears the sobriquet Juana la Beltraneja. For the case for Joan's illegitimacy, the most important book is still A. Paz y Melia, *El cronista Alonso de Palencia* (Madrid, 1914). Modern historiography sustains Joan's legitimacy; see Gregorio Marañon, *Ensayo biológico sobre Enrique IV de Castilla* (Madrid, 1930), and Orestes Ferrara, *L'Avenement d'Isabelle la Catholique* (Paris, 1958).

CHAPTER FIFTEEN

The Ordering Of Hispania by the Catholic Monarchs

In 1479 the civil war ended in Castile. John II of Aragon had died at the beginning of that same year. His son Ferdinand and his daughter-in-law — the Catholic Monarchs, as they were called [1] — began to govern jointly, under the same dynasty, the Kingdoms of Aragon and Castile (1479-1504). Nothing more, but nothing less. It is futile to apply romantic adjectives to so renowned an event. Viewed from abroad, ancient Hispania (only Portugal was still separated) had now only one voice and one will. And that summed up the matter.

The peoples united under the same scepter enjoyed a certain climate of fellowship which shaped the course of this government. The feeling was more intense — it must be stated — along the Mediterranean than on the central plateau, particularly during the years when Ferdinand was regent (1504-1516).[2] In any event, a joint

---

[1] Ferdinand and Isabel received the title of "los Reyes Católicos" from Pope Alexander VI (the Spaniard, Rodrigo Borja) in 1494, two years after the capture of Granada from the Muslims; the title was thus ostensibly a reward for their services to Christendom. But the Pope had also calculated that bestowal of a title equal in prestige to that of the French kings ("le Roi très Chrétien," first conferred on French kings in the fourteenth century, was reserved exclusively for them in the fifteenth) would secure for him Spanish support of his campaign to oust the French forces of Charles VIII from Italy.

[2] From Isabel's death in 1504 until his own death in 1516, Ferdinand acted almost continuously as regent in the Kingdom of Castile. The law-

policy on military, domestic, and foreign affairs benefited the two kingdoms equally. For Castile it resolved that centuries-old frontier problem with Aragon which had held her down until then, and left her free to strike a telling blow against Islam's last redoubt on the Peninsula.

In the course of eleven years of crude warfare, the Castilian army (which acquired its definitive military formation in this obstinate enterprise) conquered the Nasrid dynasty's territory of Granada. In 1492 the city of Granada capitulated, releasing Castile's potential at the very moment in which France once again brought up the problem of Italy. This enabled Ferdinand the Catholic to carry out excellent stratagems in the European diplomatic game.

Without a struggle, Ferdinand secured from Charles VIII the return of Roussillon and Cerdagne (1493), counties that France had occupied since the reign of John II. He thereby closed up the dangerous gap in the Pyrenean frontier of the Crown of Aragon. Thereafter, with Castilian support, he could throw himself into the Italian expeditions with a freedom to maneuver that his Aragonese predecessors (including his uncle, Alfonso the Magnanimous) had lacked. Either by allying himself with the kings of France, or by scheming against them with the Holy See and with Italian potentates, Ferdinand in 1504 succeeded in retrieving from the bastard Aragonese branch the Kingdom of Naples, the eastern bastion of the Catalan-Aragonese expansion in the Mediterranean.[3] A decisive factor in this operation was the appearance of the Castilian army in the war theatres of the Continent, where it would dominate for one and a half centuries.

A short time later, the Italian problem created a set of circumstances that enabled Ferdinand to intervene in Navarre and to claim it for Castile (1512). The new development ensured Hispanic

---

ful heir of Isabel was their daughter Joan, who was adjudged mentally incompetent.

[3] Alfonso V had, at his death in 1458, left the Crown of Aragon (including Sicily) to his brother, John II, but willed the Kingdom of Naples (which he had conquered) to a bastard son, Ferdinand.

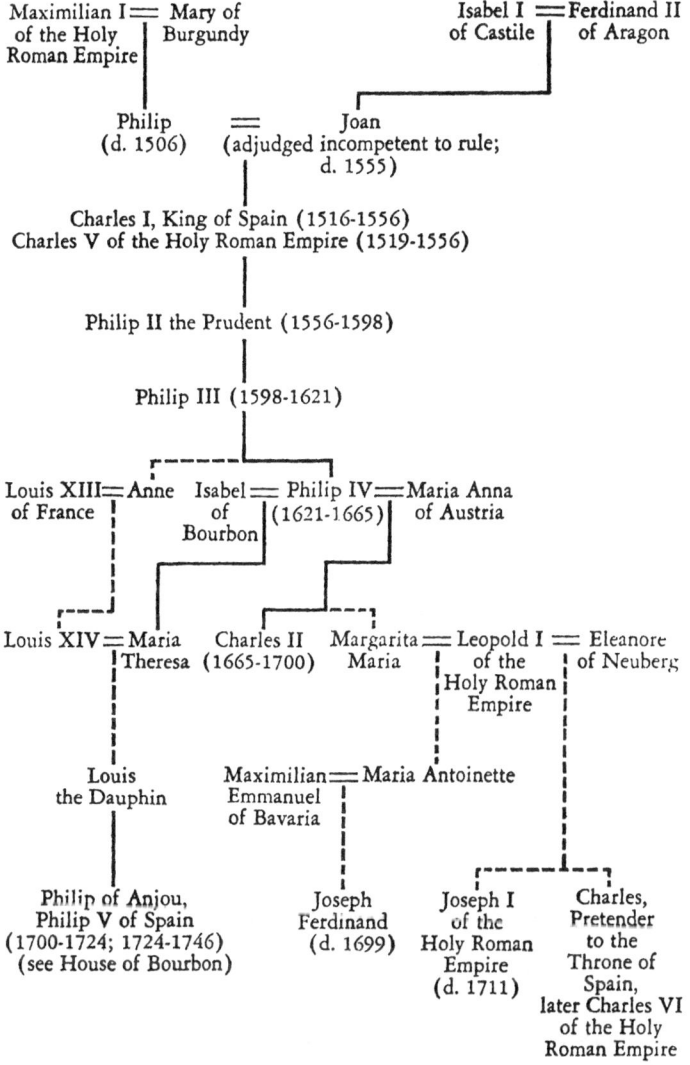

TABLE 4. The House of Austria (the Spanish Hapsburgs), which ruled in Spain from 1516 to 1700. (Broken lines indicate branches of the family that were not of the ruling line).

security in the Pyrenees, by eliminating a propitious terrain for French maneuvering. Navarre did not, however, lose her distinctive regime — an exception to the policy of the Crown of Castile; her incorporation left her with the autonomy that had characterized the policy followed by the great monarchs of the House of Barcelona.

Lured by the Mediterranean policy of the Catalan-Aragonese Crown, Castile adopted a course of action on the European problem that was diametrically opposed to that which she had followed during the Middle Ages — that is, the new course opposed the interests of France, her faithful ally since the time of the Trastámara King, Henry II. The Catholic Monarchs concluded an active alliance with the Dukes of Burgundy and, through them, with the German Empire — in brief, an alliance with the Hapsburgs, who at that time, in the person of Maximilian, had seized control of both the Duchy and the Imperial Crown. Within the total policy of the Spanish monarchs, this pact with Maximilian — teeming with grave omens — was only one of the master threads of their diplomatic web; the others were tied to England and to Portugal.[4]

Theoretically the monarchy of the Catholic King and Queen offered equal opportunities to all the peoples on the Peninsula within the newly ordered Hispania, as I noted in reference to the incorporation of Navarre into the Crown of Castile. It is important to say that the spokesman for this policy was Ferdinand. Isabel felt a loyalty to the Castilian monarchy's policy of integration, as she demonstrated by subjugating Galicia at the beginning of her reign.

---

[4] The foreign policy of the Catholic Monarchs was consolidated by a series of dynastic alliances. One alliance was with Portugal: their oldest daughter, Isabel, was married to the heir to the throne (first to Afonso, then to Manoel). When Isabel died, the Catholic Monarchs' younger daughter, Mary, was married to Manoel. An alliance with England was also consolidated through a marriage: the Monarch's youngest daughter, Catherine, was married to the heir apparent (first to Arthur, then to Henry VIII). The third alliance, with the Hapsburgs, was reinforced by marrying their only son, John, to a Hapsburg princess, and a daughter, Joan, to the Hapsburg heir, Philip. The deaths of John and Mary left Joan as the heir of the Catholic Monarchs. Thus Joan's son, Charles, inherited the Spanish as well as the Hapsburg and Burgundian domains.

Her husband pursued a policy of administrative dualism vis-à-vis Aragon and Castile (the creation of the Council of Aragon, 1494), while in Catalonia and the Crown of Aragon he consolidated the system of government by means of a contractual relationship. In this respect his political game was far superior to that of the other monarchs of his era, because he combined a true respect for the institutions of his patrimonial states with a full exercise of his royal authority (monarchic authoritarianism). Ferdinand's concept of Hispania as a pluralistic monarchy did not prevent him from encouraging Catalan and Aragonese families and institutions to amalgamate with their counterparts in Castile. One such case was that of the Tribunal of the Holy Office of the Inquisition, the only institution whose jurisdiction extended throughout Spain. Another involved the spread in Castile of various Catalan mercantile and guild institutions, such as occurred in the foundation of merchant guilds (*consulados*) in Burgos and Bilbao.

Despite these efforts it was difficult to overcome the traditional forces that delimited each Crown's sphere of influence. Thus there was an oceanic policy linked to Castile, and a North African policy limited to Aragon and Catalonia. Although the court indiscriminately employed Castilian and Aragonese men and resources to achieve its objectives, the discovery of America (1492) was conceived as an enterprise of the Castilian Crown, as a monopoly that the latter must defend on behalf of her subjects at any cost. During his regency Ferdinand provided a more just and natural interpretation of the problem, not only in the case of America, but also in that of North Africa. Even though the conquest of Oran, Algeria, and Tripoli (1509–1511) was carried out under Aragonese auspices, this did not preclude the participation of numerous military contingents from Castile, mobilized by Francis Cardinal Jiménez de Cisneros in his role as Archbishop of Toledo. Castile's presence in the Mediterranean expeditions showed that the country was able to take maximum advantage of the opportunities offered by the Catholic Monarchs. From the first moment Castile held the dominant position in the Hispanic monarchy because of her territory and population and also because of the contemporaneous decadence of

Catalonia, still convalescing from the obstinate revolutionary fury that had dissipated her resources.

Valencia, rich, prosperous, and cultured, might have assumed the commanding role on the Mediterranean façade of the Peninsula exercised until then by the Catalan principality. Instead she limited her activities to serving as the Hispanic gateway to the Renaissance and to emptying her generous purse into the eternally exhausted coffers of the royal treasury. Moreover, Valencia quickly succumbed to the aura of Castilian culture, an act of awed submission that was a premature example of what was to become a reality in all Hispania during the seventeenth and eighteenth centuries.

These basic conditions induced the Catholic monarchs to center their activity in Castile, as did, even more so, the legal barriers that restrained the monarchy's freedom to act in Navarre and in the Crown of Aragon, but that were not present in Castile. This policy had enormous consequences: throughout the territory of Spain the monarchs began to apply political remedies for problems that affected only the Kingdom of Castile, or that had reached a virulent stage only in Castile.

One of these — the problem of the continued existence of Jewish communities and its corrollary, the problem of the Conversos who had infiltrated the executive branch of the nation — instigated the establishment of the Inquisition during the first years of the Catholic Monarchs' reign and, subsequently, the decree expelling the Jews from the Hispanic monarchy (1492). The first great Spanish purge secured unity of faith based on the Catholic Church, which had been exhilarated by its three centuries as the spiritual and military director of the reconquest. However, it eliminated from the social life of Castile the only groups that might have responded to the stimulus of an incipient capitalism; it undermined the prosperous economy of many municipalities; it mobilized an enormous quantity of wealth, a large part of which was used to finance the foreign policy of the Catholic monarchs, another part of which was dissipated in the hands of the aristocrats and functionaries who were in charge of the embargo on the goods of those who fled or were expelled. The wave of terror aroused by these measures would affect the Castilian mentality within a short time — that time necessary for Judaizers and pseudo-converts to dig catacombs, and then for there to emerge upon the public scene a need, linked with the sense of honor, to prove the legitimacy of one's blood.[5]

The same principles of rigid vigilance and inexorable intransigence were applied both to longtime converts from Islam and to the newly incorporated Mudejars of Granada. For some years drastic measures were avoided. But in 1502 the Muslims of Granada, together with those of Castile, ceased to exist as a legal minority; they were ordered to convert to Christianity or leave the country. Needless to say, they converted en masse: the inevitable result was the creation of an enclave that could not be assimilated and that was predisposed to subversive activity. In all, there were three hundred thousand Muslim converts to Christianity (Moriscos) in the kingdoms of Spain, half of these in the lands of the Crown of Aragon.

At this moment we are unearthing the foundations of the social policy of the Catholic Monarchs. Ferdinand gave evidence of a liberal policy in the arbitral Sentence of Guadalupe in 1486, through which he resolved the dispute of the Catalan serfs, though to some degree he had been forced to act by a bloody peasant uprising. But

---

[5] Vicens is referring to two consequences of the fact that after 1525, juridically speaking, all Spaniards were Catholics (either "Old Christians," or converts from Judaism and Islam, "New Christians"). First, he accepts the premise that those Jews who converted did so in order to remain in Spain and hold public office but secretly remained true to their faith, which they transmitted in a sub-culture from generation to generation. This crypto-Judaism is extremely controversial. Secondly, from 1547 on converts were officially excluded from office in Church and state: candidates had to produce a certificate of "clean blood" (*limpieza de sangre*) proving that they had no Muslim or Jewish ancestors. Recent research has shown that because so many prominent families had intermarried with Jewish converts, individuals resorted to subterfuge (falsified certificates) and became hypersensitive about the honor of their family. The new emphasis on the fact that orthodox Catholicism did not suffice for public office has caused historians to reevaluate the expulsion of Jews and Moriscos and the Inquisition less as religious than as social and possibly racial problems.

this was a molecule lost in the ocean of the pro-aristocratic measures that characterized his reign in Castile.

Despite the attempt of royalty to stimulate the middle classes, Castilian nobles continued to be sacrosanct in their privileged political positions and landholdings. True, they did have to renounce all spoils seized from the royal patrimony since 1466, but in exchange they received absolute security for previous spoils (which were the more important). In like manner, they renounced their capricious manipulation of national affairs, their fierce separatist independence, and their redoubts in the military orders. But behind the façade of monarchic authoritarianism, behind their apparent political submission to the Crown, the nobles made themselves the great dominating force in the country. They did so through their lands and privileges (*encomiendas, señoríos,* and latifundia),[6] which were reinforced by continuous grants of the title of Grandee, by distribution of lands (in the Kingdom of Granada), and by the establishment of entailed estates (*mayorazgos*).

These developments jeopardized the future of Castilian agriculture. The ease of the wool business, in which the aristocracy had accumulated so many economic interests and for which the court had contrived so many fiscal measures, led to the consolidation of the privileges of the Mesta, with its inevitable sequel: an increase in land left uncultivated and the exclusion of agriculture from enclosed pastures. From 1502 on, it was necessary to set a fixed maximum price on grain, because the countryside could not meet the needs of the population; from that time on, Castile was constantly threatened by the specter of famine.

On such a weak agricultural base, it was impossible to erect a solid economic edifice. Although the Catholic Monarchs favored industry and commerce by protective measures, they did not pursue a coherent mercantilist policy. But even if they had, such a policy

---

[6] *Encomiendas* consisted of the territory, income, and title granted by a military order to a lord, theoretically for a limited period of time. *Señoríos legos* were lands over which the Crown granted laymen the rights of lords, although not necessarily legal title to the land.

Ordering by the Catholic Monarchs 95

was impossible in a land that lacked capital to invest in production. The discovery of the lands in America was still too recent for their hidden treasures to be considered for use in industrial expansion. Later, foreign wars and agricultural misery would squander the gold that fortune bestowed so prodigiously upon Castile.

In summary, the reign was complex and interesting, far removed from the monolithic character it is usually judged to have had by extremists of one side or the other. Splendid in its foreign enterprises, especially in carrying out the discovery of America, it was nevertheless a reign that vacillated in its domestic objectives, for there were many conflicts — and notable ones — among the various kingdoms that constituted the new monarchy, and among the different social classes within each of the kingdoms.

But at the end of the reign, the promising rhythm of the first wave of economic recovery in Europe generated a sensation of wellbeing and of wealth that would affect even devitalized Catalonia. This spirit opened the way for the architectural achievements of the period (the initial Plateresque) and for the cultural initiatives of a Cisneros in Alcalá de Henares.[7] Contemporaneous with the establishment of the Hispanic monarchy, Castilian Humanism flourished and colored it with raptures of imperial grandeur.

---

[7] The University of Alcalá de Henares (the parent institution of the present-day University of Madrid) opened officially on October 18, 1509, under the patronage of Cardinal Cisneros. Alcalá was to specialize in theology reflecting the fact that, in contrast with secular Italian Humanism, Spanish Humanism, like that of northern Europe, was primarily religious. Renaissance scholarship and the printing press were to be used to educate clergy, thereby strengthening the Church. Because Cisneros wanted students at Alcalá to study the original text of the Bible, he began in 1510 to subsidize preparation of the *Biblia Poliglota Complutense* (from Complutum, the Latin name for the town of Alcalá); he gathered scholars, procured manuscripts, and bought a printing press. The six-volume work, with texts in Hebrew, Aramaic, Greek, and that of the Latin Vulgate, was printed 1515-1517. But not until 1520 did it secure a papal imprimatur; nor did it go on sale until 1522, an event obscured by publication of a third edition of Erasmus' far more inexpensive translation of the New Testament.

CHAPTER SIXTEEN

Hispania Under the Hapsburg Monarchy

For three generations — those of Charles I, Philip II, and Philip III — the Hispanic monarchy continued on the course set by the Catholic King and Queen. In doing so it was influenced as much by a sense of the grandeur of the Catholic Monarchs' international achievements in Europe and America as by the administrative structure that they had fashioned for governing and dispensing justice in their possessions. During this era no one doubted that the best of all possible regimes for Spain was a system of dynastic unity combined with broad regional autonomy, nor did anyone interfere with the preponderant role that Castile played in the politics, the economy, and the culture of Hispania.

While Aragon was experiencing a period of relative prosperity, Catalonia and Valencia vegetated in somewhat gloomy isolation; only extremely grave problems such as the Turkish menace stirred them and succeeded in evoking the heroic efforts of old. The character of the Catalan principality was being transformed at that same time by the slow but continuous infiltration of persons from the south of France who promoted agriculture along the coast and banditry in the interior.[1] Lacking any collective aspiration, Catalans dispersed their energies in petty conflicts.

In this era the Hispanic ideal became identified with the ideal represented by Castile. The recent shift of geopolitical importance

---

[1] On this subject see Jorge Nadal Oller and Emilio Giralt y Raventós, *La population catalane de 1553 à 1717: L'immigration française et les autres facteurs de son développement* (Paris, 1960). See also Juan Reglá, *El bandolerisme catalá* (Barcelona, 1962).

The Hapsburg Monarchs

from the Mediterranean to the Atlantic had reinforced Castile's mission as the axis of the monarchy. Despite the deficiencies in her agricultural system, which plunged the land into great famines and made it necessary to purchase wheat in the Baltic Sea area; despite the meager output of an industry whose products could compete neither in quality nor in price with those of France, Flanders, and Italy; despite the financial incompetency of a court constantly on the verge of bankruptcy — despite all this Castile stood firm, in conflict with a Europe that vacillated in the face of the successive onslaughts of the Protestant tide.

True, Castile did rely upon the injection of precious metals from America at critical moments in the struggle: the decisiveness of this factor was shown in 1575 at the fair in Medina del Campo, when financial operations collapsed and brought on the bankruptcy of the Castilian wool trade. But America was also a constant drain; the enterprising individuals who departed for there were not replaced in the mother country.

On the whole, Castile became obsessed with her task. In order to fulfill her mission, she pruned any noble elements that burgeoned in her midst — the bourgeois ideal in the War of the *Comunidades*,[2] the offshoots of the Humanism of Erasmus and of the Renaissance — in her tenacious struggle to maintain orthodoxy. This harsh sacrifice found its compensation in the profound spirituality discovered within a Church that was able to synthesize the buoyant splendor of the dynasty and the democratizing collectivism of the people. Theologians and missionaries, mystics and ascetics, enriched this golden age of Spanish ecclesiastical life.

The profound scorn for terrestrial matters, the ideal of an ecumenical mission for Spain, definitively interred any program for the economic recovery of Castile. Genoese bankers monopolized the profits from the exploitation of American mines; Genoese outfitters

---

[2] Between 1519 and 1521, Charles I and the nobility fought against the *Comunidades*, the great incorporated municipalities of Castile — that is, they fought against the bourgeoisie and the urban gentry. At the Battle of Villalar in 1521, the Comunidades were defeated and their leaders (Juan Padilla, Juan Bravo, and Francisco Maldonado) were executed.

controlled the provisioning of the fleets. Meanwhile, Italian, Flemish, and French merchants seized control of the colonial trade by means of the fairs at Medina del Campo and the embarkations from Seville and Cádiz. Far from reacting, the monarchy became more and more involved in dangerous financial disorders that tied it to the capitalist machinery on the far side of the Pyrenees; at first this tie was indispensable, then ruinous, and finally sterile.

Philip II, with his state paternalism, exhausted Castile's economic potential by his shortsighted mercantilist policies. The only signs within the country of this economic potential were the relative prosperity of cloth manufacturers in the provinces, the unrestrained and oppressive splendor of Seville, and the munificent buildings constructed by a few Andalusian and Extremaduran gentry enriched by American holdings (*encomiendas*).[3] We find no capital invested in the country either to increase the productivity of the agricultural soil or to form commercial companies to exploit the oceanic world — not even to exploit the slave trade, which was left in the hands of the Portuguese and the French.

Castile's failure to comprehend the capitalist world made it impossible for her to compete with Europe. Here is the key factor in the central problem of the history of Spain today. And it must be clarified, going deeper not only into the mechanics of European and colonial trade, but also into the Castilian mentality of Philip II's era. If the bourgeoisie were a transitory phenomenon in Castile, they were even more so if the industrial sector is considered. Despite the fact that they were protected by a monopoly, the industries of Segovia, Cuenca, Toledo, Córdoba, and Seville never acquired any momentum of their own. And because they lacked capital, technicians, and stockpiles of raw materials, they collapsed at the slightest upset caused by a cyclical crisis or by the unleasing of a new wave of inflation. From 1590 onward the cloth and silk industries of Castile were paralyzed, and the workers, left without employment, went to Madrid to augment the legion of beggars and day laborers.

---

[3] For a discussion of encomiendas, see *n*. 3, p. 108.

The Hapsburg Monarchs

Precisely those who did possess money (aristocrats, gentry in Andalusia and Extremadura, and retired government officials) petrified it in construction (churches, palaces, and monasteries) or sanctified it in works of art. But none of them succumbed to the temptation to engage in industry, or even simply in commerce. Behind this mentality one can detect not only Castilian haughtiness, but also a fear of risking one's honor — in a case such as this, honor would be distinguished from a supposedly Judaic ideal of usury and of illicit gains. And once again this brings to the fore the theme of the "New Christian" that fills so many pages of the history of Castile's inner life during the sixteenth and seventeenth centuries.

Only later would Castile learn from experience that the wealth of a nation is the basis for a successful foreign policy, that a sound economy compensates for a thousand lost battles. Charles I, an ecumenical monarch educated in the commercial atmosphere of Flanders, might have led the Hispanic monarchy in this direction (and attempted to do so in 1529, when he liberalized trade with America), but his multiple ambitions forced him to plunder the wealth of Castile. The wars which Charles waged against Francis I of France revealed the extent of his resources: he established Spanish hegemony in Italy after the Battle of Pavia (1525) and dazzled the Continent with the splendor of his Caesarean coronation in Bologna (1529). But Charles' wars did not make a vassal of France, or terrorize the German Protestants, or halt the Ottoman Turks, or even put an end to the arrogance of the Berbers along the Mediterranean coast. Charles I formulated his own policy, one often based on a Burgundian sense of heroism or on the liberalism of Erasmus; it was therefore unintelligible to the upper ranks of Spanish society. As a result of this grand excursion into Europe on the arm of the Emperor, Castile returned home with an accentuated Francophobia, with a concentrated hatred of heterodoxy, and a tremendous scorn for the perverse and dazzling society of Europe.

The Calvinist onslaught — with a creed, dogma, and mentality as absolute as those of the Catholics — found a Castile in full spiritual reaction. The rigid cordon set up by Philip II (1556–1598) made it possible to convert Castile into the European center of orthodox resistance, although her course of action often diverged from the Pontificate's own objectives. Castile sealed herself off to influences from abroad, and was meticulously scrutinized by the Inquisition and administrative tribunals; Spaniards were even prohibited from studying in foreign universities, except at Bologna. This was the *volte-face* of 1572 that made Spain impermeable. It destroyed the compromise worked out by intellectuals during the preceding two generations, during which time a defense of the purity of the faith and an unyielding orthodoxy had not hindered richly rewarding excursions into the field of Western Humanism; I might cite the examples of Cardinal Cisneros, Luis Vives, and Francisco de Vitoria. Throughout that period religious unity had served to cover over the gaps that were clearly apparent in the Catholic Monarchs' structure of political pluralism.

Now that the Hispanic monarchy had taken upon its shoulders the burden of defending Catholicism — from Malta to the North Sea — it perfected the rudimentary attempts at centralization initiated by the Catholic Monarchs and by Charles I. The instrument used in this process was a system of Councils, meeting in permanent session, in a fixed capital — in Madrid, which at the end of the sixteenth century achieved its rank as the historic capital. Even if Madrid's geophysical location is taken into account, its designation as the capital effected nothing per se. The important thing was the system: the network of Councils — a concert of aristocrats and lawyers, bureaucrats and employees of all levels — which Philip II pressed into the service of his Crown. A wave of paper spread from throughout the entire land, inundating the Councils themselves and exhausting their administrative resources, bewildering even the ranking bureaucrat of the state — the scrupulous reigning monarch. Yet Philip kept tight hold over the Councils, and so his political directives were only delayed, not distorted, by administrators.

The formulation of high-level policy decisions was strictly limited

The Hapsburg Monarchs

to the inner circle of those who worked directly with *El Prudente*.[4] Under Antonio Pérez' direction[5] this circle was still somewhat liberal, but it became absolutely intransigent following the crisis of 1580, the dangerous turn in foreign affairs, and the clear demonstration (in the great famine of 1582) of the malfunctioning of Castile's agrarian economy.

And yet with all this, the dynamism and faith of the Castilian people allowed the monarchy to live through hours of universal euphoria: the Turks were contained in the Mediterranean after the victory at Lepanto (1571); the Kingdom of Portugal was joined to the Hispanic Crown after 1581,[6] together with her immense African and Indian colonial world, and the land of spices in the Far East; the Lowlands, in revolt since 1566, again and again were retained within Spain's defensive ramparts; France, carefully supervised during her dangerous religious meanderings, was brought back to the fold of orthodoxy by the stern attention of El Prudente. Only England — and acting in England's favor, Castile's defective economic and naval preparation, her financial bankruptcy, and the specter of misery — embittered the successes of *Hispania Magna*.

---

[4] "The Prudent," the sobriquet of Philip II, still connotes in Spanish the cardinal virtue of making decisions on the basis of reason alone, avoiding the extremes to which emotions might lead. It has not acquired the overtones of the English word, of weighing the expediency as well as the wisdom of a decision.

[5] Antonio Pérez (1540–1611), as Secretary to the Council of Castile and Secretary of State for Northern Affairs (that is, Flanders, England, and so on), enjoyed the complete confidence of Philip II until 1580, when he was implicated in a very important political murder. Because of the foreign and domestic consequences Pérez was arrested. After eleven years in prison he escaped, first to Aragon (where he incited a rebellion in defense of Aragonese privileges) and then to France. In 1594 he published the famous *Relaciones*, which purportedly reveals secrets in the life of Philip II.

[6] In 1580 the last of the House of Beja (descendants of the House of Avís) died in Portugal. Philip II claimed the kingdom on the basis of rights inherited from his mother, Isabel of Portugal. In 1581 the Portuguese Cortes acknowledged the legality of his claim.

The disaster of the "Invincible Armada" (1588) had both immediate and long-range consequences: the Netherlands could not be reduced to submission, France would recover as a great European power, and the separation of Portugal became inevitable.

At the death of the great monarch, who had imposed so exhausting a pace upon his kingdoms without achieving any concrete practical results, the edifice of the Hispanic monarchy did not collapse immediately, because a fervent desire for peace dominated the West after that turbulent period of conflict: peace was concluded with France in 1598, with England in 1604, and with the Netherlands in 1609. It was a propitious occasion to rectify errors, to modify systems. But the Councils continued to function in accordance with their habitual bureaucratic traditionalism. They definitively forced upon the incompetent Philip III (already but a shadow of the primitive biological stock of the Hapsburgs, the House of Burgundy, and the Trastámaras) a system of a prime minister with plenary jurisdiction (*valido*).

With the new century the great landholders of Andalusia — extravagant, infatuated, impetuous, proposing reckless political and financial schemes — inaugurated their political supremacy. The Duke of Lerma,[7] prisoner of the omnipotent administrative councils, tolerated the corruption of the bureaucracy — that process by which those who purchased public office took over the government. An evil in Europe in that era, it reached its uttermost extreme at the Court of Madrid. Under such circumstances the state apparatus limited itself to a passive role; it considered all old institutions venerable, and considered excellent any scheme that made it possible to maintain intact the Buddhistic splendor of the monarchy.

No one can be surprised, therefore, at the drastic measure that ended the religious diversity of Las Españas. The Moriscos of Valencia and Andalusia, and in their wake those of Aragon and

---

[7] Don Francisco Gómez de Sandoval y Rojas (1553–1625), fifth Marquis of Denia and fourth Count of Lerma, was created Duke of Lerma by Philip III in 1599.

Castile — numbering in all some three hundred thousand — were expelled from 1609 onward. This measure was intended to eliminate any threat that might move inland from the Mediterranean shore (such as that experienced in 1568 by Philip II's generation, during the very grave crisis caused by the uprising in the Alpujarras). In addition, the measure established complete religious unity, the final blow in a struggle begun six centuries earlier; this objective was supported by all the Spaniards of that era, mainly because the society of "Old Christians" lacked sufficient flexibility to assimilate the closely knit and traditionalist "Moorish nation of New Christians," still in contact with the Muslim world abroad (whether that of the Berbers of Algeria or that of the Ottoman Turks.) The only measure which could remedy that problem was expulsion, and so it was decreed.

The banishment of the Christian Moors was a ruinous business, carried out without the preparations needed to solve the difficult problem of replacing those agricultural workers. The banishment also cut off, with no legal recourse, the agricultural commodities trade, a large number of loans outstanding, and the obligation to pay the interest that encumbered the estates of the Moriscos.[8] Some few prominent individuals profited from this transfer of goods, property, and leases; but the country lost a potential source of energy at the very moment when it had to confront the great economic, social, and political crisis of the seventeenth century.

---

[8] Juan Reglá's research has disclosed that the credit system of Aragon and Valencia was based on loans made by the bourgeoisie and some religious communities to the aristocracy; they in turn used the money to work their land through Morisco tenant farmers or employees. When the Moriscos were expelled and much of the land left untilled, the aristocracy refused to pay the interest on their loans and the Duke of Lerma supported them. See Reglá, "La expulsión de los moriscos y sus consecuencias: Contribución a su estudio," *Hispania*, XII (1953), 215–267, 402–479.

CHAPTER SEVENTEEN

The Overthrow of Hispania and the Bankruptcy of the Hapsburg Dynasty's Policy

In the auroral decade of the seventeenth century, symptoms of a very grave crisis could be discerned within the recesses of the Hispanic monarchy. Everywhere the economy lost momentum, even in the trade with America, which until then had been so prosperous. Cities were depopulated and looms fell silent; only Madrid grew gigantic, because of the influx of *pícaros* and beggars. Famine came from the south and pestilence from the north, and both maddened a population already severely chastised by the implacable blows of destiny. In belles lettres, the tranquil voice of the Humanist was muted, while the appearance of the *Quijote* showed the conscience of a writer torn between the reality of the present and the rhetoric of the past.[1] Faced with disaster, the government resorted to the very serious measure of devaluating the currency, which was carried out at the expense of the country. This initiated a century of financial adventures that would end in the collapse of 1680.

Viewing this panorama, Castile's partners in the Hispanic enterprise began to ask themselves what they had accomplished and whether it was possible to continue. The Portuguese waited for an opportune moment to act. Although they had by now definitively ensconced themselves in positions of command in the American empire and in economically advantageous places in Madrid, they grieved over the loss of the East Indies. Emerging from the drowsi-

---

[1] The first part of the masterpiece by Miguel de Cervantes (1547–1616), *El ingenioso hidalgo don Quijote de la Mancha*, was published in 1605, the second part in 1615.

ness of the sixteenth century, Catalonia was a land divided by banditry, but she found no alleviation for her concerns in the court. There were murmurings that the king was "Castilian"; that he was planning to impose a different "order" in Catalonia, abolishing government by contractual agreement; that in the future, Castile would send bishops and abbots, viceroys and soldiers, to subjugate the country and to prepare an uprising of the people that would justify conquering Catalonia. Andalusia, Aragon, the Cantabrian coast, and Galicia languished. Thus in the seventeenth century the peoples of Hispania entered an era of contraction, influenced by a basically pessimistic intuition; Philip III (1598-1621) and his favorites had the same intuition. It was necessary to close ranks and wait for better times.

In 1621 a new generation came to power in Spain — that of Philip IV (1621-1665) and the Count-Duke of Olivares.[2] Through the latter, one of their most characteristic representatives, the large landholding grandees of Andalusia retained their power at court. But the new royal favorite, an euphoric and vital man, gave a different orientation to the policies of the monarchy. Acting as though he were capable of deflecting the inevitable course of events, the Count-Duke of Olivares replaced the Duke of Lerma's Pharonic pessimism with imperialistic dynamism.

His first move was to subjugate the entire bureaucratic organization to his omnipotent power. Purged and terrorized, the Councils submitted to him unconditionally and thereby upset the administrative equilibrium the Catholic Monarchs had devised as the means for combining authoritarianism with the interests of privileged groups. This important step in the centralization of power in a single person was followed by another, no less decisive: that of forcing the autonomous territories of the monarchy to march to a policy sent down from the government in Castile.

Considering that the principal obligations of the Count-Duke of

---

[2] Gaspar de Guzmán y Pimentel (1587-1645) inherited the title of Count of Olivares; Philip IV granted him the title of Duke of Sanlúcar la Mayor.

Olivares were to reconstruct the economy of Castile, to set the state treasury in order, and to save the American empire from disaster, his policies are open to controversy. Instead of involving himself in the troublesome European conflicts, where the full power of France and Holland awaited him, Olivares should have stanched the first wounds of empire inflicted by the Dutch in the Caribbean Sea, and should have placed the American colonies on a war footing. Instead, with the gold he had collected in Andalusia to carry out that sound policy, he paid for the military operations of the Thirty Years' War.

The result was that the future of Spain's American empire was liquidated in Europe. This could be clearly seen in 1628, immediately after the naval disaster at Matanzas, Cuba. The communication lines of the empire had been shattered; from that time on, even the pirates from the island of La Tortuga dared to challenge the old-time Colossus of the Seas. There, in America, is to be found the key to the Count-Duke's failures in Europe; it caused naval reverses (Battle of the Downs, 1639) and military reverses (Rocroi, 1643), and it was the reason for the secession of Portugal and of Catalonia. The arrival of the treasure from America would increasingly become more hazardous, and in the crucial year of 1639 the fleet could not cross the Atlantic from the Indies.

But leaving to one side the senseless jugglings of the Count-Duke (brought to light by recent research), one cannot fail to recognize that this Andalusian nobleman's program had certain beneficial aspects: one long-range benefit was to prepare for the inevitable participation by men from the periphery of Spain in the colonization of the Americas. Yet Olivares' efforts were frustrated from the first by the threatening tone with which he applied the law (as early as 1622 there was a vigorous argument in Barcelona concerning the limits of royal authority) and, above all else, by the devious paths which he followed in reducing Portugal and the Crown of Aragon to his governmental dictatorship.

Neither the Portuguese nor the Catalans could match the Castilians' sacrifices in behalf of the needs of the monarchy, nor had either of them suffered a bloodletting of economic and human resources such as the Castilians had. But neither had they obtained the colossal compensations bestowed upon Castile: exploitation of the American continent; cultural and political primacy within the heart of Spain. Therefore, when Catalans felt upon their flesh the lash of the Count-Duke of Olivares — who offered them only participation in the responsibilities of the chimerical enterprises of the future but no share in the profits — it was quite logical for them to fortify themselves, distrustfully, behind the solid ramparts of Ferdinand's autonomous legislation.

The war of nerves between the central power and the peripheral territories might perhaps have ended in a compromise, more or less satisfying to all parties, had it not been that France's intervention in the Thirty Years' War and her declaration of war upon Spain (1635) rapidly widened the breach in Hispanic political unity. In Paris, Catalan and Portuguese malcontents found the foreign support that they needed in order to rebel openly against their monarch.

In Catalonia, where the theory of government by contractual agreement still persisted, the schism was markedly traditionalist in nature; it was preceded by two phenomena which one must consider in order to have some concept of the complexity of ideas at that crucial moment. One was the development of propaganda on behalf of the Hapsburg dynasty, fomented from Madrid with gold from the Count-Duke of Olivares; amid furious trumpeting, this propaganda proclaimed the universality of the Hispanic monarchy (on the very edge of collapse) with the added flourish of an infantile, provocative arrogance. The other phenomenon was the unrest among peasants everywhere in Spain. In Catalonia this unrest incited movements where violent desperation resulted from the inevitable clashes with mercenary troops and, above all, from the very dangerous attitude of the central government, which was disposed to allow the gunpowder to explode in the hope that, once Catalonia had shattered into a thousand pieces, it might gather up absolute power.

This suicidal policy led to armed revolt in the Catalan countryside from the end of 1639, and to the ferocious explosion of peasant discontent in the events in Barcelona on Corpus Christi day in 1640.

Even so, this outburst of feeling might possibly have been contained and then suppressed if the Count-Duke of Olivares had not decided to use that occasion to carry out his program in Catalonia, and if France (on the alert for any opportunity) had not proposed to take thorough advantage of the situation. In this fashion the conflict that had divided the Catalan principality during the quattrocento was revived — a conflict between Castilian pressures and French ambitions. And synchronizing with that conflict — giving yet another wrench to the sundered unity of the Hispanic monarchy — Portugal declared herself in rebellion and selected her own sovereign from within the Braganza family (1640).

After twenty-two years of vainglorious omnipotence, the Count-Duke of Olivares was dismissed by the king (1643) in view of the fatal outcome of his political experiments. While the poorly equipped Spanish army was leaving the glory of its flag in shreds upon the battlefields of Europe (Rocroi, 1643; Lens, 1647; the Downs, 1658), on the Peninsula Catalonia obtained recognition of her special liberties (1653) and Portugal succeeded in consolidating her independence (1668).

At the end an exhausted Castile subsided into an ominous pessimism. Catalonia, in reaction against the Count-Duke's program, clung tightly to a legal order that signified political security for her, but that also fossilized an already defective economic and social structure. The most serious aspect of the affair was that the triumph of Catalonia and the loss of Portugal had so vividly impressed the court and its organisms that, throughout the reign of Charles II (1665–1700), the official doctrine was one of profound respect for the privileges of territories and individuals (even those of the "meritorious" *encomenderos*[3] of America). Paradoxically, this new

---

[3] An encomienda was "the patronage conferred by royal favor over a portion of the natives concentrated in settlements near those of the Spaniards; the obligation to instruct . . . and defend them in their persons and property; coupled with the right to demand tribute or labor in return for these privileges." C. H. Haring, *The Spanish Empire in America* (New York, 1947), p. 44. In general, the royal policy was to abolish these semifeudal holdings; its success is a matter of controversy.

Overthrow and Bankruptcy 109

respect for regional charters coincided with the development of vital economic interests on the periphery, and with reiterated petitions from those regions to the monarchy for administrative reforms.

Catalan effervescence was not stifled by the miserable results of governmental action — which for Catalonia were exemplified by the loss of Roussillon and part of the Cerdagne in the peace treaty of 1659 (Treaty of the Pyrenees). Catalonia supported the first coup d'etat in the modern age that originated on the periphery of the Peninsula — the coup led by John Joseph of Austria in 1669.[4] The objective was to reform the policies and administration of the monarchy, but neither the circumstances nor the personalities involved made it possible to fulfill the desire for renovation; instead, the attempt was rendered sterile by the frivolous actions of John Joseph, the would-be Messiah.[5]

Spain, a pawn in the international politics of armies and in the economic life of Louis XIV's merchants, became an easy victim of Versailles' absorbing ambitions. During the contredanse of war and peace that characterized the reign of Charles II (1665–1700), the inability of the Hapsburg bureaucracy to provide the monarchy

---

[4] John Joseph of Austria (1629–1679) was born of Philip IV's brief affair with a famous actress, María Calderón; the word Austria merely signifies his Hapsburg lineage. Officially recognized by Philip as his son, John Joseph served as the commander of the forces in Naples, Flanders, and Portugal from 1647 to 1664, where he proved to be valiant and competent. His military fame served as the basis for his attempts after the death of Philip IV to govern Spain, by exiling the Queen Regent and ruling for Charles II.

[5] The coup of 1669 was important less because of the ambitious John Joseph than because he was the first man to seek support in Catalonia for a plan to reform the government in Madrid. Specifically he proposed tax reforms, more power for the army, a more just legal system, and — to please his Catalan supporters — participation by the peripheral provinces in the trade with the Indies. But in the coup of February 1669 John Joseph showed that he had the will neither to impose his policies by force nor to renounce all political ambitions and retire. In 1669 he was outmaneuvered by the Queen Regent. In 1677 he made a second, successful attempt and ruled until his death in 1679, probably saved by this premature death from being overthrown by army, nobles, the populace of Madrid, or the Catalans, who had expected so much of him.

with relative military efficiency, or even with a precarious but viable peace, reached its culminating point. In successive stages Spain's possessions were detached: Artois, the Franche-Comté, the great fortified towns that guarded the frontier of Flanders. But far more serious than these reverses was the absolute loss of prestige. Anyone could defeat Spain, not only on the battlefield but in business competition, which degenerated to such a point that the monarchy was converted into a mere colony of the great European powers. And yet during all these events, despite the fact that one hundred years of governmental frivolity had spread corruption and self-interest throughout the various social classes, one can see that the potential of the country still far exceeded the capacity of the state apparatus.

Catalonia fared worst in the new wake of suffering, because she was the principal theater of operation during the wars with France. But on this occasion her loyalty to the monarchy was unimpaired; indeed, she willingly accepted her Hispanic responsibilities, acting in the name of a devoted love for the reigning dynasty that centered specifically in the person of the ailing Charles II.

Because Spain was powerless to maintain her territorial possessions in Europe — key possessions such as Flanders and Milan — Europe decided to proceed with the dismemberment of the Spanish monarchy. This involved the security of Europe and, quite obviously, satisfaction for many historic ambitions. Charles II's lack of an heir facilitated the plans of the European courts: France and Austria each desired for herself the fabulous inheritance, while England and Holland wanted to prevent either of those powers from establishing an absolute hegemony on the Continent. Intrigue followed intrigue around the deathbed of the King until finally, after the failure of solutions that seemed satisfactory (such as the candidacy of Prince Joseph Ferdinand of Bavaria),[6] Charles decided in favor of the plans of the pro-French party. The decisive factor in his choice was the desire to maintain the unity of the Hispanic monarchy in the world. Therefore Charles II designated Philip of

---

[6] Prince Joseph Ferdinand of Bavaria (a grandson of Philip IV's daughter, Margaret Theresa) was generally acceptable, both in Spain and abroad, but he died in 1699 at the age of seven.

Overthrow and Bankruptcy

Anjou [7] as his heir, and initially Philip was accepted by the country without any opposition.

International quarrels launched Spain on her long War of Succession. The adversaries of the Bourbons employed all their resources in an effort to weaken the monarchy; among other measures, they stirred up the deep-rooted political traditionalism of the Crown of Aragon. It must be stated that Philip V, either because he was sagacious or because it was the expedient thing to do, had introduced himself to the Catalans as a zealous supporter of their liberties. The work of the Cortes of 1701–1702 (the first Cortes since 1599 to complete its term of office) was not in vain; not only did it consolidate the fueros of Catalonia, but it opened a doorway to the future by acknowledging the latter's right to trade with America. However, the difficulties created by the War of Succession encouraged among some Catalans a legitimist spirit, and among others a desire for revenge — revenge for the situation created in 1660. Entwined with these was the eternal social unrest of peasants and artisans.

In 1705 a successful plot prepared by England allowed the Austrians to gain control of the city of Barcelona, which thereupon became the Hispanic capital of the Hapsburg pretender, Archduke Charles.[8] This time Catalans were fighting stubbornly to defend their pluralistic concept of the ordering of the Spanish monarchy. They did not realize that this was precisely the system that had led to the agony of the last Hapsburg kings, and that without a broad margin of reforms (both of the laws and of the traditional regional fueros) it would be impossible to put the country back on its feet. The Catalans were fighting against the current of history and the price for this is usually very high.

But public opinion in Catalonia was not unanimous, nor did the government established by Archduke Charles in Barcelona prove equal to the task for which it would be responsible in the Spain of

---

[7] Philip, Duke of Anjou (1685–1746), later Philip V of Spain, was a great-grandson of Philip IV. His claims to the Spanish throne were clouded by the fact that when his grandmother, Marie Theresa, married Louis XIV (1660) she renounced her rights to the throne.

[8] Archduke Charles of Austria was a great-grandson of Philip III and the brother of the Austrian Emperor, Joseph.

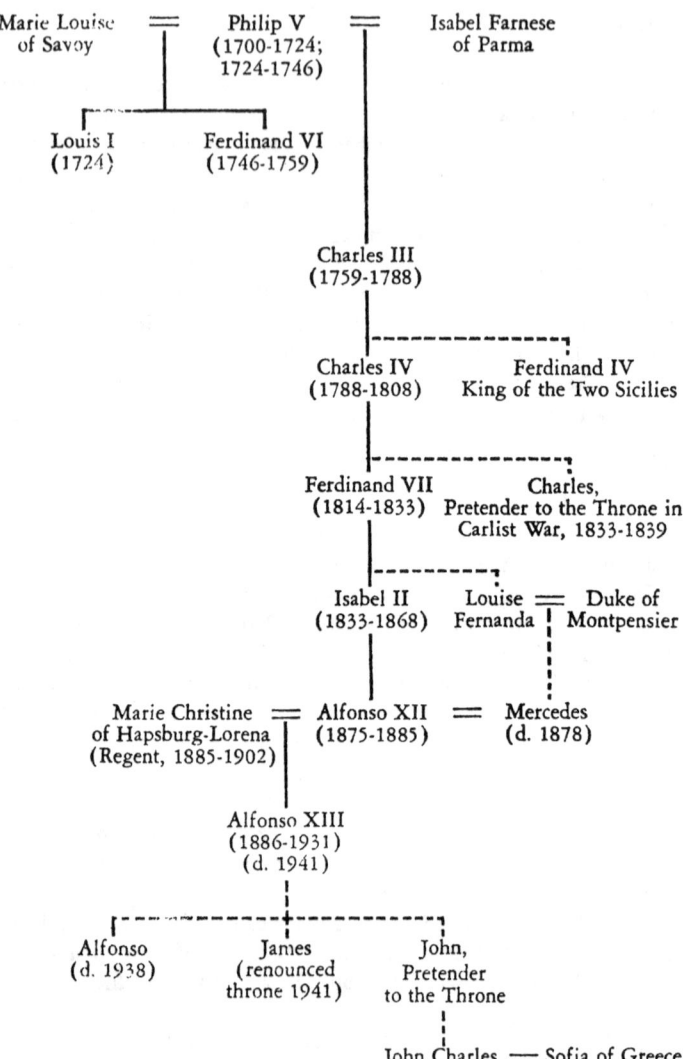

TABLE 5. The House of Bourbon, which ruled in Spain from 1700 to 1931. (Broken lines indicate branches of the family that were not of the ruling line.)

the future. On the contrary, the vices and defects of the former administration were perpetuated, making impossible any systematic organization of the resources of the Crown of Aragon. Without aid from abroad, that government would have collapsed in a matter of months. But the Catalans who supported the Archduke sincerely believed — and therefore were completely convinced — that they were defending the true cause of Spain, not simply a handful of privileges.

Castile, initially somewhat refractory because of the presence in Madrid of a Bourbon monarch and French ministers, ended up enthusiastically embracing the cause of Philip V. Although high-ranking personnel in the court and in the administration helped bring about this change, the objectives that prompted them to act were basically supported by the people in general. In one of those inexplicable twists in her history, Castile became one of the firmest props of the Bourbon dynasty — especially when Louis XIV found himself obliged to beg for peace from the victorious enemy coalition. Another possible influence upon the change in Castile was the development of efficient propaganda, directed not only against the Archduke but also against the Catalans, who were accused of secretly planning to enslave Castile.

In summary, at Brihuega in 1710 the Franco-Castilian army defeated the Anglo-Austro-Catalan army.[9] Four years later Barcelona surrendered to the troops of Philip V, and Spain was left flat as the palm of a hand, ready for the application of an objective, realistic policy (1714). Instead, the mystique of regional charters was merely replaced by a mystique of centralization at any cost — centralization not only of the administration but of the way of thinking. And in this enterprise the Bourbon dynasty and its collaborators (like their predecessors) would fail.

---

[9] In 1711, in the middle of the War of the Spanish Succession, Emperor Joseph of Austria died and was succeeded by his brother, Archduke Charles, the pretender to the throne of Spain. England thereupon threw her support to the French pretender with the proviso that Spain remain independent of France. The peace of Utrecht (1713–1715) was negotiated on this basis.

CHAPTER EIGHTEEN

Bourbon Reforms

In the course of one century, from 1700 to 1808, the new Bourbon dynasty carried out a series of thoroughgoing reforms. Some grew out of the need to liquidate the Hapsburg regime. Others were the product of arbitrary ministerial action, inspired by European examples during that age of Enlightened Despotism. The majority of the reforms attempted to remedy the acute domestic problems created by the recuperation of Spanish vitality, evident in an increase in population and in a rapid acceleration of trade and manufacturing. On the whole, Bourbon reform was successful insofar as it reactivated the power of Spain in Europe and in America; but it channeled the state into a rigid rationalism that ran counter to the historic Hispanic character. Moreover, the reforms themselves helped to create new problems: for example, that of a bourgeoisie on the periphery eager for commercial expansion, and that of a peasantry in the interior avid for lands to cultivate.

In the Crown of Aragon, which had supported the Austrian pretender, the historic system of privileges and fueros was jettisoned in favor of a "new ground plan" (*Nueva Planta*). In contrast, Navarre and the Basque country, regions loyal to the cause of Philip V (1700–1746), conserved their fueros; for this reason they were entitled the Exempt Provinces.

Catalonia became a field for experimentation with the new procedures of a unified administration: the Captaincy General, the provincial high court (*audiencia*), the intendant, and royally appointed chief magistrates in the towns (*corregidores*). The purpose of all these measures was to insure that the province paid for the army of occupation, which, in turn, was responsible for supervising the collection of the single tax (*catastro*). This transformation was so violent that Catalonia hovered on the verge of ruin for fifteen years. But with time the elimination of privileges and fueros produced unexpected benefits: Catalans not only were forced to look toward the future but, under the auspices of a common monarchic regime, were offered the same opportunities open to Castilians.

Although the adjective "hard-working" had first been used to describe the Catalans in 1680, it was during this period that the usage became widespread; for one and a half centuries it would be a ritualistic stereotype. Catalonia actually did carry out the fourth great stage of agricultural colonization during that era. The symbol was the vine, and its product — brandy — stimulated an active international trade that benefited the entire coastal population, especially the Catalan merchant fleet, which within a few decades renewed its withered laurels. For industry, the decisive factor was the introduction of cotton cloth manufacturing, financed by the surplus capital accumulated in agricultural operations and commercial expansion.

The presence of tutorial organizations, such as the Board of Commerce of Catalonia, stimulated an industrial revolution along the entire periphery of the Peninsula: Valencia, Málaga, Cádiz, La Coruña, Santander, and Bilbao came vibrantly to life once more. By 1760 the coastal regions surpassed those of the interior in population, in resources, and in their standard of living. It was inevitable that the center of economic gravity should change; the influence of this factor explains the measure of 1778, decreed by Charles III (1759–1788), which abolished Andalusia's monopoly on the trade with America and opened it up to various Spanish and American ports. Within a decade exports increased tenfold, while a flood of money made possible not only new investment in industry but the luxury of an independent foreign policy based on an efficient navy.

This process of the social integration of the various peoples in Spain was far more substantive than any legislative measure devised since the time of Philip II: Catalonia played a decisive role because of her triple expansion — in population, commerce, and the textile industry. Nevertheless, the court persisted in its determination to consider all matters from the viewpoint of an administration extremely jealous of its rights and prebends, and also from the viewpoint of the interests of the Andalusian and Extremaduran aristocracy. The latter continued to hold power or to influence it through the personnel of the administrative bureaucracy, and through their widespread contacts in state organisms — royal factories, chartered trading companies, the Bank of San Carlos, and so on.

Only under Charles III, between 1770 and 1788, was equality of opportunity finally extended to all Spaniards. But this carried with it a grievous obligation to relinquish handsome segments of their individuality in deference to a sacrosanct state-imposed uniformity. Depending on their region, the common people reacted in diverse ways against such an aristocratic, superficial, cold ambience. They tried generally to capture the most vital elements and incorporate them into their folklore. But the impossibility of breaking down the barrier that separated the two worlds gave birth to the concept of Hispanic cultural purity (*casticismo* [1]). From the mid-eighteenth century, popular culture was triumphant: from the vacuum of the era of the last Hapsburg kings emerged the official seal of folkloric (*costumbrista* [2]) Spain — bulls in the foreground and grouped around them flamenco artists,[3] gypsies, and *majos*.[4]

---

[1] The concept of *casticismo* (from the Latin *castus*, purity) is linked both to ethnic and cultural purity, the latter being defined very vaguely as the "Spanish tradition." Miguel de Unamuno (1864–1936) has analyzed the dangerous Spanish tendency to honor the form of casticismo rather than the spirit: *En torno al casticismo* (1895).

[2] The Spanish term *costumbrista* signifies the customs of the people. Although the English word *folklore* has been incorporated into Spanish, it is often used in a pejorative sense to signify things, such as flamenco, which foreigners consider typical of Spain but which actually characterize only Andalusia.

[3] Flamenco, since the mid-nineteenth century, refers to the native songs and dances of Andalusia which gypsies popularized but did not create. It connotes also the flamboyant way of life associated with gypsy artists.

[4] *Majos* were men and women of the lower class of Madrid who dramatized their folkways (a style of bravado; long cape and broad-brimmed hat) in reaction against the French fashions of official circles. During the reign of Charles IV particularly, aristocrats affected majo styles, in part

The obverse of this movement was the controversy over French ideas that developed in the highest echelons. The philosophy of the Enlightenment introduced into Spain the concept that educational and social reform of the country was needed to raise it to a level of economic, scientific, and technical achievement comparable with that of other European nations; it also introduced a spirit of criticism with regard to the religious legacy of the West embodied in the work of the Catholic Church. These ideas were diffused by four generations of intellectuals, represented respectively by Benito Jerónimo Feijóo (1676–1764), Friar Enrique Flórez (1702–1773), Pedro Rodríguez Campomanes (1723–1803), and Gaspar Melchor de Jovellanos (1744–1811). They were slowly accepted by a minority of aristocrats, gentry (hidalgos), clergymen, intellectuals, and university students. The central agency for the dissemination of these new ideas was the Societies of the Friends of the Country; using as a model the Basque Society (founded in 1765), the government organized these societies from 1774 on. The bourgeoisie barely responded to this movement because in reality no such social class as yet existed in Spain.

The ministers who governed during this period came from the nobility or from the prosperous middle class, and most of them were natives of the periphery (the Marquis of Ensenada was from Logroño; Campomanes and Jovellanos were from Asturias; the Count of Aranda from Aragon; the Count of Floridablanca from Murcia; the Gálvez family from Málaga). They devoted their efforts to resolving the decisive problem of the Spanish economy — the agricultural system of the south. A population increase of three million persons made it necessary for the ministers to train their microscope on this problem. Various remedies were applied: a program of providing capital equipment for the communication system by opening up canals and developing a network of highways;

---

to oppose Bourbon reforms and the Enlightenment. Francisco Goya (1746–1828) painted these aristocrats: his most famous portraits are the *Maja Desnuda* and the *Maja Vestida*, which are commonly believed to be of the Duchess of Alba.

a program of colonizing the interior, such as that undertaken by Pablo de Olavide in the Sierra Morena: projects to disentail the estates of the aristocracy and to disamortize the lands of the clergy. One measure was decisive: an end to the privileges of migratory grazing held by the powerful livestock organization, the Mesta. To gauge the significance of this change of direction, one must take into account the economic mentality that had prevailed in Castile since the twelfth century.

But this policy did not get to the roots of the problem — of short-term rural leases; of agricultural communities impoverished by the abuse of still extant seignorial privileges; the uncultivated lands of the latifundia; lands held in mortmain by the clergy. A solution required economic resources and a benevolence far beyond the realities of Spain in that period. Castile had land for the army of 150,000 beggars who swarmed through the country. But the obstacles were unsurmountable, and even the reforms proposed by Jovellanos in his *Report on the Agrarian Law* (1795) were nothing more than a testimony of his patriotic foresightedness.

No one was ignorant of the fact that Spain was living on a volcano, or at least of the fact that an explosion of popular discontent could happen. In 1765 the free trade of wheat was decreed — a measure well calculated to encourage agricultural progress but not one that ensured a bread supply for the cities. In the following year a small crop, reflected immediately in the price of wheat, aroused urban masses in Madrid and in various cities of Castile and Aragon.

In Madrid this movement, channeled into a protest against the power exercised by the royal favorite, the Marquis of Esquilache (1766),[5] revealed the seriousness of the problem and prompted the

---

[5] Leopoldi di Gregorio, Marchese di Squillace (*Esquilache* in Spanish) (?–1785), came with Charles III from Naples. As secretary of state for war and finance, he enacted reforms of taxes (which made him unpopular) and public works. He set off the insurrection in Madrid in 1766 by a relatively minor order forbidding residents to wear slouch broad-brimmed hats and long capes; such dress allegedly enabled conspirators and criminals to conceal themselves from the police. *Madrileños*

first law of agrarian reform known in the history of Andalusia and Extremadura. But the very complex vicissitudes of its application and final failure (1766–1793) remain hidden behind the diversionary measures employed by the Enlightened ministers of Charles III. They attributed the responsibility for the popular uprising to the Society of Jesus. Expelled from Spain and from America in 1767, the society was subsequently dissolved by the Holy See in the wake of a campaign organized by the Bourbon governments of Spain, France, and Italy. This action did not succeed in pacifying the country, but it did put an end to the monarchy's fight with the papacy in defense of its rights to intervene in Church affairs. And it did so advantageously — that is to say, by subordinating the Church to the interests of the state — for the first step had consisted of winning the battle of public education by eliminating the Jesuits who had gained control of secondary and university education.

Because a large part of the desire for reform was polarized under the aegis of Charles III, this monarch has been converted into the paradigm of Enlightened Despotism in Spain. His very personality revealed the amplitude of the objectives proposed and the timidity of the means used to achieve those objectives. Charles clearly gave the country a tone of political modernity and economic well-being; at the same time he provided a sense of power in the maritime wars that he waged against England in defense of Spain's American empire. The first war ended adversely (1761–1763) but in the second war, in which Charles supported the English colonists in North America in their struggle for independence (1779–1783), the outcome was advantageous.

Even taking into account that Charles IV (1788–1808) was not the man his father had been, the work of Charles III might have been continued if the French Revolution had not caused a radical change within Spain that endangered domestic policy.

Discarding the reform program, Manuel Godoy, the minister of Charles IV, retained only the external apparatus of Enlightened

---

resented this interference with their traditional garb, especially from a foreigner.

Despotism: ministerial omnipotence and administrative dictatorship of the country. For two decades (1788–1808) a revolutionary spirit smoldered in the souls of many Spaniards; in 1808, when a crisis occurred in the monarchy, it exploded. Some people drew their inspiration from the flame of dynastic tradition; others from an elated desire to plunge into the turbulent ocean of illusionary hopes aroused by the French Revolution.

CHAPTER NINETEEN

Politics and Economics in Nineteenth-Century Spain

The uprising at Aranjuez (March 17, 1808) was the first obvious symptom that the political and social climate of Spain had changed. This intervention by the people — incited by provocateurs — in behalf of Prince Ferdinand brought about the abdication of Charles IV and the end of Godoy's dictatorial regime. A mere anecdote in history textbooks, it should really be assessed as the sign of a profound change in the times: a monarch had been dethroned as the result of action by the people. A new era was dawning, albeit under the protection of Napoleon's bayonets.

But Napoleon had other plans. The first of these was to seize control of the Spanish state and to impose upon it an efficient administrative apparatus, a maneuver that was not discerned either by his Francophile collaborators or by the Spanish people. But there was a group of conspirators who were afraid that Godoy might return to power, and so within a few weeks after the uprising at Aranjuez they took advantage of aroused public feeling to lash out against the French. This led to the tragic events of May 2, 1808, the most remarkable feature of which was the dramatic emergence of the masses as a prime figure in the political life of Spain.

With the collapse of the bureaucratic apparatus of the monarchy — in part because the kings had been forced to abdicate, in part because of the bungling of governmental organisms — the full force of this public pressure was revealed in the decisive events of the last week of May and the first week of June in 1808. During those days the middle classes, the intellectuals, and the gentry assumed power, supported by fervent artisans and peasants disposed to sacrifice their lives in order to combat government officials who — following the example set in Madrid — were collaborating with the French. The specific objective of this struggle was not to expel Napoleon's troops but to liberate Spain from Godoy's supporters.

But when Napoleon's troops stayed in Spain in order to impose Joseph I and the Constitution of Bayonne, then the movement concentrated — although it was very far from being unanimous — on recklessly opposing the invader and all that he represented in Europe.[1] But it had another, no less apparent motive; to take advantage of the circumstances in order to so reorient the monarchy as to make impossible any reoccurrence of the ministerial despotism and humiliation that had made the entire nation suffer.

In the revolution of May 1808, the factor of least interest was the phenomenon of Separatism — a product of the circumstances in which the movement originated. The decisive factor was the desire for reform which appears in the aims set forth by each of the Provincial Juntas and subsequently by the Supreme Central Junta. The popular uprising had so profoundly shaken the regime that political and social reform became a principal objective of the struggle, as important as the obvious desire to maintain the independence of the country. The people were organized with varying degrees of efficiency by a few commanders of dubious military ability. Constantly engaged in guerrilla warfare, or in giving up their lives to defend strategic strongholds, they fought for certain concrete ideals: for their home, their God, and their king — in

---

[1] In theory, two governments existed in Spain from 1808 until 1814 (that is, from the time that Napoleon forced Ferdinand VII and his father, Charles IV, to abdicate and installed his own brother Joseph as King of Spain, until Ferdinand returned to Spain to rule). On the basis of the royal abdications, Joseph Bonaparte laid claim to the principle of legitimate succession. In June 1808, after the people rebelled against the French, a second government was organized, based on Provincial Juntas, which were later (September 1808) nominally subject to one Supreme Central Junta. They claimed to act as regents in behalf of Ferdinand, a "captive" of Napoleon; not until the Cortes at Cádiz (1810–1813) did the leaders of this government publicly base their right to act upon the principle of national sovereignty.

short, for their country. It would be a gross error, however, to ignore the ferment of social renovation, including a current of antiaristocratic feeling, that motivated the bull goaders of Bailén in Andalusia (*los garrochistas*), the armed vigilantes of Bruch in Catalonia (*los somatenes*), and the guerrilla fighters of Saragossa.

The élite of the country, in contrast, apparently divided into four large groupings. One — the smallest of all — was composed of those who accepted the state of affairs prior to the movement of May 1808. Another was the traditionalists who sought a panacea for the reconstruction of the state among the ancient modes of the monarchy (either to defend a system of regional fueros or a system of centralization). Still another group paid homage to Joseph Bonaparte in the belief that the best system for Spain was an imitation of Napoleonic France (these men were called *Afrancesados*).[2] Finally there were the reformers who fought against the French because they were the invaders, but who also believed it was an opportune moment to draw up a constitutional charter that would be revolutionary in nature: intellectuals, priests whose background was more or less Jansenist, big landowners, and one sector of the middle classes from the periphery of the Peninsula.

Aid from the English and extraneous developments (the offensive campaigns waged by the *Grande Armée* from 1809 to 1812) helped the reformers to carry out their proposals. They succeeded in arranging a meeting in Cádiz of a general Cortes unconditionally devoted to their cause. There they proclaimed national sovereignty and freedom of the press, and then followed this up by giving to the country the Constitution of 1812 — more Spanish in essence

---

[2] *Afrancesado* refers specifically to those persons from the upper classes who collaborated with the French during the War of Independence (1808–1812) in the expectation that through the power of an enlightened despot (Joseph Bonaparte) they could impose the eighteenth-century Bourbon program for the economic and administrative reform of Spain. This collaboration tended to discredit all reforms as being "foreign-inspired." After the war and exile, alienated from most liberals by their rejection of national sovereignty, the Afrancesados would eventually (from 1827 on) work out a tenuous alliance with Ferdinand VII based on an absolute monarchy committed to certain reforms.

than its form would indicate. The diverse criteria applied to many of the issues debated in the assembly at Cádiz solidified in two principal ways of thinking: one was termed Servile, the other Liberal. The controversy over the suppression of the Inquisition — the first public polemic about Spain's past — opened up an insuperable chasm between Serviles and Liberals, particularly after the bishops absolutely refused to consent to the measure.[3]

The ousting of the French from Spain and the return of Ferdinand VII (1814–1833) combined to create a difficult political situation. In the struggle between Serviles and Liberals, the monarch chose the most comfortable solution: restoration of pure absolutism. He thus turned a deaf ear not only to the demands of the Liberals (which was logical at that moment) but also to the demands of the Persians — royalists who, although traditionalist by nature, advocated reforms in the monarchy in order to avoid ministerial despotism.

Ferdinand's decision drove the Liberals into secret sects, where they reached an agreement with army officers who had returned from French prisons and with the men who had commanded the guerrilla forces. Both of the latter groups had become deeply disillusioned when they were relegated to a secondary position, while sinecures were given to the survivors of the Old Regime — enthusiastic supporters of Godoy who had been soundly defeated by Napoleon's troops. Thus it was that Liberal army officers prepared

---

[3] Liberalism in Spain has both a political and a religious content. As elsewhere in Europe (where the term Liberal was adopted), its adherents defended a limitation on the absolute power of the monarch through a written constitution that safeguards the right of the Cortes to legislate as the representative of the people, and the right of the individual to defend his private interests against state intervention by guaranteeing freedom of speech, press, and assembly. But the *Dictionary of the Royal Academy of Spain* (16th ed., 1956) does not mention these tenets and instead defines Liberalism as a "political-religious system which proclaims the absolute independence of the state, in its organization and actions, from all positive religions." The Liberals' religious policy was one factor, but not the only one nor the most important one, in the Carlist wars (see pp. 127–128) and in the subsequent struggle to establish constitutional government in Spain.

for their long period in power in Spain within the recesses of Masonry and of the *Carbonari* — evils endemic in that era.

In 1820, after various thwarted attempts, Liberal army officers led the troops in Andalusia who were waiting to embark for America in a successful *pronunciamiento*[4] against absolutism. Names and episodes lack importance. The salient factors are the triumph of the movement in garrisons along the periphery, the eventual defection of the Army of Central Spain, and the monarch's acceptance of the Constitution of 1812. Amid an astonished Europe, Spain became a lighthouse for the Liberal Revolution and emitted rays that ignited similar movements in Portugal and Italy. And yet, with the exception of the urban masses, Spain remained committed to her traditionalist creed. This explains why the political battle waged in Madrid by the two nascent branches of Spanish Liberalism — those who supported the Constitution of 1812 (*los Doceañistas*) and those who advocated a more radical policy (*los Exaltados*) — failed to spread to other cities.

Meanwhile, peasants in the countryside of northern Spain, who were showing their growing restiveness, found an outlet in the royalist uprising of the summer of 1822 — an uprising that was particularly violent in Catalonia and Navarre. A regency was set up in Catalonia — the Regency of Urgel[5] with a program whose origins can be traced, not to the capricious absolutism of the recent

---

[4] A pronunciamiento (a term incorporated into the English language) is defined in the Dictionary of the Royal Academy of Spain as a military rebellion. Usually it consisted merely of subverting all or part of the army, and sometimes the police force, thereby depriving a government of the means to defend itself. Many writers have pointed out the complexity of this phenomenon: the use of the armed forces of a nation to defend one party or one politician or one viewpoint; the paradoxical combination of justifying the right to act in defense of the "national will" (against an arbitrary monarchy or corrupt politicians) and the use of force (but with a minimum of bloodshed or even of fighting).

[5] Entitling itself the Supreme Regency of Spain during the Captivity, the Regency of Urgel issued a manifesto on August 15, 1822, exhorting the people to release King Ferdinand, a "captive" of the Liberals (using the argument set forth during the wars against Napoleon).

experiences under Ferdinand, but to the tendencies toward reform and regional fueros shown in the 1814 Manifesto of the Persians.

With the Exalted Liberals in power, constitutional government lost favor with landlords, nobles (whose seignorial rights were threatened), and the bourgeoisie. Some capitalists were threatened by the first attempts to organize labor agitation recorded in Spanish history. A simple military promenade in 1823 — by a French army called the "Hundred Thousand Sons of St. Louis" — sufficed to demolish the apparatus of Spain's second experiment with constitutional government. Once again a wave of persecution and purges engulfed the Liberals, a sharp retort to the one that they themselves had just concluded. Following an example set by so many other Spanish political movements, the majority went into exile. But the group of 1823 was particularly significant because these constitutionalists were young people, avid for novelties. And among other things, they were to discover the Romantic movement at the height of its creative power. In France, and above all in England, Liberalism and Romanticism went hand in hand — and this is the way they would return to Spain in 1833.

On the Peninsula, meanwhile, something had changed at the heart of the Royalist party. Its most important faction, led by the audacious group of Apostolics, began to lose confidence in Ferdinand VII. It reproached him for his excessive indulgence of the moderate elements within the army; for placing confidence in high-ranking state officials with Afrancesado tendencies; for refusing to admit en bloc the officers and troops of the Royal Volunteers of 1822–1823; for his suspect position on rehabilitating the Inquisition. The group fastened its gaze upon the person of Charles of Bourbon, brother and probable successor of Ferdinand VII. It hoped that he would endorse the entire movement, which by now was definitely committed to a defense of the Spanish Catholic ideal and of an absolutist form of government that would be compatible with the country's tradition of regional fueros. The Apostolics broke with Ferdinand VII in 1827, on the occasion of an uprising of Catalan peasants, the *malcontents*. From that moment on the Carlist party began to take shape. High-ranking monarchist officials anxiously began to seek a formula which would make it possible to form a government midway between the extremist groups — the Carlists to one side, the Liberals to the other. Ferdinand, who was unwilling to cast in his lot with one side or the other, preferred to continue governing dictatorially with the support of an "enlightened" bureaucracy which was very loyal to him. The tentacles of this bureaucracy reached out in one direction to Afrancesado bankers in exile and in another direction to cotton manufacturers in Barcelona, to merchants in Cádiz, and also to no small number of Moderate Liberal groups in exile.

Moderate Liberalism — that is to say, a program of a properly defined liberty — was precisely the formula supported by the bourgeoisie in coastal cities and by businessmen who began to appear in Madrid in response to the incipient development of a national economy. Therefore, the court's preference for the Moderate Liberal band represented not only a position in defense of the rights of succession of Princess Isabel (born in 1830) [6] but also the intention of Ferdinand's bureaucracy to avoid what they sensed was coming — a violent clash between the Exalted Liberals and the Carlists. The proclamation of Isabel as heir to the throne was, therefore, not the work of a cabal of courtiers. The bourgeoisie everywhere welcomed the event with extraordinary applause.

The Carlists rose up in arms in 1833, after the death of Ferdinand VII and the establishment of a regency of the state in the person of his widow, Marie Christine of Bourbon. The uprising was confined to those regions where the spirit of regional fueros was most intense and where the peasants enjoyed relative economic independence — the Basque provinces, Navarre, Aragon, and Catalonia. It forced the government to accentuate its Liberal tendencies. Power was entrusted to the Moderates (that is, Liberals who supported the principles of 1812, together with "enlightened" bureaucrats), who

---

[6] By 1829, despite three marriages, Ferdinand VII had no surviving children, and it was assumed that his brother, Charles, would inherit the throne. But in that year he married again (a niece, Marie Christine of Naples), and in 1830 a daughter, Isabel, was born; in 1832, a second daughter, Marie Louise Fernanda, was born (d. 1897).

thought they had found a panacea for the conflicts dividing the nation in the promulgation of a Royal Statute (1834) — a kind of charter conferred by the Crown which, while safeguarding the monarchic principle, enabled the wealthy classes to participate in the government of the country. This was precisely the ideal of the bourgeoisie, and so the Royal Statute was received with effusive gratitude by a social class that entered upon a period of free enterprise with the introduction of the first steam-powered machinery (Barcelona, 1833).

But the moderate regime forecast in that legislative instrument was thwarted by the virulence of the passions unleashed by the civil war that ravaged the north of Spain. The Carlists held at bay the disorganized columns of Marie Christine's army, while in the major cities there were outbursts of a ferocious anticlericalism motivated by obscure resentments of the populace and by the demagogic propaganda of the Exalted Liberals. In 1834 and 1835 numerous convents were burned and sacked; their occupants were persecuted and, in some cases, assasinated. The same thing occurred at the great monasteries that still dominated the rural life of the nation, but in this case it is easier to understand the attitude of the peasants, for whom life had been very hard during the preceding years.

Taking advantage of this situation the Prime Minister, Juan Álvarez Mendizábal, put into effect a project harbored by bureaucrats since the time of Charles III and Charles IV, and vigorously defended by the Liberal movement since the Cortes of Cádiz in 1812 — the nationalization and sale of clerical property. This measure (1837) is of the greatest importance within the framework of the political and social developments of the nineteenth century. It might have constituted a true agrarian reform that would have provided some basis for stability in the lives of the peasants of Castile, Extremadura, and Andalusia. Instead, it did nothing more than transfer property from the Church to the economically strongest classes (large landholders, aristocrats, and bourgeoisie) — a development from which the state derived the least benefit and one which did grave harm to the agricultural workers. One immediate consequence of this measure was the consolidation of the Liberal regime; conservatives who had purchased national property were now bound by their own interests to the cause of Isabel II. The second immediate consequence was the expansion of a new system of latifundia that was far more powerful and, above all, far more egoistic than the system created between the thirteenth and fifteenth centuries.

A new shift to the left (prompted by some sergeants at the palace of La Granja) inspired the Constitution of 1837, one of the most liberal of that period. It was the expression of a discontented minority of Progressives (the old-time Exalted Liberals) who could count on support from some few intellectuals, from various senior military officers, and from the ranks of a recently created industrial proletariat.

A few successes in the civil war (following the deterioration of the Carlist party) and its oblation to the country of an end to hostilities (the Agreement of Vergara, 1839) made Progressivism a decidedly ambitious party. Its chief, General Bartolomeo Espartero, felt bold enough to confront Marie Christine and force her to renounce the regency. This was essentially a victory of the lower classes — concretely, of the workers and artisans of Barcelona — over the urban bourgeoisie.

But on the political scene of Spain it raised the curtain on an episode that had not been foreseen: government by the sword arm of a political party (*espadones*). Given the fact that no one had any authority — neither the Crown, nor the parties, nor the people — someone had to introduce order into the government and back it up with army bayonets. And at this point — under General Espartero — Spanish romantic militarism began a career embellished with numerous and at times bloody pronunciamientos.

Government by the Progressives and General Espartero (1840–1843) was not convincing, especially to the bourgeoisie of Barcelona, who could not forgive Espartero for supporting the workers and they, in turn, would not forgive him his failure to keep his promises. By this time the economic vitality of Catalonia's capital city had transformed it into the hub of Spanish political developments. The situation very soon degenerated into an open conflict between the Espartero regency and the citizens of Barcelona, whose city was bombarded by government troops in 1842. This led to Espartero's fall in the following year, for Barcelona made herself the leader of the faction which — in the wake of a pronunciamiento at Torrejón de Ardoz (1843) — turned power over to the Moderate elements.

Catalonia emerged disillusioned from this experiment. She had thought that she could direct Spanish politics by means of a Central Junta, and she had found herself besieged, defeated, and muzzled by a permanent state of martial law. The only compensation was that under the conditions of martial law, the bourgeoisie had a free hand to industrialize the region.

Politically speaking, the long period of Moderate governments (1844–1868) was a grey era. Under the aegis of the Constitution of 1845 — conservative and based on a high property franchise, as was to be expected — government succeeded government. Presiding directly or from behind the scenes was General Ramón Narváez, the sword arm of the Moderates. Whenever he deemed it necessary, Narváez did not hesitate to resort to a dictatorship, the procedures for which could be found in the Constitution itself, embedded in its misleading provisions.

The episode at Vicálvaro (1854) — a pronunciamiento of Liberal origins — had an unforeseen consequence: the abrupt appearance upon the Spanish political scene of the urban masses, a movement of such dimensions that it can only be evaluated in relation to the precedent of 1808. This gave rise to a new and brief experiment with Progressive Liberalism, a reflection of the democratic movements of 1848 in Europe. One of the most interesting developments in this period was the beginning of an unexpected surge of prosperity, a result of the Crimean War and of a general upward trend in the economy. Another interesting development was the appearance of widespread organized workers' movements. In 1855 Catalonia witnessed her first general strike, declared by workers who intended to wrest from the government (where General Espartero was again in power) the right to organize. Andalusia and Castile were the scenes of demonstrations by peasants protesting against the horrible lot that had befallen them since the Church had lost her property, which had passed into the hands of unscrupulous capitalists. Espartero's government was unable to resist either the pressures from below or the intrigues from above. And so the biennium of the *Vicalvarada* (1854–1856) faded away.

In the reaction that followed, restraints were applied by an army whose devotion to Liberalism facilitated the formation of a new political coalition, an intermediate step between the Progressives and the Moderates — the Liberal Union, in which General Leopoldo O'Donnell was the star performer. The Unionists considered themselves the authentic representatives of the Moderate Liberal tradition, in opposition to the conservative deviations of Narváez and his faction. Actually such disputes constituted an amusing game of personalities in which base ambitions, stimulated by the unsavory intervention of Isabel II and of her advisors, were played out.

The country stayed out of this farce. The political bosses (*caciques*) undertook to testify on its behalf. Political intermediaries between the people and the state, the caciques emerged because of the apathy of the neutral masses — that is, of those who had nothing to gain by betting on the cards of reform or on those of reaction. The faltering parliamentary government of Spain had to rely upon these bosses in order to make their purportedly constitutional arena look authentic.

In other respects, the activities of this Isabelline generation of Moderates turned out to be far more interesting. In the first place, it guaranteed the new agrarian order by reaching an agreement (the Concordat of 1851) with the Papacy on the expropriated clerical property: through annual compensatory payments, the state — that is, the Spaniards as a whole — obligated itself to pay for the upkeep of the Church as well as of the clergy. Later, by means of a juridical usage based on specious legal texts, Moderate governments encouraged breaking up the lands owned in common, or owned by a local town government — lands that were the basis for the economy of many rural municipalities. This redistribution of property doubled the area of land under cultivation, and so for the moment the country was assured of a sufficient food supply, but for the great majority of peasants it did not contribute anything to improving their standard of living or their position in society. On the contrary, a very rapid population increase created an expanding agricultural proletariat, especially in Andalusia (*braceros*) and in Extremadura (*yunteros*). Lack of capital made it impossible to apply on a large scale such concrete solutions to the agrarian problem as the irrigation of dry lands. However, it was during this period that an efficient policy of hydraulic power had its first great beginnings (the Urgel canal, 1860).

The same lack of capital jeopardized the future of the Spanish railroad system, which from 1840 onward was the basis for tempestuous financial manueuvers that involved a working partnership of the bank, politics, and foreign capital. The first installations were financed by local companies, which laid down tracks of guaranteed performance (Barcelona to Mataró, 1848). But far greater investments were needed to establish a national network. At this point foreign capital (French, Belgian, and English) under the guidance of the Rothschilds or Pereires entered the scene, and financed part of the construction of the Spanish railway lines; the rest of the money came from Catalonia. Despite the economic errors committed, the railroads linked the regions of Spain together with ties far stronger than those created by the Liberals' distinctively French policy of centralism. From 1880 on, this new system of communication made it possible to move people about on a large scale, and also strengthened the reciprocal relationship between a policy of protection for Castilian wheat and one for Catalan industry. Although this criterion was contrary to that which prevailed in Europe at the time, it was necessary in Spain in order to avoid a disastrous collapse of the price of wheat or of textiles.

And as a matter of fact, in Catalonia, following in the wake of cotton textiles, light industry gained a firm foothold. Although it was almost entirely a small-scale enterprise, dispersed and barely rationalized, light industry made headway because of the enormous sacrifices of individuals and because of an indomitable will to triumph. Steam took over everywhere in the country, prompting

The Nineteenth Century

a rush of people from rural areas to the city. Barcelona grew in an unorganized fashion amid riots and turmoil.

But Catalonia found it far more difficult to develop heavy industry because coal and iron supplies were far distant and very insufficient. In a display of creative enthusiasm, some firms were established in Barcelona, but by that time the principal centers of the heavy industry of Spain were located along the Cantabrian coast, in Asturias and Vizcaya, where an abundance of coal and iron ore, respectively, explains the presence of big furnaces and metal foundries.

The Moderate governments of the Isabelline era paid relatively little attention to the capital equipment needed by industry. For its part, the only thing industry asked of a government was that it meddle as little as possible in the economy except to guarantee its future by protecting it against foreign competition. On the other hand, Moderate governments did take advantage of the pacification of civil discord to provide a new administrative structure. They worked out the bases for the treasury, for national education, and for public order. The most important measure of that era was the foundation of the Civil Guards (1844). In the countryside as in the city, Civil Guards maintained order not only against bandits and criminals, smugglers and highwaymen, but against peasants whom years of misery had stirred into rebellion, and against workers kept down by iniquitous labor conditions.

The organization of provinces, initiated in 1833 as an instrument to combat Carlism,[7] gained vitality and efficacy through its financial, educational, militia, and administrative duties. The province was the quintessence of centralized Liberalism. In it public officials assumed their final form as a social group distinguished by a specific mentality, one that during this era was not renowned either for

---

[7] In 1833, Spain's historic territorial divisions were somewhat arbitrarily reorganized into forty-nine provinces (forty-seven on the Peninsula, two more for the Canary and Balearic Islands). Provincial administrative officials were usually appointed by, and directly responsible to, their ministries in Madrid, so that a uniform administrative system prevailed throughout the nation.

its education or for its integrity. Discharged with each change of government, a public official had to use his term in office to advantage in order to balance the family budget for the future.

The Moderate regime deteriorated because of a lack of grandeur in both its domestic and its foreign ideals. The War of Morocco (1859–1860), the intervention in Mexico (1861), and the pompously entitled War of the Pacific (1866–1868)[8] were campaigns of patriotic propaganda that glossed over the tremendous lack of military preparedness. The Moderates' systematic refusal to broaden their horizons, their persistent elimination of all possibility of change either to the right or to the left, their administrative corruption, and the political irresponsibility of the throne reduced their party to a few already exhausted men and to a skeletal bureaucratic structure.

The fall of the Moderates, instigated by an army that was still Liberal, dragged royalty down with it. Not even the highest-ranking members of the conservative group (including, among others, Antonio Cánovas del Castillo) would agree to carry out any further dealings with the Crown. But the pronunciamiento of 1868 that triumphed at Alcolea bridge went far beyond what had been foreseen by its leaders: Juan Prim, Francisco Serrano, and Juan Bautista Topete. The movement of a "Spain with Honor"[9] gave way to a general revolutionary uprising that attempted a singular experiment in nineteenth-century Spanish life: to give the country

---

[8] Spain's War of the Pacific originated in her failure to recognize Peruvian independence and therefore to resolve conflicting territorial claims, particularly to the Chincha Islands. Peru, allied with Chile and Ecuador, declared war in 1866 and completely routed the token Spanish fleet in 1868. An armistice was not signed until 1871.

[9] On September 19, 1868, Generals Serrano and Prim and Admiral Topete, together with other officers, published a manifesto entitled "Spain with Honor" defending their action. They declared, among other matters, that "the person charged with the defense of the Constitution should not be its irreconcilable enemy" — a barely disguised reference to Isabel's interference in government. Implicit in the manifesto was a criticism of Isabel's indiscretion about her rather scandalous private life.

The Nineteenth Century

an opportunity to govern itself. Such was the profound significance of the "September Revolution."

Spain's first experiment with democratic government made manifest the good intentions of a minority and the lack of discipline in a people subjected to pressures far greater than those needed to make them participate, by means of universal suffrage, as a simple coefficient in public life. Government officials had to combat a new outbreak of Carlism — the direct inheritance of the dissatisfied Catholic peasantry of the north — which took hold in Navarre and Catalonia. They also had to combat an atmosphere of factionalism that crushed any joint effort, the mental lethargy of the bureaucracy, and the mystical infantilism of new ideologies that expanded in the warmth of an unexpected liberty. Within a few years Federalism had seized control of the Mediterranean and Andalusian coast, followed close behind by labor extremism — a reflection of the First International. This movement was certain to find generous support among Andalusian laborers and one group of Catalan workers, who had already fallen under the influence of Proudhon's doctrines through the works of Francisco Pi y Margall.

The country was suffering from political vertigo brought on because she was overwrought and because of the type of problems that confronted her — especially the problems of agriculture and labor. Spain moved from a provisional government under Juan Prim to the monarchy of Amadeo of Savoy (served by inefficient and punctilious ministers), and then from this monarchy to the First Republic.[10] Within a few scant months, the Republic exhausted all solutions and ended up in a frenzy of Separatism — the apex of Pi y Margall's Federalism and the counterpart of Carlist regionalism.

After the manifestation of such discrepant viewpoints, in the midst of a full civil war on the Peninsula and in Cuba, the only

---

[10] The First Republic lasted eleven months (from February 11, 1873, to January 3, 1874). During this time it had four presidents (or, more exactly, presidents of the executive branch): Estanislao Figueras (1810–1882); Francisco Pi y Margall (1824–1901); Nicolás Salmerón (1838–1908); and Emilio Castelar (1832–1899).

possibility was to negotiate a formula for a state that would be viable and that would bring together under one roof all Spaniards, regardless of their political opinions — a formula of legitimate monarchy with a broad constitutional government. This was the idea that Antonio Cánovas del Castillo proclaimed and then imposed, after General Manuel Pavía's *golpe de estado* (1874) had abolished the Republic, and after the Bourbons — in the person of Alfonso XII (1875-1885) — were restored to the throne.

The Restoration was, essentially, an act of faith in Hispanic coexistence. Even today one can admire the tact with which Cánovas proceeded to draw up the Constitution of 1876 and the impartiality with which he directed the preparation of the great legal codes — the civil law code, the mortgage law, the legislation governing civil and criminal trial procedures. Cánovas wanted to establish a legal state, not an arbitrary one, but one that would be backed by the vital forces of the nation — agricultural landowners, industrialists, and bourgeoisie — and by an army with no capricious desires for a pronunciamiento. Thus his policies were conservative, making only such concessions as were necessary to provide the machinery for an active dialectic in the parliamentary game, but limiting any concession to minor issues. In establishing a peaceful rotation of office, Cánovas was able to secure the cooperation of the old-time chief of the Liberals, Práxedes Mateo Sagasta — an achievement that enhances still further his sagacity as a statesman.

Coinciding with the great stage of bourgeois expansion, the Restoration governments decidedly stimulated the acquisition of capital equipment for industry. Using as a point of departure the free trade legislation imposed in 1869 by Treasury Minister Laureano Figuerola, the country emerged from the blind alley into which it had been led by the protectionism of the preceding decade. Free trade opened up the mineral wealth of the Peninsula to the voracity of foreign financiers: copper, lead, and iron were loaded on ships headed for France, England, and Belgium. But no one can be condemned for considering the welfare of his country within the framework of the ideas of his era. And indeed it was necessary to begin all over again. By means of a policy of free trade, Spain was able to confront the problems of installing new railroads, developing public utilities, expanding the Catalan textile industry, and creating and expanding incredibly the industrial and financial complex of Vizcaya. With the profits obtained from the sale of iron ore, the Basques climbed within twenty years to first place in Hispanic heavy industry, maritime transportation, and banking.

Catalonia demonstrated her financial potential in the International Exposition of 1888 and in the expansion of Barcelona beyond her medieval walls. But this expansion was always limited by an important factor: the very limited capacity of the consumer — the agrarian masses. The results were a demand for protectionist measures, the meager growth of capital, the impossibility of any large-scale reconversion of her industry or installation of new equipment. All the bold efforts of the Fomento del Trabajo Nacional of Barcelona — the bastion of the haute bourgeoisie of Catalonia — as well as the distinterested projects of some few intellectuals such as Joaquín Costa, were dashed to pieces against the barrier of a limited consumer demand. Only with great parsimony did agriculture mobilize its resources, thus creating a fatal obstruction at the heart of Spain's economic life.

Peasant passivity — maintained, of course, by Cánovas — explains why the Restoration had to resort to a legal fiction in order to keep in motion the parliamentary mechanism that served as its fulcrum. With or without universal suffrage, a people of impoverished agricultural workers had to disengage themselves from public affairs and concentrate their efforts on a direct, sterile, and exhausting struggle to obtain greater returns for their labor. This is the principal cause of the development of bossism (*caciquismo*) in this period. For one entire generation the general Spanish superstructure conceived by Cánovas was undermined at its base by a primitive organization of family clans that was completely detached from the great exigencies of the nation and, even more significantly, that was unstable — quick to revolt at the side of the first agent provocateur or the first subversive propagandist.

Under the quiescent mantle of the Restoration, Spanish activism flourished grandly. In first place was the intellectual activism.

Groups appeared who were dissatisfied with Spain as she was, not in her political aspect (of secondary importance to them) but in her historical essence and in her relationship to European culture. One such group was that of the Free Institution of Education (Institución Libre de Enseñanza),[11] founded by Francisco Giner de los Ríos and by other disciples and admirers of Julián Sanz del Río, who had introduced the philosophy of Krause into Spain. This Krause-inspired intelligentsia prepared the dissatisfied Spanish intellectualism of the twentieth century with its desire for new horizons of knowledge and for incorporation into Europe. Anti-traditionalists, they regarded Spain as an uncomprehended world that should refashion herself, in accord not with Catholic tradition but with a singular past which they sketched only in bare outline. Europeanizers, they dumped onto Castile an alluvium of literary novelties that renewed and revolutionized university education. Nationalists, they practiced a Castilian creed, tending (as had the Count-Duke of Olivares) to confuse Spain with Castile.

The Catalanists were another activist group, heirs to the eighteenth-century Catalans' pride in their region, to the literary spirit of their Romantic generation, and to the moral debacle of Federalism and Carlism. Catalanism did not reject Spain as a historic reality. It did reject the way Spain's history had been interpreted by Liberal centralism, the adjustment of the national pace to the rhythm of Castile, and the political and economic consequences that these developments had entailed. Thus, although

---

[11] The *Institución Libre* was founded in 1876 by Francisco Giner de los Ríos (1839–1915) as a private school (the term *free* in its title indicates nonofficial). Determined to remain independent of state supervision, Giner abandoned the original program of secondary and university studies (requiring an official curriculum) and concentrated on an experimental elementary school inspired by the neo-Kantian philosophy of Karl Krause (1781–1832), disseminated in Spain by his student, Julián Sanz del Río (1814–1869), a professor at the University of Madrid. Influential because it rallied a group of politicians and intellectuals to attempt the renovation of Spain through educational reform, it continued its work after Giner's death under the direction of Manuel Cossío (1858–1935). A declining momentum merged with the Civil War to end its existence.

Catalanism was the expression of a mentality and language different from those of Castile, it was not therefore necessarily less Hispanic. And although it did react negatively insofar as the tonic of the Restoration was concerned, Catalanism was from the beginning a movement of youthful optimism.

The proletarian movement was still another source of activism. This phenomenon occurred in the country as an outgrowth of the general European socialist movement, with the differences appropriate to the economic conditions of Spain and to the idiosyncracies of her working-class masses. Beginning in 1830, workers in the textile industry of Catalonia had organized trade unions (*sociedades de resistencia al capital*) which maintained an uncertain existence, more or less complicated by the political disturbances of the era. The period of maximum expansion of unionization in Catalonia occurred in the years 1854–1855. It gathered momentum under the stimulus of a subversive ideology that was an adaptation of Etienne Cabet's utopianism and, above all, of Proudhon's anti-state individualism. This explains both the acceptance of Bakunin's creed, disseminated in Spain in 1869 by Giuseppi Fanelli (Bakunin's disciple), and the foundation in Barcelona in 1870 of a Spanish Regional Federation of the International that openly declared its anarchist orientation. This movement spread through Valencia, Murcia, and Andalusia, while the group in Madrid (in accord with its bureaucratic and rigid spirit) took its bearings from the authoritarian Marxist position. With the breakup of the International in 1874, the group in Madrid founded, successively, the Spanish Socialist Party (1879) and the General Union of Laborers (1888). Pablo Iglesias was the organizer. Although socialism attracted few adherents along the Mediterranean and Andalusian periphery, it did secure some in the heavy industry areas of the north (Vizcaya and Asturias).

A syndicalist ideal continued to prevail in Catalonia, Valencia, and Andalusia.[12] But anarchist groups (whose origins varied)

---

[12] Syndicalism means simply a labor movement whose objective is to force the government and employers to grant better wages and working conditions. In the nineteenth century, particularly in Catalonia, the most

superimposed themselves on this ideal; they were prepared to liquidate the bourgeois world by acts of personal violence. Between 1892 and 1897 Barcelona was the stage for an endemic manifestation of terrorism that, long before the street warfare of 1917-1922, gave it sad fame in the annals of world subversion. The expansion of anarchism cost Cánovas his life — the first of the Presidents of the Council to be sacrificed upon the altar of social conflict.

---

common term for a trade union was "society of resistance to capital," a term that persisted into the twentieth century. But gradually after 1900 it was replaced by syndicalism, in imitation of the French, when referring to the national labor movement that scorned politics (specifically, the Socialist party) and was willing to resort to violence in support of its demands. Because of its apolitical tenet and use of violence, syndicalism acquired the connotation of a labor movement intent upon revolution, particularly after anarchists gained control of the national syndicate organization (described by Vicens Vives in the paragraph above and again on p. 146). But the Franco regime has made the term respectable by using it as the official name for the twenty-six national organizations (which include employers and state officials as well as workers), grouped according to industry.

CHAPTER TWENTY

The Crisis of the Twentieth Century

During the first half of the twentieth century Spain was convulsed by a profound crisis. That it can be considered a regional version of the general European crisis in this century does not diminish its importance. Granting that many problems were identical and developed along parallel lines, some facets affected Spanish life exclusively.

The very first of these was that malaise had been manifest in Spain far earlier than elsewhere in Europe, at the height of the gilded and prosaic *fin du siècle*. Although there had been many indications of a profound spiritual change, it crystallized under the impact of Spain's defeat by the United States in 1898. The frivolous official optimism and the facile patriotism of the man in the street gave way to universal consternation, which some felt as simply a level stretch before Spain moved on to another inconsequential era; others felt it as humiliation and shame, as an avowed determination to change, either along the paths of exalted nationalism, or along those of revolutionary internationalism. Both groups agreed that if the situation — the government, the society, the vulgar and silly way of life, the deceit, the routine, the lethargy — continued, it would lead to the extinction of Spain.

But what was Spain? The question was answered in a great variety of ways: Spain was Castile, Spain was Africa, Spain was an entelechy, Spain was the sum total of the autonomous regions in the era of the Catholic monarchs, and so on. That generation did, however, set forth two unanimous and incisive affirmations: they

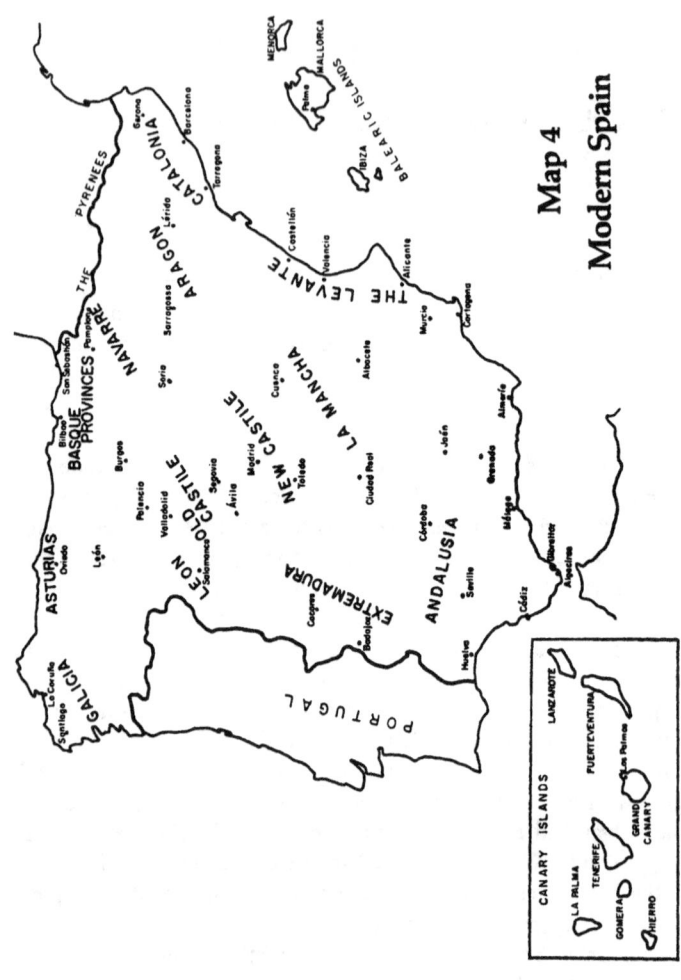

Map 4
Modern Spain

did not like Spain as she was at that moment, and they believed it necessary to Europeanize her at any cost.

On the form to be given to the future Spain that those men so ardently desired, there was a divergence of opinion. This was the second specifically Spanish facet of the European crisis. Those on the periphery, especially the Catalans, predicated an optimistic solution — one that was constructive, bourgeois, and historically oriented. Castilians, in contrast, were characterized by pessimism, by a break with the past, by an aristocratic tenor, by a tendency toward abstractions. Both groups found their *razón de ser* in an ardent nationalism that longed to burn intervening stages and to restore the grandeur of Spain. If that were not possible — if Spain were dead — then the Catalans, the Basques, and the Galicians would have to refuse to continue shouldering the added burden of Castile. Therein lay the entire problem. The effect of this restless regional mentality on the Spanish structure as a whole was to stimulate an intellectual and literary revival of the first order, one that maintained its momentum throughout the following two decades. But the ideas that it contained — explosive ideas, capable of shattering the country — did not reach the political scene until 1917, by which time the revival had undergone a philosophical process of defining its ideology and a historic process of gaining public support.[1]

The fact that there were two different generations — which we express in a double code, 1898 for Castile, 1901 for Catalonia — stimulated dissension between Castile and Catalonia on the question of how the Spanish state should be organized. Fundamentally the dispute involved not only the possibility of accepting the indigenous and authentic culture of Catalonia as representative of one mode of the Hispanic essence, but also the possibility of providing the state with an efficient and modern structure whose leaders, instead of playing politics, would seek solutions for the country's most urgent and dramatic problems. In order to present both tendencies in the best possible light, Catalan nationalists asked for an autonomous

---

[1] For a more detailed expression of Vicens Vives' ideas on the crisis of 1917, see his *Historia social y económica de España* (Barcelona, 1959), V, 409–412.

regime. Their proposal was encumbered by its own antiquated concepts and by the fear that it would lead either to the breakup of the Spanish state that had emerged at the Renaissance, or else to the decline of Castile's historic mission as the national entity that had founded that state.

At the height of the intellectual controversy and of the political game, theoretical positions were established that verged, ideologically, on mutual separatism; such positions were used to advantage by those who captivated facile enthusiasms. But the strict reality of the events reveals that, as part of the nationalist tendency mentioned previously, Catalans participated in the scientific, social, and economic life of Spain far more than they ever had in the past.

The third facet of the Spanish crisis concerned religion. The attacks upon Catholicism and the alienation of the masses from the Church were of course general throughout Europe. But the manner in which the problem was presented — entwined with politics and even with war — was specifically Spanish.

The aristocratic and bourgeois Liberalism of the nineteenth century had been moderately secular and had favored a Church subject to state controls. Its great objective was to eliminate the religious orders and acquire their property; but the secular Church was to be defended and protected by the state itself (the Constitution of 1845 and the Concordat of 1851). Meanwhile Democratic, Republican, and Federalist movements were preaching not only anticlericalism in general but also — and for the first time in Spain — an atheistic point of view. Beginning in 1868, anti-religious propaganda opened wide cracks in the old-time bloc of Spanish Catholicism, especially in the proletarianized industrial zones. The schism created within the country in 1869, at the time of the arguments over the Catholic unity of Spain, had of necessity profound repercussions in the succeeding era.

If we except the group of apologists led by Jaime Balmes, the reaction of the Church was quite weak throughout the nineteenth century. At its close only one individual, Marcelino Menéndez y Pelayo, was able to rise above the vulgarity and defend the Catholic roots of Hispanic life. However, during those same years the generous policies of the Restoration governments benefited the Church by allowing new and old religious congregations to expand their educational activities. A new factor that should be pointed out is that regionalist movements were supported by a large sector of the clergy on the periphery, and this in turn stimulated a powerful current of religious revival. Thus the Spanish Church also had its "Generation of 1898." From those focal points (particularly Catalonia, Valencia, Asturias, and the Basque provinces) came a surge of liturgical revival that secured new and fervent public support for the Church, especially among the nobility, the bourgeoisie, and the middle classes. Because Catholicism was thus revitalized, its clash with the first anticlerical wave of the century — unleashed in 1901 in the wake of the French and Portuguese campaigns — was more violent.

This wave of demagogy inundated the proletarianized masses and prepared a break between them and the Church, which it accused of being an instrument used by the bourgeoisie and the landowners to oppose the demands of labor. This psychology of having been defrauded might explain the assaults upon the church buildings that have been so rife in recent Spanish history, beginning with the Tragic Week of Barcelona in 1909. The Church, however, did not abandon the course that she had set for herself: the reconquest of society by means of education.

Although many and varied, the Church's efforts in the social field were very timid, in both the industrial and the agrarian zone. Unfortunately, those who directed these activities, even high-ranking members of the hierarchy, did not find the support that they deserved. In 1917 — in the general crisis of labor relations — the Catholic labor movement was sacrificed and left to its fate. "Yellow syndicalism" gained support within this group and diverted it into combat positions that promoted neither social peace nor religious tolerance.[2]

---

[2] "Yellow syndicalism" was the term used for company unions in Spain. The term originated in France where, during an important strike of miners, the members of the company union pasted yellow paper on the windows of their office after strikers had smashed all the panes. In Spain

Far more than in other Western European countries, the conservative classes of Spain were intransigent in their attitude toward labor demands, because of the presence of a violent and destructive anarchist movement. It still remains to be clarified whether anarchism developed as a consequence of the lack of vision and the harshness of Spanish employers, or whether employers adopted a position of strong resistance when confronted with anarchist syndicalism's tendency toward lawlessness or avowedly revolutionary action. In either case, whereas the bourgeoisie and even the government reached a stage where they were able to negotiate with the UGT (Unión General de Trabajadores, the Socialist labor organization), and while the Socialist party participated in Spain's national and municipal politics, anarchistic syndicalism remained intractable.

As a matter of record, one must distinguish between the two components of this movement: pure syndicalism and militant anarchism. Syndicalism [3] — an imitation of the French movement, apolitical and advocating direct action — began to organize in Barcelona in 1901. It gave rise to Solidaridad Obrera (first a federation of labor societies of Barcelona, and then a regional confederation of Catalan labor), the National Confederation of Labor (CNT — Confederación Nacional del Trabajo), and the Single Syndicates (Sindicatos Únicos, 1918). The second component was militant anarchism. Weakened by the failure of individual terrorism at the

---

as in France, the company unions themselves as well as their opponents used the term. Initially Spanish employers supported the craft unions organized by Catholic workers from 1906 on, but these were not successful because the hierarchy did not support them and because workers denounced them as company unions. Beginning in 1919 employers encouraged the organization of completely secular Free Syndicates (Sindicatos Libres); however, many members of the Free Syndicates were also members of the Catholic labor movement. The Free Syndicates purported to be strict labor unions as against the anarchist-dominated National Confederation of Labor (CNT). During the years 1920–1922 their armed members fought alongside the police and employers against CNT members.

[3] For a discussion of Spanish syndicalism, see p. 139n.

end of the nineteenth century, anarchism slowly gained control of organized labor and finally, after 1909, imposed upon it the ideals of a cataclysmic and definitive social revolution. This is the way that anarchism and syndicalism consolidated; the street fighting in Barcelona from 1919 to 1923 made their symbiosis indissoluble.

During these years syndicalists, theoretical anarchists, professional terrorists, and hired gunmen mingled in one of the most explosive, destructive movements — and until now the least studied — of that general European social complex which emerged from World War I. They were people disposed to wrest power from the hands of the bourgeoisie and their coercive forces, to annihilate the state in one great revolutionary blow, and to initiate a life of collectivized property organized into free municipalities and based on an agrarian and patriarchal economy. An enervated utopia, with no possible counterpart in the world, it was purely the reaction of an illiterate peasant transformed into the mechanized worker of an urban enterprise.

Finally, the last of the Hispanic features of the twentieth-century crisis concerned the agrarian problem. Although not exclusive to Spain, for she shared it with other nations in Eastern Europe and the Balkans, it was a differential factor inasmuch as it did not occur in other Western European nations. This difficult problem (simultaneously a moral, economic, technical, and social problem) was circumvented by the parties who alternated in office (*los partidos turnantes*) and who were selected from the great landowners. The First World War had momentarily provided a solution because of the demands of belligerent nations for rural products and for raw materials, but the subsequent decline in prices and the resulting unemployment darkened the already stormy horizon of the Spanish countryside.

The remaining facets of the Hispanic crisis were identical with those of Europe in general: diversity of opinion as between directed and free economies; between authoritarianism and democracy; between private property and collectivization of the means of production; between a humanistic and a materialistic concept of life. But given the Hispanic temperament and the magnitude of these problems, the differences of opinion developed on Peninsular soil into an extremely violent conflict.

Prior to 1936, there were three attempts to overcome the difficulties that obstructed the organization of Spanish society. The first solution, attempted during the actual reign of Alfonso XIII (1902–1931),[4] consisted of implementing the parliamentary system correctly, exactly as it had been set forth in the Constitution of 1876, but as Cánovas, its author, had not wanted it to develop. Antonio Maura was the architect of this policy. His grand idea was to reform local government, in the belief that this would have a twofold result: it would uproot bossism (caciquismo) and it would provide an outlet for Catalonia's desire for autonomy. But Maura's policy was doomed to failure by the workers' explosion in Barcelona in 1909 — an explosion that had been foreseen since 1901, but that nothing had been done to avoid, because the labor problem was considered only in terms of public order. A shift to the left, proclaimed publicly by José Canalejas, made some further progress for a little while, but his assassination in 1912 and the declaration of World War I canceled this promising experiment in reforming the parliamentary system.

Although Spain remained neutral, the war began to undermine her nineteenth-century society. The process of transformation was stimulated by the two torrents from the battlefields of Europe — money for supplies, and ideas to maintain faith in the struggle. Even the army felt the impact of subversion from within; officers organized *Juntas de Defensa*. Their activities and proclamations helped demolish the principles that were the basis for the parliamentary governments — purely caretaker governments harassed by demands for redress of political and social grievances, and for regional autonomy. In 1917 this situation turned into a crisis. The labor strike of that year was quelled by the army and by the Catalan bour-

---

[4] Alfonso XIII, born after the death of his father, Alfonso XII, was nominally king from the day of his birth in 1886, but until 1902 his mother, Marie Christine, acted as Regent.

geoisie, who, although themselves leaders of a movement for political renovation, allowed themselves to be detoured into the attractive, sheltered harbor of positions in the government.

The crisis of 1917 led to years in which grievances were exacerbated. Disjointed and invertebrate was the way that José Ortega y Gasset defined this juncture.[5] Each sector of society sought a drastic solution: labor syndicalism blindly devoted itself to fighting in the streets, precisely the site preferred by the most reactionary bourgeoisie, who specialized in summoning the army to their aid; Catalan regionalism, which had achieved its first administrative structure (*la Mancomunitat*, 1913),[6] demanded a definitive legal document as part of its campaign for self-determination, which was derived from President Wilson's principles; Castilian radicalism spied out the slightest occasion for an attack on any government whatsoever. And in chorus, all of these groups exclaimed that a new political solution must be sought.

Contrary to the forecasts of many persons, the solution — the second one attempted — was the establishment in 1923 of a dictatorship under General Miguel Primo de Rivera. The Constitution of 1876 was suspended and the very principle of the Crown's legitimacy was transgressed. But given the circumstances — terrorism, ill-starred colonial campaigns, the disintegration of the state — the monarch and the army believed that they should intervene and reorganize the life of the country. It was a propitious moment to attempt such a project, for Western Europe was reorganizing in a conservative fashion and Mussolini had already carried out his march on Rome. Primo de Rivera set up a system of purely defen-

---

[5] José Ortega y Gasset, *España invertebrada* (Madrid, 1921).
[6] The *Mancomunitat* was established by a Royal Decree (December 18, 1913) because opposition within the Cortes prevented it from being enacted into law. It was an association that superseded the legislative assemblies of the four Catalan provinces (Barcelona, Lérida, Tarragona, and Gerona). It was unable to expand its original limited legislative jurisdiction because of internal dissension over social and economic policies and because the central government zealously guarded its powers. The Mancomunitat was dissolved in 1925.

sive, paternalistic government that lasted as long as the wave of general prosperity that followed the end of the First World War. The economic crisis of 1929 removed him from power. His fall revealed the immensity of his failure: aside from the pacification of Morocco and the construction of some public works, everything still remained to be done. What was even worse was that the problems had become inflammatory because they had been going on for so long and because of the wave of radicalism that the Great Depression had prompted throughout Europe.

The mystique of revolutionary reform, the general feeling of a large majority of the Spanish population in 1931, gave rise to a third solution — the Second Republic. Swept into power by an initial movement of popular enthusiasm, the Republic proclaimed a state that was democratic, regionalist, secular, and receptive to broad social reforms. Such a program would benefit leftist businessmen, a professional middle class, and skilled workers — precisely the classes which (except in such peripheral territories as Catalonia) were the least vital ones in the Spanish panorama. For this reason the progress of the Republic was totally obstructed by the demands of labor (the syndicalists of the CNT inspired by the mystique of the Third Revolution, and the socialists of the UGT inspired by revolutionary Marxism) and the opposition of great landowners (the revolt of General José Sanjurjo, 1932). Catholics also harassed the government because their consciences were threatened; instead of democratically and sincerely attempting to take over the places of command, they helped to undermine the Republic.

To these deep gashes in the hide of the Hispanic bull, no other balm was applied than the apologia of violence — learned in the Germany of Hitler, the Italy of Mussolini, the Austria of Dollfus, the Russia of Stalin, and even the France of February 1934. Europe fell upon Spain, obscured her vision, and plunged her into the tremendous crisis that occurred in Catalonia and Asturias in October 1934. From this she emerged with a revolutionary mentality, both on the right and on the left. And thus it was that, just as many drops of water form a torrent, the Hispanic peoples allowed themselves to be propelled toward the dramatic vortex of July 1936.

Commentary on Bibliography

CHAPTER ONE   In the first edition of this book, I omitted the prehistoric period. Since the end of the Civil War, many prehistorians have been content to write only popularized accounts, and I did not feel that I could overcome my distrust of their archaeological research. And I felt this even more keenly because, as a student of Pedro Bosch Gimpera,[1] I had followed with insatiable eagerness the intellectual and personal careers of the prehistorians. Although I was criticized by my good friends, the archaeologists, I made no promise to amend my position.

To be specific, it seems to me that Spanish prehistory functions on the basis of very limited documentation and that the subjects of its monographs are even more limited. A simple calculation suffices to show that the deposits of stone artifacts cover barely one-thousandth of the time and space needed to formulate a theory that would have any chance of being successfully defended. One glance at the archaeological map is enough to demonstrate that the distribu-

---

[1] Pedro Bosch Gimpera (b. 1891), an ethnologist and archaeologist now living in exile in Mexico City, deeply influenced the study of Spanish prehistory through his chair at the University of Barcelona, his work in the Institut d'Estudis Catalans, and his writings. His great ability to systematize and synthesize has been invaluable; some prehistorians, however, would dispute his chronology. Throughout his long career, Bosch Gimpera has stressed the importance of contact with North Africa in the cultural and ethnological prehistory of Spain. See his *Etnología de la Península Ibérica* (Barcelona, 1932) and *Los pueblos de España: Ensayo de etnología* (Barcelona, 1946).

tion of these deposits has much more to do with their proximity to a university center, or to a government-supported archaeological team, than with the possible diffusion of a culture. In short, in Spain as elsewhere, the role of the prehistorian is very difficult.

In this second edition I have decided to include two chapters on prehistory. I have done so mostly to prove that I am indifferent neither to the remote past of Spanish lands nor to the work of my colleagues and friends, the prehistorians. Although at this moment their contributions may be valuable only as collections of data, they have helped to open a window on those six-hundred-thousand-odd years that separate us from the first hominids. Such depth in time is enough to make us grateful for their enthusiasm and to pardon them for the intuitions that have so often led us astray along the bypaths of Spain's most remote past. Meanwhile a certain tendency to unify criteria, which always signifies important progress, can be discerned in the most recent work of the archaeologists.

In my account, totally free from the direct influence of any group or school, I have followed the moderate line laid down by the mature authors: that is to say, that which might be represented by Luis Pericot,[2] Martín Almagro,[3] and Julio Caro Baroja.[4] The objection will be made that given such names, one cannot trace a mini-

---

[2] Luis Pericot García (b. 1899), a professor in the University of Barcelona, defends the existence of a homogeneous cultural region along the coasts of the western Mediterranean during the Upper Paleolithic, thus stressing the cultural and racial exchange between the Iberian peninsula and North Africa. See *La España primitiva* (Barcelona, 1950) and *El arte rupestre español* (Barcelona, 1950).

[3] Martín Almagro Basch, archaeologist and professor at the University of Madrid, has devoted his attention to the dating of cultures and peoples. See *Origen y formación del pueblo hispano* (Barcelona, 1958). He has also written exhaustive reports on his excavations: *Las necropolis de Ampurias*, 2 vols. (Barcelona, 1953–1955), and *El poblado y la necropolis megalíticos de Los Millares* (Madrid, 1963).

[4] Julio Caro Baroja (b. 1914), Director of the Museo del Pueblo Español in Madrid from 1944 to 1955, has written on the ethnology, linguistics, and culture of the prehistoric era. He attempts a synthesis, trying to relate isolated incidents, peoples, and theories. See *España primitiva y romana* (Madrid, 1957) and *Razas, pueblos y linajes* (Madrid, 1957).

Commentary on Bibliography

mum common line; but since I am neither a prehistorian nor an anthropologist, I am able to consider matters from a more flexible viewpoint, although not so flexible as to convert Hispanic prehistory into a matter of political controversy.

In the general presentation of the theme, I have relied upon the recent works of André Varagnac.[5] For the details, I have followed the classic writers cited above (and in addition, Bosch Gimpera). The entire chapter suffers from a lack of authentic, concrete, and reliable data, but this is not my fault.

The great problem now under debate is whether or not Africa influenced the development of the first Spanish populations. Thirty years ago, everything was profoundly westernized and Africanist;[6] ten years later, the African element was still accorded importance and prestige;[7] today, almost no one believes in it.[8] Mysteries of prehistoric science! We do not know, therefore, if the Pithecanthropi were able to reach Spain by crossing the Straits of Gibraltar, a most difficult undertaking, or if they had to go around by the Caspian Sea, which would indeed have been a circuitous route. The same problem exists for the itinerary of Solutrean man.

---

[5] From the viewpoint of Spanish prehistory, the most important work of André Varagnac (b. 1894), the French historian, is the first volume of his ambitious history of the world: *L'Homme avant l'ecriture* (Paris, 1959). Varagnac and his collaborators (including Bosch Gimpera) assign the Iberian peninsula a major role in the prehistoric world. See also Varagnac's *De la Prehistoire au monde moderne: Essai d'une anthropodynamique* (Paris, 1954).

[6] A staunch defender of the African origins of the Iberian people was Adolph Schulten (1870–1960), the German prehistorian who devoted his career to Spanish prehistory. See *Hispania* (Barcelona, 1920), which was expanded and published under the title *Iberische Landeskunde: Geographie des antiken Spanien*, 2 vols. (Strasbourg, 1955–1957).

[7] Both Bosch Gimpera and Luis Pericot sustain the importance of North Africa in Spanish prehistory, beginning in the Upper Paleolithic.

[8] A younger generation of prehistorians — Miguel Tarradell, Francisco Jordá Cerdá, Eduardo Ripoll Perelló — reject completely or minimize the importance of North Africa as an ethnic or cultural factor. They believe the decisive element to be European or Mediterranean in origin, and point specifically to the Gravettian or Périgord culture of the Upper Paleolithic.

Without Africa, the weight of foreign influence shifts to Europe and the Mediterranean. In the text I have pondered the role of the men of the Magdalenian culture, because it seems to me that they were really the first to consider the "know-how" of things, and that they mechanized the world from that point on. Possibly this was not so. But in any event, we would all like the archaeologists to stop pasting nametags on earthenware pots and enlighten us about the life of the men who fashioned them. This too might result in some errors, but how much more interesting they would be than those errors that are to be found, layer upon layer, scattered through books which no one consults any longer.

And let us not even mention the problem of Mediterranean art, with which the chapter ends.[9] Even today no one knows how to classify it precisely. Oh, for those happy student days when we thought that *Homo capensis* from Africa was the bearer of that art form. Later we realized that all such ideas had been unwarranted, a mistake due to *horrorem vacui* — so perceptible among prehistorians.

CHAPTER TWO   This chapter could be written with far greater ease than the preceding one; there is more documentation — some of it historical — while random affirmations and the whimsies of those who work by intuition can be more easily isolated. The theme is in accordance with the purest Mediterranean doctrine. In my youth, the neophyte historian had to be a pro-Westerner, especially in

---

[9] The art of eastern Spain (Mediterranean, or Spanish Levant), discovered in the last fifty years, shows hunters as well as animals on open-air paintings on rocks; Cogul and Albarracín are the most famous sites. Although difficult to date because there are no accompanying artifacts in identifiable strata, and the animals pictured could live in warm or cold climates, most scholars today believe it post-glacial (Mesolithic, 12,000–5,000 B.C.). Still controversial is its relation to the art of Africa. See Pericot and Eduardo Ripoll, eds., *Prehistoric Art of the Western Mediterranean and the Sahara* (Chicago-Barcelona, 1964).

Commentary on Bibliography 155

the question of megaliths.[10] Now it is completely the reverse; everything comes from the East. I am the first to be convinced of this.

What I would not affirm with equal certainty is the theory, sustained by the most prominent authors, of a series of migrations.[11] The Mediterranean is too large to require that so many people move from one site to another; the maintenance of good relations between one coast and another would be enough. If in the eighteenth century B.C., the techniques of the *bou* [12] took only half a century to advance overland from the Gulf of Rosas in Catalonia to Vizcaya, then we have reason to suspect that everything was possible in the western Mediterranean with twenty oars and a square sail. In short, it is a question of patience, of research *in situ*, and of great monographs. At present, we lack these. Thus the problems of the early Neolithic and that of the peoples of the *Cardium* pottery remain completely unresolved. These have simply been noted, but I would not put my hand into the fire to defend any one of the theses. It would be dangerous.

In contrast, the picture of the plenary Neolithic seems to me almost definitive. The bell beakers are the disturbing element. Such an expansion seems to me not only strange but inconsistent with any other Hispanic manifestation in more recent history. But there is a solid doctoral thesis to support the theory,[13] and no one — least of all myself — would dare be the first to question it.

---

[10] Because so many megaliths (collective underground tombs of the Neolithic) were found in Iberia, this was believed to have been their place of origin. It is now accepted that the concept came from the East (Mycenae) by sea to southern Iberia, brought by traders or colonizers, and then spread to Western Europe.

[11] See, for example, the book by V. Gordon Childe (1892–1957), the English archaeologist who was very interested, and very influential, in the Iberian peninsula: *Prehistoric Migrations in Europe* (Oslo, 1950).

[12] *Bou* is fishing by dragging a net between two boats.

[13] For the controversy over Bell Beaker pottery (was it carried to Europe from southern Iberia ca. 2250 B.C. or vice versa; did it diffuse through trade or did colonists carry it together with a knowledge of metal working), see H. N. Savory, *Spain and Portugal: The Prehistory of the Iberian Peninsula* (London, 1968), pp. 166–189.

The point at which the controversy hardens is when it reaches the first millennium. In the text I have not given even a remote idea of the pitched battle being waged. On the subject of colonizations, I need only point out that, despite the famous biblical references, there are some people who deny even the existence of Tartessus.[14]

The Celts and the Iberians, however, are the *casus belli*. Following a phase of overflowing Iberianism (the Bosch Gimpera stage), a truly demolishing Celtic offensive was unleashed (the Martín Almagro stage) that coincided with a draconian readjustment of the chronology of Iberian art (the theory of Antonio García y Bellido).[15] All of this was undoubtedly intended to proclaim the warlike nature of the primitive *gens hispanica* and to establish the possibility of a sense of unity predating Roman colonization. The latter position is absurd because, by definition, all primitive peoples are individualists. They are transformed into an intellectually united population only by collective psychological pressures — re-

---

[14] Despite extensive excavations and research, the site of Tartessus has not been found. Adolph Schulten initiated the scientific search, first in written sources and then by means of archaeological excavations in western Andalusia, near the Guadalquivir river; he came to the conclusion that Cretan navigators had founded Tartessus, only to be superseded (before 1000 B.C.) by Etruscan colonizers. See Schulten, *Tartessos: Ein Beitrag zur ältesten Geschichte des Westens* (Hamburg, 1922; Spanish trans., 1945; 2d, rev. ed., 1950). Antonio García y Bellido and Bosch Gimpera consider the founders of Tartessus to be primitive or proto-Iberians who had grown prosperous from the Atlantic tin trade (1100–800 B.C.) and had developed a rich culture ("Atlantic Bronze Age Culture") in response to eastern Mediterranean and Celtic stimuli.

[15] Antonio García y Bellido maintains that Iberian art is a product of the Hispania which was fully organized as a Roman province (first century B.C.). For example, he denies the Greek origins of the famed piece of sculpture, la Dama de Elche, and sets its date in the last few decades of the pre-Christian era (in contrast with the American archaeologist Rhys Carpenter, who believed it Greek in origin, dating from the fifth century B.C.). See García y Bellido, "Arte ibérica," in Menéndez Pidal, ed., *Historia de España*, vol. I: *España prehistórica*, part 3 (Madrid, 3d ed., 1963). For Rhys Carpenter's viewpoint, see *The Greeks in Spain* (Bryn Mawr, 1925), 61–64.

ligious, juridical, historical, and linguistic — and these imply an already very evolved historic process.

CHAPTER THREE   This chapter encompasses numerous problems. Without any doubt, the principal one concerns the survival of the Roman element in the later Hispanic world. Granting that the mirage created by an excessive emphasis on continuity has been one fraught with emotion, Américo Castro's affirmation turned out to be explosive: Castro denies any relationship between the Roman mentality and the Spain of the Reconquest.[16] In opposition to this position, Ramon Menéndez Pidal has taken a stand,[17] as have Claudio Sánchez Albornoz and Luis G. de Valdeavellano. The latter is perhaps the most convinced that Romanization was a unifying force (even socially, as when he writes "the indigenous settlers merged with the Italic colonists, unifying the social organization of Roman Spain").[18] Sánchez Albornoz vacillates far more. However, after affirming that "those who believe it to be decisive are as mistaken as those who believe it to be inoperative," he writes on the following line "that the domination of Rome was fecund in the making of Spain . . . because it encouraged, among the peoples of the Peninsula, an understanding of a higher Hispanic unity." [19]

After having thoroughly reviewed my classics, and having followed the trajectory of the economic history of Hispania under Rome, I find myself in a position (an empirical one) not far dis-

---

[16] Américo Castro, *Structure of Spanish History*, trans. Edmund King (Princeton, 1954), viii.

[17] Menéndez Pidal opposes the idea that the transmission of a culture can be completely cut off by any military or political defeat. In 1959 he published a new book reiterating his theory that a culture, like a literature, can exist in a "latent state," can be maintained, uninterrupted, by tradition or by "poesía cantada": *La Chanson de Roland y el neotradicionalismo: Origines de la épica romana* (Madrid, 1959).

[18] G. de Valdeavellano, *Historia de España* (Madrid, 2d ed., 1955); I, 17–19, 201.

[19] Sánchez Albornoz, *España: Un enigma histórico* (Buenos Aires, 1956), I, 117.

tant from that of Américo Castro, yet one approaching somewhat more that of Julio Caro Baroja.[20] Therefore I was forced to do over a good part of this chapter, because, with certain modifications, I had formerly accepted the conclusions of Menéndez Pidal.[21]

But in any event, the final word has yet to be said. We all long for the development of a school of classical historians capable of answering the questions that we are asking. It would be interesting to discuss the role in the Romanization of Hispania of local bourgeoisie and retired Roman civil servants; the contrast between countryside and city; the effect (a demolishing one) of the Frankish invasions during the fourth century and the peasant uprisings in the following century; the role of the Church in this era. At present we can only waver between generalizations that are always gratuitous, and minute details that are solid but as yet lacking any context.

CHAPTER FOUR   Nothing is more open to revision in these times than the history of the Visigoths. Disregarding the inevitable controversy over the nature of Spain and of Castile, a series of medievalists of great integrity have turned to the documents and the archaeological material of the Visigothic era, and have begun to demolish the rhetorical edifice constructed by Romantic scholarship and Germanic institutional history. As work progresses and the field cleared away, it can be verified that the Visigoths constituted only a superstructure of power. Thus my general working hypothesis concerning the "epigonism" of the Visigoths, a theme advanced in the first edition of this book, has been confirmed.

It is of fundamental importance to change our ideas on certain key issues. For example, the Goths did not remain on the central plateau after the Muslim invasion.[22] Sánchez Albornoz offered an

---

[20] See Caro Baroja, *España primitiva y romana*, pp. 113–117.
[21] For a resumé of the ideas of Ménendez Pidal, see "Hispania, Provincia del Imperio Romano, su personalidad," *España y su historia* (Madrid, 1957), I, 131–173.
[22] The theory of E. Gamellscheg, as quoted in Ramón de Abadal y

Commentary on Bibliography 159

interesting theory about the origins of the Castilian people in the intermarriage of Visigoths with Basques and Cantabrians,[23] but archaeology and linguistics have now swept this into a corner.

The famous process of a fusion of the Gothic and Hispanic races has also been discarded. Even after the promulgation of a juridical regulation authorizing mixed marriages, they remained few in number. Lists of ecclesiastical authorities often designate them specifically as Goths, Romans, Greeks, or Africans. The idea of any artistic [24] or juridical [25] legacy from the Visigoths has also been discounted. The conclusions are always negative.

"No one can survive who has never lived," writes Ramón de Abadal, a specialist in this question of the Visigoths.[26] Nevertheless, the sheer weight of the Goth's state superstructure did bequeath an important principle: political unification under a monarchy. Only very slowly would the chanceries of León and Castile be able to assert their claim to this legacy.

CHAPTER FIVE   The problem of the continuity of Hispania reaches its climax in these pages. Did the Islamic avalanche completely destroy all the traditions which the Romans and Visigoths had established on the Peninsula? This is Américo Castro's theory,

---

Vinyals, "A propos du legs visigothique en Espagne," *Caratteri del secolo VII in Occidente* (Spoleto, 1958), II, 553.

[23] Sánchez Albornoz, "The Frontier and Castilian Liberties," *The New World Looks at its History*, (Austin, Texas, 1963), p. 27.

[24] José Antonio Maravall, *El concepto de España en la Edad Media* (Madrid, 1954), pp. 177–179.

[25] Alvaro d'Ors, *Estudios visigóticos*, vol. II, *El Código de Eurico* (Rome-Madrid, 1960).

[26] Ramón de Abadal y Vinyals (b. 1888), "A propos du legs visigothique," 570. De Abadal has written on various aspects of the Visigothic kingdom: *Del reino de Tolosa al reino de Toledo*, (Madrid, 1960); "El paso de Septimania del domino godo al franco a través de la invasion sarracena," *Cuadernos de historia de España*, XIX (1953), 5–54; *La batalla del adopcionismo en la desintegración de la iglesia visigoda* (Barcelona, 1949).

to which Claudio Sánchez Albornoz and others have taken exception.

The first edition of this book has already stressed my ideas about the catastrophic nature of the Islamic invasion, which, in one blow, destroyed the social structure. However, at that time I was convinced of the validity of Manuel Gómez Moreno's theories about the role played by Mozarabs in reconstructing the cultural values of Hispanic Christianity.[27] With the discoveries of the kharjas,[28] and with José Antonio Maravall's brilliant account of Mozarab influence in the north,[29] Gómez Moreno's ideas appeared to gain new strength. But Millás Vallicrosa's criticism [30] of Sánchez Albornoz' theories has convinced me that the truth is to be found by understanding two phenomena: the conversion of the peasants to Islam, and a reduction of the role attributed to the Mozarabs as a dissident element in the south and as a nationalist element in the north.

Whether the break between prehistoric–colonial Spain and Christian–seignorial Spain occurred in the eighth century, or in the tenth century, does not appear to be of any great consequence. The important thing is to point to some kind of continuity between the traditions of the two worlds. And yet even in this case, all due reservations must be made concerning the possibility of uninterrupted economic, social, and psychological developments. In history

---

[27] The classic work of Manuel Gómez Moreno (b. 1870) is *Iglesias mozárabes: Arte español de los siglos IX a XI* (Madrid, 1919). See also his *Perfiles de la España bárbara, siglos V a X* (Madrid, 1952), pp. 35–46.

[28] Kharjas are lyric poems, written about 1040 in the Mozarab dialect of Latin, that served as the refrains of Arabic or Hebraic poetry; they constitute the earliest lyric poetry written in a Romance language. In 1948 M. S. Stern discovered the first twenty kharjas in manuscripts in Cairo, and published his findings in the very important article, "Les vers finaux en espagnol dans les muwassahs hispano-hebraiques," *Al-Andalus*, XIII (1948), 299–346. See also Stern's book, *Les Chansons mozarabs* (Palermo, 1953).

[29] Maravall, "El factor mozárabe como sustrato hispánico," *El concepto de España en la Edad Media*, pp. 163–203.

[30] The comments of Millás Vallicrosa are in "La Roma cristiana y el auténtico ser de España," *Nuevos estudios sobre historia de la ciencia española* (Barcelona, 2d, rev. ed., 1960), pp. 31–48.

Commentary on Bibliography 161

there are not, nor can there be, doors that are closed and sealed off; in ways that are at times imperceptible, a tradition that is apparently broken can be repaired and a piece that has broken off can be grafted on.

CHAPTER SIX   With respect to the former edition of this book, I have made no essential innovation in subject matter or in interpretation, except for reducing the Mozarabs' role in the origins of the Asturian kingdom and assigning a larger role to members of the Visigothic military oligarchy and administration.

Obviously I could speak at length about the vexatious controversy over the invention of the sepulcher of St. James the Apostle (Santiago).[31] But here I agree with Sánchez Albornoz that the important thing was neither the event, nor the process of discovery, but the spiritual force which in the course of the ninth century invoked St. James as commander of the Christian forces.[32]

Another problem that arises in the ninth century concerns the titles used by the monarchs. Inspired by Germanic scholarship, the Castilian has devoted great care to reconstructing, interpreting, and evaluating chancery formulas. Once and for all I declare that I absolutely do not believe in the efficacy of this method. Nevertheless, in order not to make it too uncomfortable for myself, I have accepted within the text the possible historical consequences of the legitimacy of the Asturian monarchy.

The French orientation of Catalonia, which Maravall has attempted to deflate,[33] has been absolutely proven in Ramón de Abadal's recent publications.[34]

---

[31] See Américo Castro, "The Belief in Saint James of Galicia," *Structure of Spanish History*, pp. 130–158.
[32] Sánchez Albornoz, *España: Un enigma histórico*, I, 265–287.
[33] Maravall, *El concepto de España en la Edad Media*, pp. 179, 186–190.
[34] De Abadal, *Els primers comtes catalans* (Barcelona, 1958); see also his great unfinished work, *Catalunya carolingia*, 4 vols. (Barcelona, 1925–1955).

CHAPTER SEVEN   Any account of the realities of the Caliphate in the tenth century always reduces itself to an outline of the great works of Évariste Lévi-Provençal.[35] This is unfortunate because that eminent historian of Spanish Islam never concerned himself (and from his viewpoint we can readily understand it) with problems of the social and economic structure, the relationship between countryside and city, and so on. And therefore we still do not know today precisely why militarism developed in Islamic Spain; on what social bases it rested; how it was possible to reinstate slavery in the milita and in agriculture; and so on.

The same thing can be said about the excessive literature on the imperial titles of León, which neglects the economic and social conflicts that precipitated the downfall of that monarchy. Researchers might possibly achieve a more direct approach to historical knowledge if they took into account problems such as that of the frontier, as Claudio Sánchez Albornoz, the principal authority in this field, has so often indicated.[36] Let us recall briefly that the departure of the Goths to Galicia in the ninth century invalidates

---

[35] Évariste Lévi-Provençal (1894–1956), professor at the Sorbonne and organizer and director of the Institute of Islamic Studies at the University of Paris, devoted his research almost exclusively to Islamic Spain. For the most detailed summary of his work, see *Histoire de l'Espagne musulmane*, 3 vols. (Paris, 2d, rev. ed., 1950–1953). At the time of his death he had completed only the period up to the end of the Caliphate (to 1031). Two of these volumes have been translated into Spanish by Emilio García Gómez, professor of Arabic at the University of Madrid, and published as vols. IV and V of the *Historia de España* edited by Menéndez Pidal (Madrid), vol. IV (1950) and vol. V (1957). See also Lévi-Provençal's *La Civilisation arabe en Espagne: Vue génerale* (Paris, 3d ed., 1961).

[36] Sánchez Albornoz has repeatedly stressed the concept of the Duero valley as a frontier region that was not occupied during the early Middle Ages because it was the corridor for attacking Muslim and Christian armies moving north and south. When repopulated in the tenth century, it produced the same type of democratic institutions as the American frontier, thus preventing the growth of feudalism. See "The Frontier and Castilian Liberties," pp. 27–46. See also his major work *En torno a los origines del feudalismo*, 3 vols. (Mendoza, Argentina, 1942; Buenos Aires, 2d rev. ed., 1945).

the tripod upon which that distinguished author based his theory concerning the abrupt historical inception of Castile.

CHAPTER EIGHT   Although in my judgment the working hypotheses set forth in this chapter offer satisfactory explanations for many phenomena, they will not be readily accepted. The cultural force developed by Europe penetrates all of the Hispanic kingdoms; Navarre benefited first and, immediately afterwards, Castile. I must point out that there is a center that propels this wave — the Papacy. Millás Vallicrosa has clearly emphasized the spiritual and political significance of this point.[37] However, this does not diminish the role of Cluniacs and Cistercians in renovating agrarian structures.

From the eleventh century on, the Papacy and Europe strongly influenced the outcome of Hispanic events. It seems to me that this has been too often overlooked in the distorting light of Castilian nationalism (Ramón Menéndez Pidal)[38] and of the polemic over Castile's past and future (although Américo Castro and Claudio Sánchez Albornoz have concerned themselves with the route to Santiago de Compostela,[39] which was the least they could do).

In any event, it is a definite fact that Castile emerged with a powerful personality, which I have tried to characterize by consulting the person with the best knowledge of her primitive spirit — the already cited Sánchez Albornoz. However, my presentation does include certain anthropological and sociological reservations which can be evaluated in the text.

Alfonso VI's policies have caused a flurry among those concerned

---

[37] Millás Vallicrosa, *Nuevos estudios sobre historia de la ciencia española*, pp. 32–33, 38–42.

[38] Menéndez Pidal has written a history of this era, *La España del Cid* (1st ed., 1929; 4th, rev. ed., 1940; 5th ed., 1956). He has also published a definitive edition of the epic *El cantar del mío Cid*, 3 vols. (Madrid, 1906–1911).

[39] For a comprehensive summary of the pilgrimages, see Luis Vázquez de Parga, José María Lacarra, and Juan Uria, *Las peregrinaciones a Santiago*, 3 vols. (Madrid, 1948–1949).

with the mechanics of medieval chancery imperialism. We must seek their structural basis in the displacing of communities with a livestock economy from the north (Navarre, the Cantabrian area, and Castile) to the south and east coasts of the Mediterranean. But as yet we know very little about this (although we have the prospect of a monograph that a prominent medievalist has promised us), and are bewildered by the interpretation of texts, which has no other value than that of perpetuating a shallow rhetoric.

With respect to the figure of El Cid, it seems to me that after the contributions of José Camón Aznar,[40] which guided me in the first edition, and of Professor Antonio Ubieto Arteta's studies of the chronology of the *Cantar del mío Cid*,[41] the moment has now come to carry out a substantial revision of Ménendez Pidal's thesis.

CHAPTER NINE Having plunged into the very core of the central problem in the history of Spain, I have weighed each word of the text in order not to lead astray either the researcher or the reader. Nevertheless, I would once again call attention to the following events:

1. The appearance of the ideal of a Crusade (which seems to me a good basis for interpretation and one which has been verified) seems to conflict with the subsequent tendency of Christians, Moors, and Jews to achieve a harmonious accord within a common social and intellectual abode. The contradiction does exist; the explanation is that Christian-Islamic integration was an urban event, while the antagonism between Christians and converted Muslims (Moriscos) was a rural phenomenon. Royalty oscillated between the two camps, protecting now one and then the other, until the decision of the

---

[40] José Camón Aznar, "El Cid, personaje mozarabe," *Revista de estudios políticos* (Madrid, 1947), pp. 109–141. For Menéndez Pidal's reply, see *La España del Cid* (5th ed.), II, 976.

[41] Antonio Ubieto Arteta (b. 1923), "Observaciones al Cantar del Mío Cid," *Arbor*, XXXVII (1957), 145–170.

Catholic Monarchs — a decision that is dramatic from so many points of view.[42]

2. Perhaps the intervention of the Papacy has not been stressed sufficiently. Rome responded to the invasions from North Africa with a spiritual offensive, based on the white monks of Cîteaux (the Cistercian monks).[43] The Papacy is unitary, the result of her catholic orientation and also of her inheritance of the rights of the Roman Empire (here are more vestiges of the Roman chancery). Yet on the Peninsula, the Papacy followed a policy of supporting territorial pluralism (in the case of Portugal, of León, of Aragon, and of Catalonia). This is another contradiction that must be kept in mind.

3. The exhaustion of Castile in the twelfth century, disguised by the chancery and by the chroniclers of Alfonso VII, contrasts with the vitality of the small states in the Pyrenees and even with that of the Galician *finisterre*.

4. The southern half of the central plateau, which was awarded to the pure and simple warriors of the military orders, suffered an unhappy fate. These warriors deformed the original character of the repopulating of Castile, erected a barrier of social prejudices between the north and the south of the country, and created a new image of the Castilian — a prodigal, anarchistic, and domineering individual.

CHAPTER TEN   This chapter presents more difficulties than are apparent at first glance. One reason, far outranking all others, is

---

[42] In 1492 the Catholic Monarchs, Isabel and Ferdinand, ordered the expulsion of all Jews (which forced them to convert or to emigrate). In 1502 they decreed the expulsion of all Muslims from Granada and Castile (those who converted became known as Moriscos); the order was subsequently extended to the Crown of Aragon in 1525.

[43] The Cistercian order, a severely austere adaptation of the Benedictine order, was founded at Cîteaux in 1098. Nominally, the Spanish military orders were under the rule of the Cistercians. The introduction of Gothic architecture into Spain is usually attributed to the Cistercians.

that Catalonia makes her appearance as one of the protagonists in the history of Spain. Neither for good nor for bad has this development been understood. One has only to view the lack of knowledge about Catalan history among even the most eminent professional historians of Castile. Their procedure has been to resort to the very antiquated and deforming interpretation offered by Andrés Giménez Soler.[44] At least today they can find a better version of the problems in the *Historia de Catalunya* by Fernando Soldevila.[45]

My hypothesis rests on the work of José María Lacarra,[46] Antonio Ubieto Arteta,[47] and Percy Ernst Schramm,[48] who have reformulated the problems from an absolutely documented viewpoint. It also rests upon a theory that I myself have formulated about historical developments in Catalonia, one likewise based upon documentation and concrete historic situations. The most recent publications agree with the affirmations set forth in the text.

Two other questions, intimately related to one another, are still pending: the nomenclature of the union formed by the Aragonese and the Catalans, and the value of each people's participation in the common enterprise. With respect to the first question, it is impossible to restrict the name to any one single term except in specific cases: for the maritime expansion, the term Catalonia or Catalans (in accordance with the documentation); for the enterprise as a whole, the term Catalan-Aragonese or the Crown of Aragon. Even with absolute good will, it is easier to analyze this question than

---

[44] Andrés Giménez Soler (1869–1938), *La Corona de Aragón en La Edad Media* (Barcelona, 1930).

[45] Fernando Soldevila Zubiburu (b. 1894), *Història de Catalunya*, 3 vols. (Barcelona, 1935; 2d, rev. ed., vol I, 1962).

[46] José María Lacarra, *Aragón en el pasado* (Saragossa, 1960).

[47] Antonio Ubieto Arteta, *Navarra-Aragón y la idea imperial de Alfonso VII de Castilla* (Saragossa, 1956).

[48] Percy Ernst Schramm (b. 1894), Joan F. Cabestany (b. 1930), and Enric Bague (b. 1900), *Els primers comtes-reis: Ramon Berenguer IV, Alfons el Cast, Pere el Catòlic* (Barcelona, 1960); Schramm wrote the section on Ramon Berenguer IV. See also his "Der König von Aragon: Seine Stellung im Straatsrecht," *Historisches Jahrbuch* (Munich, 1955), pp. 99–123.

Commentary on Bibliography 167

to arrive at the correct answer. With respect to the second question, it is better not to arouse petty antagonisms; the fact that Aragon contributed the institution of the monarchy and Catalonia provided the mechanism which made it effective, demonstrates collaboration in the same communal dynamics.

CHAPTER ELEVEN   The events which occurred on the Peninsula during the thirteenth century, especially those related to the mobilization of infra-structures, have given rise to many conflicting viewpoints. Thus Sánchez Albornoz interprets as similar in nature the repopulating of Andalusia and of Valencia,[49] despite the essential differences that I have emphasized in the text and that are supported by the recent findings of Henri Lapeyre in his geographical study of the Moriscos.[50] This means that we do not possess all the documented resumés that we might desire or, rather, that we excessively subdivide our knowledge.

I might possibly have inserted into this chapter various considerations on the economic and social repercussions of the Hispanic monarchies' territorial and political expansion. After rereading the chapter, I did not consider it opportune to do so. I have preferred to introduce a new chapter that describes the possibilities open to Hispania at the beginning of the fourteenth century — that is to say, before the era of the great civil wars in the late Middle Ages.

CHAPTER TWELVE   As I noted in the preceding commentary, this chapter did not appear in the first edition. I believe that it will serve not only to simplify Chapter Thirteen (the organization of which did not completely satisfy me) but also to call attention to a problem that is economic, social, cultural, and political — a prob-

---

[49] Sánchez Albornoz, *España: Un enigma histórico*, II, 38–42.
[50] Henri Lapeyre (b. 1910), *Géographie de l'Espagne morisque* (Paris, 1959).

lem that explains the accentuation of the characteristics of a pluralistic Hispania. About this factor, it is futile to attempt to deceive oneself. In the consciousness of this era, something more than a historical experience exists; there is the indelible and irreversible stamp of collective personalities.

My desire to synthesize has possibly prevented me from expressing my position in the difficult debate initiated by Américo Castro about the injection of Islamic and Hebraic elements into the Castilian mentality. Even conceding that Castro has gone too far on certain occasions and that one cannot follow (except in a very critical manner) his spiritual itinerary — a very refined ideologism of a high school — I find his theory more acceptable than that of Claudio Sánchez Albornoz, even though the latter's facts would appear, perhaps, to be more impressive. But when he speaks of the Jewish world, this illustrious medievalist acts not only as a historian who is going to testify but as the judge — or at times, as the prosecuting attorney — of a dangerous sect. This prejudices a position that initially might have favored him.

Certainly (and this is what weighs most in my opinion), the hypothesis of Américo Castro, more than that of his opponent, fits in with the documents on the economy, society, and culture of the fifteenth century which I have examined personally during the preceding two decades. Perhaps the moment has arrived in which to publish and comment on these documents.

CHAPTER THIRTEEN When I reread this chapter, I encountered no basic difficulty. On the contrary, its keystone is very simple: in putting an end to the crisis of the fifteenth century, Castile and the Crown of Aragon used very different methods; this is to be explained by the differing weight of the bourgeoisie within their respective social structures.

This argument might perhaps have led me to refer within the text to the hypothesis of Sánchez Albornoz concerning the democratization of the Castilian Cortes — the hypothesis that between the time of Ferdinand III and Alfonso XI the Cortes was composed of representatives from all the municipal councils, not simply of delegates from the most important ones. This is a very suggestive guideline for research, but it is adorned with so many anticipatory factors, both doctrinate and pragmatic in nature, that it may possibly be tainted by projection.

In any case, the development of a theory of a contract in the Cortes of Castile comes much later than it does in Catalonia, nor does it have by any means the constitutional force that it possessed in the Principality of Catalonia. This fact leads me to suspect that an authentic bourgeois estate never existed in the Cortes of Castile. Representatives of rural farmers and sheepherders predominated in Castile's type of open Cortes until the middle of the fourteenth century. Later, when the monarchy imposed its will, delegates from the cities predominated — that is to say, the aristocrats who had gained control of the city governments. It is moreover a well-known fact that in the most active cities of their realm, the kings of Castile launched a vigorous attack against the first stirrings of a nascent guild organization.

CHAPTER FOURTEEN   In this chapter I have followed the line of my own research on the fifteenth century[51] and that of my students.[52] With respect to the first edition, I have made a few important rectifications.

The essential thing is to understand the social problem resulting from the long period of economic contraction during the fifteenth century, and to understand the spiritual conflict created in Castile

---

[51] Vicens Vives has been responsible for a radical reorientation of the history of the fifteenth century in Spain. Among his major works are *Historia de los remensas en el siglo XV* (Barcelona, 1945), *Juan II de Aragón: Monarquía y revolución en la España del siglo XV* (Barcelona, 1953), *El Segle XV, Els Trastàmares* (Barcelona, 1956), and numerous articles.

[52] See, for example, Juan Reglá Campistol (b. 1917), *Historia de la Edad Media* (Barcelona, 1960).

by the alienation of "Old Christians" from the Conversos.[53] We doubt that any true light can be shed on this development if researchers continue to write dithyrambs and to use pejorative lenses. The conflict between Catholics and Conversos is a fact that admits of no rebuttal. From a sociological point of view, the following question might be formulated: why did the immense majority of the population fail in the task of assimilating a minority, at a moment in which the latter had still not resorted to the subterfuges of the sixteenth century? [54]

Recently published works seem to me to have established the position of the nobility of Castile.[55] It was a class that was on its way up, not down. They had considerable sources of wealth, but all of these originated in the Crown, since even their landholdings were royal gifts (*mercedes*) from Ferdinand III, Alfonso X, Sancho IV, and Henry II. Great parasites of the kingdom, the Grandees also drank in a third fountain (as Richard Konetzke has revealed): booty from the Moors of Granada.[56] In this, they were abetted by the Crown. More than a few of them found a comfortable source of income in the continued existence of Granada, and therefore did not terminate the Reconquest, despite the insistence with which the Church demanded it and (as a purely demagogic or diversionary tactic) the monarchy proposed it.

My portrait of Henry IV is one gleaned from the reading of docu-

---

[53] A major work on this subject is Francisco Cantera Burgos, *Alvar García de Santa María y su familia de conversos: Historia de la judería de Burgos y de sus conversos más egregios* (Madrid, 1952).

[54] See Caro Baroja's exhaustive study of this crypto-Judaic society from the sixteenth century on: *Los judíos en la España moderna y contemporánea*, 3 vols. (Madrid, 1962).

[55] For a survey of the position of the nobility in this period, see Santiago Sobrequés Vidal, "La alta nobleza," *Historia social y económica de España* (Barcelona, 1957), II, 111–130.

[56] The campaigns for loot and enslaved prisoners of war were financed and managed by the nobles "as business enterprises" (even for capital formation). See Richard Konetzke (b. 1897), "Entrepreneurial Activities of Spanish and Portuguese Noblemen in Medieval Times," *Explorations in Entrepreneurial History*, VI, no. 2 (1953–54), 115.

Commentary on Bibliography 171

ments unvitiated by pro-Isabel propaganda. The civil war in Castile ended with a victory for the faction that did not defend the legitimate cause. But history often provides such surprises.

CHAPTER FIFTEEN   I have rounded out this chapter but without modifying its organization. At the end of eight years its working hypotheses remain useful and effective. However, I have emphasized the indications that the Catholic Monarchs conceived of a pluralistic state, because this is a reality, noted daily in research in the field of administrative institutions. Moreover, this concept of a pluralistic state would be the basic theme of the Spanish political controversy until 1714.

In addition, I have given a new cast to the paragraphs on the Moriscos of Granada. In evaluating the effects of the establishment in Spain of the Tribunal of the Holy Office of the Inquisition, I have introduced a psychological element. The orientation of modern research makes it impossible to ignore such a factor in dealing with the issues of the sixteenth century.

CHAPTER SIXTEEN   Written in 1952, this chapter on the first three kings of the Austrian dynasty has stood up under the publication of major works such as those by Henri Lapeyre,[57] Juan Reglá,[58] and Tulio Halperín Donghi,[59] and even those commemorating the

---

[57] Henri Lapeyre's major work in this period is the already cited *Géographie de l'Espagne morisque* (1959). In addition he has published *Simón Ruiz et les asientos de Philippe II* (Paris, 1953), and *Une famille de marchands: Les Ruiz* (Paris, 1955). In collaboration with Ramón Carande, Lapeyre published *Relaciones comerciales en el Mediterráneo durante el siglo XVI* (Madrid, 1957).

[58] Juan Reglá Campistol, *Felip II i Catalunya* (Barcelona, 1956), and *Els virreis de Catalunya* (Barcelona, 1956; 2d ed., 1962).

[59] Tulio Halperín Donghi (b. 1926), "Recouvrements de civilisation: Les Morisques du Royaume de Valence au xvi siècle," *Annales: Economies, sociétés, civilisations*, XI (1956), 154-182.

fourth centennial of Charles V.[60] This means that my approach — inspired by Fernand Braudel,[61] Earl J. Hamilton,[62] and Ramón Carande y Thobar[63] — has plumbed the depths of the problem. With the few revisions that I have introduced, I believe it will be valid for some years more.[64]

The most extensive revision deals with the problem of the bourgeois meteor in the sixteenth century. Everything cannot be blamed on El Prudente's financial imprudence. There was such a deficiency in the banking structure of Castile that the credit mechanism of the Spanish monarchy can only be described as infantile. Philip II's finances were in the hands of men from Genoa,

---

[60] Among the many publications on the occasion of the fourth centennial of the death of Charles V, see *Carlos V, 1500–1558: Homenage de la Universidad de Granada* (Granada, 1958). See also the mimeographed proceedings of the III Congreso de Cooperación Intelectual, held in Cáceres in October 1958 and devoted entirely to Charles V: *Clausura del III congreso de cooperación intelectual* (Madrid: Instituto de Cultura Hispánica, 1958).

[61] Fernand Braudel (b. 1902), *La Mediterranée et le monde méditerranéen à l'epoque de Philippe II* (Paris, 1949), which was translated into Spanish in an expanded version, *El Mediterráneo y el mundo mediterráneo en la época de Felipe II*, 2 vols. (Mexico City, 1953). Braudel dedicates his book to Lucien Febvre.

[62] Earl J. Hamilton (b. 1899), *American Treasure and the Price Revolution in Spain, 1501–1650* (Cambridge, 1934); *Money, Prices, and Wages in Valencia, Aragon, and Navarre, 1351–1500* (Cambridge, 1936); *War and Prices in Spain, 1651–1800* (Cambridge, 1947); *El Florecimiento del capitalismo y otros ensayos de historia económica* (Madrid, 1948).

[63] Ramón Carande y Thobar (b. 1904), *Carlos V y sus banqueros* (Madrid: Vol. I, 1943; vol. II, 1949), and *El crédito de Castilla en el precio de la política imperial* (Madrid, 1959).

[64] An important book on this era, based largely on Spanish and French historiography, published after Vicens' death, is John Lynch, *Spain Under the Hapsburgs*, vol. I, *Empire and Absolutism, 1516–1598* (Oxford, 1964). Vicens Vives had enthusiastically reviewed Lynch's earlier book, *Spanish Colonial Administration, 1782–1810* (London, 1958); see item 30361, *Indice histórico español*, V (1959). See also the excellent general account by J. H. Elliott, *Imperial Spain, 1469–1716* (New York, 1964).

Commentary on Bibliography 173

Portugal, Germany, and Amsterdam; his successor's were even in the hands of Conversos. It was Castile who failed to respond to the demands of the time, because of the military, seignorial, and religious vestiges left from the last stage of the Reconquest. And one of these, as we have indicated in the text, was the question of crypto-Judaism.

I have not involved myself in a discussion of the quality of the Hispanic empire, nor in the question of whether Charles V succumbed to Spanish influences or was a universal emperor. This is a book for adults.

I recognize that America has been left out, and that nothing which happened in Spain between the sixteenth and eighteenth centuries can be explained without the New World. But in order to understand my general approach, the reader need only remember that the entire financial mechanism of the monarchy consisted of supplying luxury and consumer products to the colonies and of importing precious metals from Peru and Mexico. This entire transaction was monopolized by the merchants of the Seville Exchange (*la Lonja*), who maintained a remunerative, vice-ridden alliance with functionaries of the official government agency (*la Casa de Contratación*) and with foreign factors (Genoese merchants and, after they went bankrupt, with Flemish, English, and French merchants).

The number of Moriscos who were expelled has been rectified in accord with the recent definitive study of Henri Lapeyre.

CHAPTER SEVENTEEN   There are interesting themes in this dramatic seventeenth century. In order to clarify the background of the political dynamics, I have prepared a few paragraphs drawing attention to the moment in which the crisis of the Hispanic monarchy begins (1604–1610) and to the moment in which it exploded before the eyes of the world (1640). Pierre Vilar has made the greatest contribution to the orientation of this working hypothesis; he relates the crisis directly to the collapse that took place during the last years of Philip II's reign.⁶⁵ Vilar's compatriots, the Chaunus, have illustrated for us the potent effect upon European affairs of the Count-Duke of Olivares' lack of concern about America.⁶⁶

Other corrections, minor ones, were inspired by the work on the seventeenth century carried out by José María Jover,⁶⁷ J. H. Elliott,⁶⁸ José Sanabre,⁶⁹ and Juan Reglá.⁷⁰ I should like to add that, for an approach to the crisis that destroyed Olivares' policy, it would be most beneficial to have a study on peasant movements in Spain and Portugal beginning in the years 1615-1620.

I have rectified my evaluation of the Cortes of Barcelona in 1701 and of the first stage of Philip V's Catalan policy. It was an extremely erroneous evaluation, the product of layer upon layer of that enduring, outdated historiography which has inspired the historians who are most prejudiced against those Cortes.

CHAPTER EIGHTEEN   The Spanish eighteenth century lives in the shadow of French influence. Bourbon reform was the adaptation of a French product to Spain. Castile broke the back of Catalonia's resistance (a development that I can describe more as it really happened because of the research of Juan Mercader),⁷¹ and then

---

⁶⁵ Pierre Vilar (b. 1906), whose article Vicens Vives published in his *Estudios de historia moderna*, has published his major work since Vicens' death: *La Catalogne dans l'Espagne moderne; Recherches sur les fondements économiques des structures nationales*, 3 vols. (Paris, 1962).

⁶⁶ Huguette Chaunu and Pierre Chaunu (the latter b. 1923), *Séville et l'Atlantique 1504-1650*, 8 vols. (Paris, 1955-1959). Lucien Febvre wrote the preface.

⁶⁷ José María Jover Zamora (b. 1920), *Historia de una polémica y semblanza de una generación* (Madrid, 1949), and *Política mediterránea y política atlántica en la España de Feijóo* (Oviedo, 1956).

⁶⁸ J. H. Elliott's major work was published after Vicens' death: *The Revolt of the Catalans* (Cambridge, 1963).

⁶⁹ José Sanabre Sanromá (b. 1901), *El tractat dels Pirineus i els seus antecedents* (Barcelona, 1961).

⁷⁰ For the works of Juan Reglá Campistol, see p. 171, n. 58.

⁷¹ Juan Mercader Riba, *La ordenación de Cataluña por Felipe V: La*

she succumbed to French influence. Yet Castile maintained a strong tendency to seek an original personality, which she looked for and found in an Andalusian way of life. This is the hypothesis of José Ortega y Gasset.[72] However, it will be necessary to develop this scientifically, in the same way that Carlos Clavería has demonstrated the popularity of gypsy folkways in the aristocratic society of that time.[73]

The other three great themes of Bourbon Spain are the economic hegemony of the periphery (about which there is today no doubt); the dramatic problem of agrarian landholdings in southern Spain (not one word has yet been uttered about the sum total of this problem); and finally, the now very controversial matter of the spread of Encyclopedism and the formation of the so-called "Two Spains."

We are becoming more thoroughly acquainted with the group of Spanish intellectuals who served the new philosophy and with the policies they initiated through the work of Jean Sarrailh,[74] Marcelin Defourneaux,[75] Luis Sánchez Agesta,[76] Carlos E. Corona,[77]

Nueva Planta (Barcelona, 1951), and *Els capitans generals: El segle XVIII* (Barcelona, 1957).

[72] José Ortega y Gasset (1883–1955), "Goya y lo popular" (1958), *Obras completas* (Madrid, 2d ed., 1964), VII, 521–536.

[73] Carlos Clavería (b. 1909), *Estudios sobre los gitanismos del español* (Madrid, 1951).

[74] Jean Sarrailh (1891–1964), *L'Espagne éclairé de la seconde moitié du xviii*ᵉ *siècle* (Paris, 1954), translated into Spanish by Antonio Alatorre as *La España ilustrada de la segunda mitad del siglo XVIII* (Mexico City, 1957).

[75] Marcelin Defourneaux (b. 1910), *Pablo de Olavide, ou l'«Afrancesado»: 1725–1803* (Paris, 1959), and *L'Inquisition espagnole et les livres français au xviii*ᵉ *siècle* (Paris, 1963).

[76] Luis Sánchez Agesta, *El pensamiento político del despotismo ilustrado* (Madrid, 1953), and *Moratin y la sociedad española de su tiempo* (Madrid, 1960).

[77] Carlos E. Corona Baratech (b. 1917), *La doctrina del poder absoluto en España en la crisis del XVIII al XIX* (Oviedo, 1962), and *Revolución y reacción en el reinado de Carlos IV* (Madrid, 1957).

Richard Herr,[78] and others. Nevertheless, it is still difficult to relate this movement to the actual circumstances of the period. What I do consider quite improbable is that Encyclopedism was linked with the bourgeoisie. I repeat for the nth time (and this, after having consulted documentation concerning the Barcelona textile bourgeoisie and the commercial bourgeoisie of Cádiz during the eighteenth century) that one cannot speak of a bourgeois revolution in the Spain of Charles III and Charles IV. When the revolution does break out, it will be the result of pressure from the people (laborers, artisans, and peasants) instigated by intellectuals.

CHAPTER NINETEEN   I have made a number of essential corrections in this chapter. During the preceding ten years, extensive work has been done on the nineteenth century and many working hypotheses have been advanced; concurrently, some have been established as definitive theses. Political history continues to prevail because there is an avid public for it, but it cannot contribute anything essentially new. In contrast, the history of ideas, of social and economic movements, and of infrastructures is being constantly enriched as stereotypes are destroyed and new horizons opened up.

In the pages of the fifth volume of *La historia social y económica de España y América*, I have synthesized the major problems that concern any historian of the modern school. I hope that the book is readily available to the reader, but if it is not, he should know that the most interesting and still unclarified problems are: (1) the relationship between demography and the economy, the society, and politics; (2) the disentailing of civil and ecclesiastic property, and its effect on agriculture and on an agrarian society; (3) the effect on the Church and on Catholicism of the change in the ideology of the country; (4) the army as a protagonist in the social

---

[78] Richard Herr, *The Eighteenth-Century Revolution in Spain* (Princeton, 1958), transl. by E. Fernández Mel as *España y la revolución del siglo XVIII* (Madrid, 1964).

Commentary on Bibliography 177

history of Spain throughout the nineteenth century; (5) the grandeur and the servility of the bourgeoisie; (6) public administration, and the bureaucracy as a social entity; (7) everything related to the social problem, but especially the labor system in the countryside, in the mines, and in the cities, as well as the way in which the proletariat lived; (8) political parties, bossism, and parliamentary life; (9) regional groups (Andalusia, Valencia, Catalonia, the Basque Provinces, Navarre, and so on) as activating agents in the national structure.

CHAPTER TWENTY   Almost the entire historiographical task still remains to be done. This chapter is, therefore, more an expectation than a reality, more a limited approach, or an unfinished symphony . . .

Nevertheless, the reader is entitled to certain reflections. That there were two generations of the disaster — one Castilian, one Catalan — is obvious. But just as the former has had good historians, the latter has slipped by almost unnoticed, despite its very clear consciousness of itself as a generation, despite the variety and quality of the elements that composed it (thinkers, poets, technicians, industrialists, and politicians), and despite the rapid and sensational triumphs that it achieved within one decade, both in the field of art and in the construction of asphalt highways. Not only did it exist, but it did so with greater power than did the generation of 1898 in Castile — limited as the latter was to a handful of eminent intellectuals and to a few politicians with more ambitions than good will. During that auroral moment in Castile, the people did not take part in the work of those individuals. Perhaps this was why their ideas were condemned in advance, when they were not misunderstood or even shunted off into channels flowing in exactly the opposite direction.

In any event, I have been concerned with outlining my thoughts on the two variants of the same generation, and I reaffirm my working hypothesis of the first edition of this book — namely, that further research will show the decisive weight that bourgeois optimism had upon the Catalan generation and professorial pessimism upon the Castilian generation.

That Catalonia should translate this situation into a demand for a theory of Hispanic pluralism was a logical development. Since 1812 she had condemned the Jacobin measures of the constitutional governments; then, in the course of the century, she continued to elaborate pluralistic positions — provincialism, commission rule (*juntismo*), federalism, regionalism. In 1901 this tendency erupted, not in pluralism, but in a controversial dualism that was essentially very stimulating — perhaps to an excessive degree, given Castile's intense emotions.

Even to outline the problem of the Church during the first third of the twentieth century is impossible. I have emphasized those elements that, in my judgment, are essential and deserve to be investigated: the reconquest of the bourgeoisie by religious orders; the revival of popular piety by means of the liturgy, and the clergy's intellectual activities; the failure of its social program among the working classes. The latter point appears to be well-established by recent research.

As for the perspective in which to view these events, I prefer to focus on the repercussions that Western European social and political movements had upon what was essentially a semi-feudal and underdeveloped nation. I do not believe in a cataclysmic development moving towards a "geological catastrophe," about which certain thinkers talk. In the same way that the upheavals in Europe caused by the First World War crystallized in the Russian Revolution, those of the Great Depression aroused in anguished Spain strong, passionate forces whose strength can only be explained by the lack of a social and administrative structure that was solid and equitable.

To place the burden of responsibility upon the shoulders of the Spanish people — when Europe was the provocateur of Spain's fatal destiny, and if not provocateur, accomplice — would seem to me to end the stirring history that we have witnessed in these pages with an infamous affront.

Index

Abadal y Vinyals, Ramón de, 158 n, 159, 161
Abd-ar-Rahman I, 29
Abd-ar-Rahman III, 36–37, 39
Acheulian culture, 2
Adoptionist heresy, 30, 33
Afrancesados, defined, 123 n
Agnano, Treaty of, 61
Ágreda, Treaty of, 62
Agricultural proletariat, 132
Al-Andalus, 31, 32, 37, 39, 42 n, 45 n, 46 n
Alans, 22
Albigensians, 59
Alcalá de Henares, 95; University of, 95 n
Aldea, defined, 16 n
Alexander IV, Pope, 69 n
Alexander VI, Pope, 87 n
Alfarrobeira, battle of, 82
Alfonso I of Aragon, 50, 51, 79 n
Alfonso I of Asturias, 33
Alfonso II of Asturias, 33
Alfonso II of Crown of Aragon, 53 n, 54
Alfonso III the Great, 31, 33, 37
Alfonso V the Magnanimous, 78, 81, 83, 88
Alfonso VI (1065–1109), 42, 43, 44, 46, 51, 163
Alfonso VII (1126–1157), 47, 51, 53, 54, 165
Alfonso X the Learned, 56, 63, 64, 65, 66, 69, 70, 170
Alfonso XI, 63, 68, 69 n, 169
Alfonso XII (1875–1885), 136, 148 n
Alfonso XIII (1902–1931), 148
Algeciras, 46, 62, 63
Algeria, 91, 103
Al-Hakam II, 37
Alicante, 62
Aljubarrota, battle of, 72
Almagro, Martín, 152, 156
Al-Mansur, 39, 41
Almería, 7, 9, 10, 11, 18, 36, 49, 54
Almizra, Treaty of, 56
Almogavars, 62
Almohads, 46, 49, 56, 57, 62
Almoravids, 42 n, 43, 44 n, 45, 46 n, 50, 57, 63. *See also* Berbers; Islam; Moors; Muslims
Alpujarras, uprising in (1568), 103
Alvarez Mendizábal, Juan, 128
Amadeo of Savoy, 135
Anarchism, 139, 146, 147
Andalusia, 9–16 *passim*, 23, 30, 56, 57, 63, 70 n, 77, 79, 99, 102, 105, 106, 115, 116, 119, 125, 130, 132, 139, 167
Annales, xi, xix n, 171 n
Anticlericalism, 128, 144, 145
Anuario de historia del derecho español, xvi n

Index

Apostolics, 126
Aquitaine-Cantabrian paintings, 5, 6, 10
Aragon, 30, 49, 50, 56, 70, 96, 101 n, 103 n, 127, 165; House of, 73; Infantes of, 81 n, 82; Council of, 91. *See also* Crown of Aragon
Aranda, Count of, 117
Aranjuez, uprising in (1808), 121
Arbor, xiv n
Armada, defeat of, 102
Asturians, 7, 15, 32, 33, 35
Asturias, 5, 30, 31, 32, 33, 37, 117, 133, 139, 150, 161
Ataulf, 22
Athens, Duchy of, 62
Atlanthropus, 1
Audiencia, defined, 114
Augustus Caesar, 15
Aurignacian culture, 4
Australopithecines, 1
Austria, 110, 111; House of, 89
Avila, 43, 82
Avís, House of, 101 n
Azilian culture, 7, 10

Badajoz, 42
Bague, Enric, 166 n
Bakunin, Mikhail A., 139
Balearic Islands, 53, 54, 58, 62, 63, 73, 133 n
Ballesteros-Gaibrois, Manuel, xiv n
Balmes, Jaime, 144
Barbarossa, Frederick, 47
Barca family, of Carthage, 14 and n
Barcelona, 22, 23, 35, 39, 53, 59, 64, 74, 79, 84, 85, 107, 111, 127; House of, 52, 59, 62, 80, 90; surrenders to Philip V, 113; first steam-powered machinery introduced in, 128; Progressivism in, 129; Fomento del Trabajo Nacional of, 137; terrorism in (1892–1897), 140; Tragic Week of (1909), 145, 148; syndicalism begins to organize in, 146; street fighting in (1919–1923), 147; Cortes of, 174
Basque Society, 117
Basques, 10, 24, 34 n, 58 n, 114, 127, 137
Bayonne, Constitution of, 122
Beja, House of, 101 n
Berbers, 29, 45 n, 99, 103. *See also* Almoravids; Islam; Moors; Muslims
Bernheim, Ernst, xv
Bible, Complutensian Polyglot, 95 n
Bilbao, 91, 115
Bishko, Charles Julian, 65 n
Black Death, 72, 75, 76
Bloch, Marc, xi n
Bologna, 99, 100
Bosch Gimpera, Pedro, 151, 153, 156
Bou system of fishing, 155
Bourbon, House of, 111, 112, 113
Bourbon reforms, 114–120, 123 n, 174, 175
Braceros, in Andalusia, 132
Braudel, Fernand, 172
Breuil, Henri, 154 n
Brihuega, battle of, 113
Brittany, 10, 85
Brugge, 74
Burgos, 44 n, 65, 69, 80, 91
Burgundy, 83, 85, 86, 90; House of, 48, 102
Byzantine Empire, 24, 62
Byzantine Spain, 23

Caballeros villanos, defined, 43
Cabestany, Joan F., 166 n
Cabet, Etienne, 139
Caciquismo, 131, 137, 148
Cádiz, 11, 56, 98, 115, 123, 124, 127, 128, 176
Caliphate of Córdoba, 31, 36, 37, 39, 42, 162

Index

Caltabellota, Treaty of, 61
Calvinism, 99
Camón Aznar, José, 164
Campomanes, Pedro Rodríguez, 117
Canalejas, José, 148
Canary Islands, 133 n
Cánovas, Antonio, 134, 136, 137, 140, 148
Cantabrian Sea, 5, 13
Cantabrians, 15, 24, 31, 32
Cantera Burgos, Francisco, 170 n
Capsian culture, 3 n
Caracalla, Emperor, 17
Carande y Thobar, Ramón, 171 n, 172
Carbonari, 125
Cardium pottery, 9, 155
Caribbean Sea, 106
Carlism, 126, 127, 128, 129, 133, 135, 138
Caro, Baroja, Julio, xii, 93 n, 152, 158, 170 n
Carolingian Empire, 34
Carpenter, Rhys, 156 n
Cartagena, 62, 72
Carthage, 14, 15
Caspe, Compromise of, 80
Caspian Sea, 153
Castelar, Emilio, 135 n
Casticismo, defined, 116 n
Castile, xxiii, xxiv, 9, 27, 39–53 *passim*, 56, 58 n, 61, 62, 63, 64, 67, 79, 82, 92, 97, 130, 174–175, 177; New, 5, 11 n, 57; Old, 11 n, 63, 65 n; Councils of, 43, 63; Mesta in, 65, 70, 78, 79, 80, 94, 118; and Granada, 68; response to European movements, 69; under Peter the Cruel, 70, 72, 73; ascendancy of *grandes* in, 72; *Conversos* in, protected by Trastámara kings, 77; civil war in, 78; end of civil war in (1479), 87; merchant guilds in, 91; wealth of, plundered by Charles I, 99; embraces cause of Philip V, 113; and Catalonia, dissension between, 143; Cortes of, 168–169
Castillo, Alberto del, 155 n
Castro, Américo, xi, xii, xvi, xxi, xxii, xxiii, xxiv, 157, 158, 159, 161 n, 163, 168
Catalan Grand Company, 62 n
Catalan Revolution, 81, 84, 85
Catalanism, 138–139
Catalonia, xxiii, 5, 9, 10, 12, 32, 34, 35, 39, 41, 51 n, 53, 54, 58, 59, 60, 63, 64, 84, 91, 92, 95, 96, 105, 107, 108, 109, 110, 166, 174; New, 58; subversive movements in, during fifteenth century, 78; unified administration in, new procedures of, 114–115; Board of Commerce in, 115; uprising in (1822), 125, Espartero government in, 129–130; first general strike in (1855), 130; light industry in, 132–133; Carlism in, 135; and International Exposition of 1888, 137; trade unions organized in, 139; and Castile, dissension between, 143; crisis in (1934), 150; pluralistic positions of, 178
Catastro, defined, 115
Catholic Monarchs, 87–95, 96, 100, 105, 165, 171
Catholicism, Hispanic, 24, 46, 68; attacks upon, 144; revitalization of, 145. *See also* Christian Spain
Cave paintings, 5, 154 n
Celts, 12, 13, 156
Cerdagne, 88, 109
Cervantes, Miguel de, 104 n
Céspedes, Guillermo, xiv n
Chanson de Roland, 34 n, 157 n
Charlemagne, 30 n, 34

Charles, Archduke, of Austria, 111, 113
Charles I, 96, 97 n, 99, 100
Charles II, 108, 109, 110
Charles III, 115, 116, 118 n, 119, 128, 176
Charles IV, 117 n, 119, 121, 122 n, 128, 176
Charles V, 172, 173
Charles VIII, 87 n, 88
Chaunu, Hugette and Pierre, 174
Childe, V. Gordon, 155 n
Chindaswinth, 26
Christian Spain, 39, 40, 160. *See also* Catholicism, Hispanic
Cisneros, Francis Cardinal Jiménez de, 91, 95, 100
Cistercians, 49 n, 165
Civil Guards, formation of, 133
Clavería, Carlos, 175
Cluniac reform, 40, 163
Communidades, War of, 97
Concordat of 1851, 131, 144
Constitution: of Bayonne, 122; of 1812, 123, 125; of 1837, 129, 149; of 1845, 130, 144; of 1876, 136, 148
Contractual state, defined, 74 n
Conversos, 77, 80, 82, 92, 170, 173
Corbeil, Treaty of, 59
Córdoba, 56, 66 n, 98; Caliphate of, 31, 36, 37, 39, 42, 162
Corona, Carlos, 175
Corregidores, defined, 114
Corsica, 61
Cossío, Manuel Bartolomeo, 138 n
Costa, Joaquín, 137
Costumbrista, defined, 116 n
Crimean War, 130
Crisis of twentieth century, 141–150
Cro-Magnon man, 4
Crown of Aragon, 45, 51, 53, 54, 54–64 *passim*, 68, 72, 80, 81, 85–91 *passim*, 111, 113, 165 n, 168; principal objectives of, during fourteenth century, 73, 74; prosperity of, 74; decline of aristocracy in, 75; Conversos protected in, 77; Moriscos in, 93; "new ground plan" in, 114. *See also* Aragon
Crusade, ideal of, 49, 164
Crypto-Judaism, 93, 173
Cuenca, 49, 98
Cultural history, xviii; defined by Vicens Vives, xviii n
Cutanda, battle of, 50

Defourneaux, Marcelin, 175
De los origines a la Baja Edad Media, xii n
Domínguez Ortiz, Antonio, xiv n
Downs, battle of, 106, 108
Duero river, 31, 37, 38, 41, 42, 43, 44, 162 n
Duero tableland, 47, 49

Ebro river, 16, 37, 42, 44, 50, 51 n
El Argar, 11, 18
El Cid Campeador, 44, 164
Elliott, J. H., 74 n, 75 n, 172 n, 174
Emporion, 12
Encomiendas, defined, 94 n, 108 n
Encyclopedism, 175, 176
England, 74, 85, 86, 90, 101, 102, 110, 111, 113 n, 119, 136; Liberalism and Romanticism in, 126
Enlightened Despotism, 114, 119, 120
Enlightenment, 117
Ensenada, Marquis of, 117
Epila, battle of, 75
Erasmus, Desiderius, 97, 99
España invertebrada, 149 n
España: Un enigma histórico, xxii, 157 n, 161 n, 167 n
Espartero, Bartolemo, 129, 130, 131
Esquilache, Marquis of, 118
Estates, entailed, 94

Estudios de historia moderna, xiii, 174 n
Euric, 23
Exalted Liberals, 126, 127, 128, 129
Exempt Provinces, 114
Extremadura, 57, 65, 72, 99, 119, 128

Fanelli, Giuseppi, 139
Febvre, Lucien, xi n, xix n
Federalism, 135, 138
Feijóo, Benito Jerónimo, 117
Ferdinand, Joseph, of Bavaria, 110
Ferdinand I of Aragon, 80
Ferdinand I of Castile, 41, 42, 50 n, 51, 53
Ferdinand I of Trastámara, 81 n
Ferdinand III of Castile, 56, 57, 68, 69, 169, 170
Ferdinand VII (1814–1833), 124, 126, 127
Ferdinand the Catholic, 87, 88, 90, 91, 93, 165 n
Feudalism, and Cluniac reform, 40
Figueras, Estanislao, 135 n
Figuerola, Laureano, 136
First International, 135, 139
First Republic, 135
First World War, 147, 148, 150, 178
Flamenquismo, defined, 116 n
Flanders, 65, 74, 80, 97, 99, 110
Flórez, Friar Enrique, 117
Floridablanca, Count of, 117
Forans, defined, 64 n
France, 81, 83, 85, 86, 88, 90, 96, 97, 99, 101, 102, 106, 107, 108, 110, 136, 150; Liberalism and Romanticism in, 126
Francis I of France, 99
Franco regime, 140 n
Franks, 21, 22, 23, 34, 35, 39 n
Free Institution of Education, formation of, 138
Free Syndicates, 146 n
Free trade, 136–137

French Crusaders, 59
French Revolution, 119, 120
Fuero, defined, 58 n

Galicia, 13, 17, 23, 24, 27, 32, 33, 37, 47, 90, 105, 162
Galinda Romeo, Pascual, xv n
Gálvez family, from Málaga, 117
Gamellscheg, E., 158 n
García IV of Navarre, 50 n
García Gallo, Alfonso, 26 n
García Gómez, Emilio, 162 n
García y Bellido, Antonio, 156
Garonne river basin, 5, 40
Gaul, 21, 23. *See also* Franks
General Union of Laborers (UGT), 139, 146, 150
Genoa, 63, 72, 73, 172
Germany, 90, 173; of Hitler, 150
Gibraltar, 3, 46 n, 61, 62, 63, 68, 153
Giménez Soler, Andrés, 166
Giner, Francisco, 138
Giralt y Raventós, Emilio, 96 n
Godoy, Manuel, 119, 121, 122, 124
Gómez Moreno, Manuel, xxiii, 160
González, Fernán, 39
Gothic art, 69
Goths, 23, 162
Goya, Francisco, 117 n
Granada, 46 n, 62 n, 63, 68, 87 n, 88, 93, 94, 165 n, 170, 171
Grandes, defined, 43 n
Gravettian culture, 3 n, 4 n, 153 n, 154 n
Great Depression, 150, 178
Greeks, ancient, 11–12, 156 n
Guadalquivir river valley, 10, 16, 24, 36
Guadalupe, Sentence of, 93
Gubern, Ramón, xiii n
Guifred the Hairy, 35

Hadrian, Emperor, 19
Hamilton, Earl J., 172

Hapsburg monarchy, Hispania under, 96–103
Haring, C. H., 108 n
Heidelberg man, 1
Henry II of Castile, 80, 170
Henry II of Trastámara, 70, 72, 74, 90
Henry IV of Castile, 82, 83, 85, 86, 170
Hermenigild, 24
Herr, Richard, xxiii n, 176
Hidalgos, defined, 43
Hinojosa, Eduardo de, xvi n, 26 n
Hisham II, 39
Hispania: Historia política y cultural de España, x n, 170 n
Hispanic March, 34
Historia de Catalunya, 166
Historia de España (Soldevila), xii n
Historia de España (Valdeavellano), xii n, 157 n
Historia social y económica de España y América, xiv n, 143 n, 176
History of the Goths, 25 n
Hitler, Adolf, 150
Holland, 102, 106, 110
Holy Roman Empire, 70
Homo capensis, 7, 154
Huesca, 50
Humanism, 95, 97, 104; and historic tradition, 79
Humiliores, defined, 17
"Hundred Thousand Sons of St. Louis," 126

Iberians, 3 n, 12, 13, 156
Ideologism: defined by Vicens Vives, xi n; shallowness of, xix
Iglesias, Pablo, 139
Indice histórico español, xiii, xiv n, 172 n
Industry, development of, 132–133, 136–137

Inquisition, 77, 91, 92, 93 n, 124, 171
Institutional history, xv n, xvi, xvii
International Exposition of 1888, 137
Isabel of Portugal, 83, 86, 101 n
Isabel the Catholic, 87, 88 n, 90, 165 n
Isabel II, 129, 131, 134 n
Isidore, St., 25
Islam, 25, 32, 33, 36, 39, 44, 45 n, 54, 88, 160; victory over, 68, 88. *See also* Almoravids; Berbers; Moors; Muslims
Islamic Spain, 28–31, 36, 43, 158, 159–160, 162
Italy, 65, 87 n, 88, 97, 99, 119, 125; of Mussolini, 149, 150

James I, 56, 57, 58, 59, 73
James II, 61, 62, 73
Jaspers, Karl, ix
Jesuits, 119
Jews, 43, 65, 66, 67, 92, 93, 164, 173; persecution of, 76–77; expulsion of, 92, 165 n
Joan, Princess (1462–1530), 86
John II of Aragon and Navarre, 78, 81, 83, 84, 85, 87, 88
John II of Castile, 81, 82, 83 n
Jordá, Francisco, 153 n, 154 n
Joseph, Emperor, of Austria, 111 n, 113 n
Joseph, John, of Austria, 109
Joseph I, 122, 123
Jovellanos, Gaspar, 117, 118
Judaizers, 77, 93
Judíos en la España moderna y contemporánea, xii n, 93 n, 170 n
Juro, defined, 78 n

Kamen, Henry, 93 n
Kharjas, 160
King, Edmund, xxi n, 157 n

Index

Klein, Julius, 65 n
Konetzke, Richard, 170
Krause, Christian, 138

La Coruña, 115
La Mancha, 77
La realidad histórica de España, xxi n, xxii
Lacarra, José Maria, 163 n, 166
Languedoc, 54, 58, 74
Lapeyre, Henri, 167, 171, 173
Las Navas de Toledo, battle of, 46 n, 49, 56
Latifundia, 16, 49, 57, 94
Leander, St., 25
Lehrbuch der historischen Methode, xv n
Lens, battle of, 108
León, Kingdom of, 30, 31, 33, 37, 38–39, 41, 42, 44, 46, 47, 53, 56, 69, 162, 165
Leovigild, King, 24
Lepanto, battle of, 101
Lérida, 54, 58, 84
Lerma, Duke of, 102, 103 n, 105
Lévi-Provençal, Évariste, 162
Liber judiciorum, 26
Liberal Union, 131
Liberalism, in Spain, 124, 125–133 *passim*, 144
Lisbon, 72
Livestock taxes, in Castile, 78
Louis IX of France, 59
Louis XI of France, 79, 81, 85
Louis XIV of France, 109, 111 n, 113
Lower Paleolithic period, 2
Lucanus, Marcus Annaeus, 19
Luna, Don Alvaro de, 82
Lusitanians, 13, 15
Lynch, John, 172 n

Madrid, 3, 43, 98, 100, 102, 104, 107, 109 n, 113, 116, 118, 119 n, 122, 127, 133 n; Socialist Party formed in (1879), 139
Magdalenian culture, 4, 5, 6, 154
Majo, of Madrid, 116
Málaga, 36, 115, 117
Mallorca, 58, 63, 64, 73, 74, 78
Mancomunitat, la, 149
Manifesto of the Persians, 126
Manual de historia económica de España, 69 n
Map: of two Spains (socio-economic view), xxx; of Roman Hispania, 18; of Spain at beginning of tenth century, 38; of modern Spain, 142
Maravall, José Antonio, xvi n, 159 n, 160 n, 161
Marie Christine, regency of, 127, 128, 129, 148 n
Marinids, 62
Martial, 19
Martin the Humanist, 80
Marxism, 139, 150
Masonry, in Spain, 125
Matanzas, Cuba, naval battle at, 106
Materialism, and historical method, xix
Maura, Antonio, 148
Mayorazgos, 94
Medina del Campo, 80, 97, 98
Megaliths, 155
Menéndez Pidal, Ramón, xii, xvi, xxiii, 44 n, 156 n, 157, 158, 162 n, 163, 164
Menéndez y Pelayo, Marcelino, 144
Mercader, Juan, xiii n, 174
Merchant guilds, in Castile, 91
Mérida, 30
Mesolithic period, 3 n, 7
Mesopotamia, 7
Mesta, 65, 70, 78, 79, 80, 94, 118
Methodology, in history, xv, xvi

Mexico, 173; Spanish intervention in (1861), 134
Middle Ages, 20, 26, 57, 58 n, 66 n, 76, 90, 162 n, 167
Middle Paleolithic period, 2
Milan, 110; Edict of (313), 20
Military orders, of Spain, 49 n, 57
Moderate Liberals, 127, 131
Monarchia Hispania, 80
Montazgo, 78 n
Montiel, Peter the Cruel murdered at, 70
Moors, 43, 44, 93, 164, 170. *See also* Almoravids; Berbers; Islam; Muslims
Moriscos, 31, 58, 63, 93, 102, 103, 164, 165 n, 167, 171, 173
Moriscos de Granada, Los, xii n
Morocco, 28, 37, 45, 46 n, 62, 150; War of, 134
Mousterian culture, 3
Mozarabs, 29, 30, 31, 33, 34, 66 n, 160, 161
Mudejars, 67, 93
Muhammad I, 30
Muladíes, 29
Murcia, 23, 28, 56, 58, 59, 63, 139
Muret, battles at, 58, 59
Muslims, 27 n, 28, 29, 30, 34, 35, 39, 43, 45, 46, 50, 51 n, 54, 58, 62, 66, 78 n, 93. *See also* Almoravids; Berbers; Islam; Moors
Mussolini, Benito, 149, 150

Nadal, Santiago, x
Nadal Oller, Jorge, 69 n, 96 n
Naples, 74, 83, 85, 88
Napoleon, 121, 122, 124, 125 n
Narrative method, in history, xv
Narváez, Ramón, 130, 131
Nasrids, 46 n, 88
National Confederation of Labor (CNT), 146, 150
Nationalism, Spanish, 141, 143, 163
Navarre, 5, 34, 37, 39, 40, 41, 50 n, 56, 81, 84, 88, 90, 114, 125, 135, 163
Neanderthal man, 2, 3
Near East, 8, 59, 155 n
Neolithic period, 3 n, 8, 9, 10, 154 n, 155
Neopatria, Duchy of, 62
New Castile, 5, 11 n, 57
New Catalonia, 58
New World, 173
North Africa, 8, 64, 72, 91, 153; invasions from, 43, 45-49, 165
Numantines, 15

O'Donnell, Leopoldo, 131
Olavide, Pablo, 118
Old Castile, 11 n, 63, 65 n
Oliba, Bishop, 41
Olivares, Count-Duke of, 105, 106, 107, 108, 138, 174
Olmedo, battle of, 81 n, 82
Oran, 91
Ordoño I, 33
Ordoño II, 37
Ortega y Gasset, Jose, xxiii, 149, 175
Ottoman Turks, 62, 99, 101, 103

Paintings, cave, 5, 154 n
Palencia, 69
Palestine, 50
Palma de Mallorca, 58, 63, 64, 73, 74, 78
Papacy, 163, 165
"Party Kingdoms," 42, 45, 57
Pau, John Cardinal Margarit, 79
Pavia, battle of, 99
Pavía, Manuel, 136
Payne, Stanley G., xi n, xiv n
Pelayo, 32 n
Pérez, Antonio, 101
Pericot, Luis, 152, 153 n, 154 n
Périgord culture, 3 n, 4, 5, 6, 7, 8, 153 n
Perpignan, 64

Index   187

Peru, 134 n, 173
Peter the Ceremonious, 73
Peter the Cruel, 70, 72, 73
Peter the Great, 59, 64, 73, 75
Petronilla, Infanta, 51, 53 n
Philip II, 96, 98, 100, 101 n, 103, 115, 172, 174
Philip III, 96, 102, 105, 111 n
Philip IV, 105, 109 n, 110 n, 111 n
Philip V, 111, 113, 114, 174
Philology, xvi, xvii
Phoenicians, 11, 12
Pi y Margall, Francisco, 135
Pithecanthropi, 1, 2, 153
Pluralistic state, concept of, 53, 171, 178
Portugal, 3, 9, 11, 23, 45, 47, 70, 72, 82, 85, 86, 87, 90, 101, 102, 165, 173, 174; secession of, 106, 108; Liberalism in, 125
Positivism, and historical method, xix
Prehistoric Art of the Western Mediterranean and the Sahara, 154 n
Prehistoric Migrations in Europe, 155 n
Prim, Juan, 134, 135
Primo de Rivera, Miguel, 149
Privilegio General, conferred by Peter the Great, 75
Progressive Liberalism, 130
Progressivism, 129
Pronunciamiento, defined as military rebellion, 125 n
Proudhon, Pierre J., 135, 139
Provence, 54
Provinces, organization of (1833), 133
Provincial Juntas, in revolution of 1808, 122
Prudence, connotations of, in Spanish, 101 n
Pueblo, defined, 16 n
Punic War, Second, 14

Pyrenean Empire, and Hispanic pluralism, 50–55 *passim*
Pyrenees, 2, 5, 7, 10, 11, 12, 22, 23, 34, 41, 50, 75, 85, 90, 165; Treaty of, 109

Quijote, don, 104
Quintilian, 19

Rahola, Federico, xiii n
Railroad system, Spanish, 132
Ramiro I, 50
Ramiro II, 37
Ramón Berenguer I, 41
Ramón Berenguer III, 54
Ramón Berenguer IV, 47, 49, 51, 53, 54
Recceswinth, 26
Reglá, Juan, xiii n, 96 n, 103 n, 169 n, 171, 174
Relaciones (Perez), 101 n
Renaissance, 76, 79, 92, 95 n, 97, 144
Report on the Agrarian Law (Jovellanos), 118
Restoration, 136, 137, 139, 145
Ripoll monastery, 41 n, 69
Ripoll Perello, Eduardo, 153 n, 154 n
Rocroi, battle of, 106, 108
Roderick, King, 27 n, 32
Roman Hispania, 14–21, 22, 26, 79 157–158
Romanticism, 126
Roussillon, 53, 73, 79, 88, 109
Royal Statute (1834), 128
Royal Volunteers of 1822–1823, 126
Russia, of Stalin, 150
Russian Revolution, 178

Sagasta, Práxedes Mateo, 136
Sagrajas, battle of, 43, 45 n, 46
Sahara Desert, 45, 154 n
Salado, battle of, 62 n, 63
Salamanca, 43, 47; University of, 69

Salmerón, Nicolás, 135 n
Sanabre, José, 174
Sánchez Agesta, Luis, 175
Sánchez Albornoz, Claudio, xi, xii, xvi n, xxii, xxiii, xxiv, 157, 158, 159 n, 160, 161, 162, 163, 167, 168
Sánchez-Barba, Mario Hernández, xiv n
Sancho III the Great, 40–41, 50
Sancho IV, 170
Sanjurjo, José, 150
Santander, 115
Santiago de Compostela, 39, 40, 163
Sanz, Julián, 138
Saragossa, 30, 34, 42, 44 n, 47, 50, 51, 74, 80
Sardinia, 61, 62, 64, 73, 74
Sarrailh, Jean, 175
Sauvetat, Raimont de, 66 n
School of Translators of Toledo, 66, 69
Schramm, Percy Ernst, 166
Schulten, Adolph, 153, 156 n
Scipio family, 14, 15
Second Republic, 150
Segovia, 43, 79, 98
Seneca family, 19
Seniores, defined, 16, 17
Señoríos legos, defined, 94 n
Separatism: in revolution of 1808, 122; and First Republic, 135
Sephardim, 93 n
"September Revolution," 135
Serrano, Francisco, 134
Serviles, and Liberals, 124
Seville, 23, 36, 42, 56, 63, 72, 76, 98
Sicilian Vespers, 59 n
Sicily, 53 n, 59, 61, 62, 64, 73, 74, 88 n
Sicroff, A. A., 93 n
Socialist Party, Spanish, 139, 146
Societies of the Friends of the Country, 117
Soldevila, Fernando, xii, 166

Solutrean culture, 4, 5, 153
"Spain with Honor" manifesto (1868), 134
Spanish-American War, 141
Spanish Empire in America, The, 108 n
Spanish Inquisition, The (Kamen), 93 n
Stalin, Joseph, 150
Statistics, in history, xix, xx–xxi, xxii
Stern, M. S., 160 n
Structure of Spanish History, The, xxi n, xxiv n, 157 n
Suevi, 21, 22, 23, 24
Supreme Central Junta, and revolution of 1808, 122
Sylvester II, Pope, 69
Syndicalism, 139, 140 n, 146, 147, 150
Syrians, 29

Tajo River, 3, 5, 12, 43
Tarifa, 62, 63
Tarradell, Miguel, 153 n
Tarragona, 54
Tarshish, 11
Tartessus, site of, 156
Thirty Years' War, 106, 107
Toledo, 23, 30, 42, 43, 45, 69, 98; Councils of, 24, 27; School of Translators of, 66, 69
Topete, Juan Bautista, 134
Torrejón de Ardoz, pronunciamento at (1843), 130
Tortosa, 36, 54, 85
Toynbee, Arnold, ix
Trade unions, 139, 140 n, 146, 147
Trajan, Emperor, 19
Trastámara, House of, 70, 71, 80, 102
Tripoli, 91
Tudilén, Treaty of, 49

Index

Ubieto Arteta, Antonio, 164, 166
Uclés, battle of, 46
Unamuno, Miguel de, xxiii, 116 n
Unions, trade, 139, 140 n, 146, 147
Upper Paleolithic period, 3 n, 4, 5, 7, 153 n
Urban IV, Pope, 59 n
Urgel, 33, 53; Counts of, 75, 80; Regency of, 125; canal in, 132
Uria, Juan, 163 n
Urraca, Queen, 47, 79 n
Usatges (legal code), 41
Utrecht, peace of (1713-1715), 113 n

Valdeavellano, Luis Garcia de, xii, 157
Valencia, 8, 42, 44, 46, 53, 56, 57, 58, 62, 63, 64, 74, 80, 92, 96, 103 n, 139, 167
Vallicrosa, Millás, 17 n, 160, 163
Vandals, 22, 23
Varagnac, André, 153
Vergara, Agreement of, 129
Viana, Prince Charles of, 84, 85
Vicálvaro, pronunciamento at (1854), 130

Vilar, Pierre, 173, 174
Villa, defined, 16 n
Villafranca del Penedés, capitulation of, 84
Villalar, battle of, 97 n
Visigothic Hispania, 22-27, 79, 158-159
Vitoria, Francisco de, 100
Vives, Luis, 100
"Vivir desviviéndose," xxiv
Vizcaya, 133, 137, 139

War of Independence (1808-1812), 123 n
War of Morocco, 134
War of the Pacific, 134
War of Spanish Succession, 111, 113 n
Wilson, Woodrow, 149
World War I, 147, 148, 150, 178

"Yellow syndicalism," 145, 146 n
Yunteros, in Extremadura, 132

Zamora, 43

www.ingramcontent.com/pod-product-compliance
Lightning Source LLC
Chambersburg PA
CBHW071204240426
43668CB00032B/2076